Elisabeth-Paule Labat

The Presence of God

Translated by David Smith

PAULIST PRESS
New York/Ramsey

Library of Congress
Catalog Card Number: 80-82089

ISBN: 0-8091-2336-3

Published by Paulist Press
Editorial Office: 1865 Broadway, New York, N.Y. 10023
Business Office: 545 Island Road, Ramsey, N.J. 07446

Printed and bound in the
United States of America

Contents

Preface

This book may well become one of the few spiritual classics of the twentieth century. The authoress, an enclosed Benedictine nun, wrote these very personal meditations over a period of many years. The text is presented here to the public in the form in which it was written. A few slight corrections, which the authoress would certainly have made herself, have been made and a number of repetitions, which she would undoubtedly have eliminated if she had lived longer, have also been cut from the text. She was so painstaking and modest that there can be no doubt that she would never have consented to the publication of these meditations until probably even more corrections and cuts had been made. We can therefore, on her behalf too, thank Father Jean Armogathe, a member of the editorial staff of the international Catholic journal *Communio*, for his careful and discreet editing of the manuscript.

Mother Elisabeth-Paule Labat received an outstanding Christian education and also apparently enjoyed many profound inner experiences as a girl, but later, like so many other young adults, she became so deeply immersed in culture—literature and especially music—that her faith seemed to disappear almost entirely.

This loss of faith was, however, only apparent. She soon became aware of the emptiness of a life led without God. Her attention was drawn back to Christ by a deeply spiritual priest and she suddenly discovered the personal presence of God in the world. This book is the story of that discovery. From the moment that she became conscious of this need to look for God, no other way of life but the monastic way could satisfy her.

She brought her musical gifts to the convent and these became transmuted into what might be called a philosophy and a poetic understanding of music. There is ample evidence of this deep understanding in her book *Mystère de la musique*, in which she examined some of the finest pieces from the repertory of Gregorian chant.

She was also and above all a fully human being and her humanity did not in any sense wither away in the convent. In being poured out, it became completely mature and she became more and more perfectly human. One is very conscious of this deep humanity in this book as well as of her communication of her experience of the total meaning of human life in this world as the sign of God's presence and the expression of an encounter with God.

She was born in 1897 at Tarbes and entered the Benedictine community of Saint Michel-de-Kergonan near Carnac in 1922. She died there, after a long and painful illness, in 1975. The attentive reader will be aware, in the serenity of these chapters, of the inner experiences that tested Mother Elisabeth-Paule's total faith and which resulted in what may be described as a pure song of joy.

The key word throughout is "presence." In her sensitive and deeply harmonious spirit, she was able to absorb and thus overcome all the discords of modern life and testify here and now to the reality of eternal peace. This unity and harmony of her life simply echoed the presence of God in her, a presence that she herself recognized and which others sensed.

Many theological treatises have been written on the subject of God's presence. Most of these are abstract and speculative and the sound that we hear from them is muffled and indistinct. Mother Elisabeth-Paule's meditation is biblical, liturgical and monastic. It is a clear song of such purity that it is profoundly moving, the song of a well-tuned Aeolian harp whose strings have been touched by the Holy Spirit.

Louis Bouyer

A Note to the Reader

Most of this book was written a few years ago in answer to a request made by a person who, like so many others, was externally very active and was anxious to preserve a deep inner life. The title that I had originally thought of using was "God in us." On reflection, however, it became clear to me that, if I really wanted to say something meaningful about the intimate presence of grace in us, I had first to go further and look beyond time at God's life in us and our life in God, through our eternal model, and the creative presence of immensity which is the basis of the presence of grace. The only suitable title for such a work seemed to me therefore to be "The Presence of God."

It is, of course, true that God is totally present in the absolute simplicity of his being for everything that he creates. There is no difference between his essence and his activity. They are one. He is universally present as the being from which everything that exists flows.

Before anything was created, however, he decided to be the object of our knowledge and love in order to be able to adapt himself to our weakness, our limitations as fallen creatures. Because of this intention, he is present for us in different ways.

We can therefore make distinctions within this one presence so that we can seize hold of it, insofar as it is possible for us poor travelers here below to do this.

God's presence—that is our immense and inexpressible joy, a

joy that cannot be lost. We cannot escape from God or from his glance, his knowledge of us or his activity with us. His presence surrounds us, invades us, penetrates to our innermost being, transfigures us, rules us and consumes us in a death that gives life. This all takes place in the movement from grace to glory. For us, the condition is faithfulness.

This is the eternal life to which we can look forward. This life has, moreover, already begun in us in this world and we can find it if we choose freely to respond to the eternal plan of the Father to lead us in, with and through Christ and in the Holy Spirit, to the heart of the realm of blessedness.

I would emphasize that this book is no more than an attempt. Despite its defects, I would hope that it will increase our immense gratitude to the one who lives and sees, as Agar the Egyptian called God in the loneliness of the desert. May it cause us to thank the one who, in his Christ who is God with his Father and man with us, formed an indissoluble covenant with us based on his promise and who continues his own incarnation in each one of us.

Introduction

The hour of the Lord, the hour of his passion, is at hand. Outside, it is night and the powers of darkness are preparing to launch their great attack. Inside, around Jesus, everything is light, intimacy and sweetness. Like a pledge of unlimited love, anticipating his sacrifice of himself, Jesus has just given his body as food and his blood as drink to his own. Then, before leaving for the garden, he also gives them his last instructions and his final promises. Everything is solemn but at the same time so simple that the apostles—first Peter, then Thomas and then Philip—have no hesitation in questioning him. Then Judas, not Iscariot, but the Faithful, asks him: "Lord, how is it that you will manifest yourself to us and not to the world?" And Jesus replies: "If anyone loves me, he will keep my word and my Father will love him and we shall come to him and make our home with him" (John 14. 22–23).

What an unheard of promise: It goes far beyond all the hopes of the people of Israel for a more inward form of religion, all the assurances given by the prophets and all the longings of the psalmist. It is so deep and so beautiful that the apostles themselves cannot as yet understand it. The Spirit of truth and love will have to come to them before the full meaning of this promise can be grasped.

When the Lord has risen again and ascended to the right hand of the Father, his disciples will know that their master is not absent from them. They will know that he is in fact incomparably more present than he was during his life on earth. And together with Jesus, in whom the Spirit that they have just received lives in fullness—he is the Son of God—the Father is also with them, because, in the embrace of this Spirit of love that they breathe together, Jesus and the Father are one. From that time onward the apostles will baptize men of all nations in the name of the Trinity and take the good news everywhere, fulfilling their great task of including all who are "destined for eternal life" (Acts 13. 48) within the family of the three who are consubstantial. Within this family, those who are thus destined will live in complete joy (1 John 1. 3, 4).

God is in us—we are in God. These two formulas seem to be quite different. In reality, they are synonymous and complementary. They contain the mystery of the kingdom of God as announced by John the Baptist and proclaimed in so much that Jesus told his own, sometimes directly and sometimes in parables. It is a kingdom that is above all interior, invisible and silent. It is a mystery that is sweet, private and full of happiness and in which God is not only master, but also father, brother, friend and spouse. It is a mystery in which one melts and merges together in the unity of a love that comes from the depths of God and goes back to him through us: "I in them and you in me, may they be completely one" (John 17. 23).

If God makes his home with us, he certainly does not do this in order to remain inactive. He makes his home with us to rouse us, carry us along in the stream of his life in the Trinity and to plunge us, poor finite beings, into the immense sea of his essence. If, then, he seizes hold of us in the depths of our being, it is only to make us live in him who lives in us. We are therefore truly present within him as he is in us in an indescribable way. It is almost impossible to describe mutual inner presence because it is in a sense similar to the existence of the persons of the Trinity in each other and because its principle is to be found in the unity of the three divine persons, toward which it is always directed.

Despite the certainty of theological data and the witness borne by those who have endured God in contemplation, this reality of God's presence in us brings us close to realities that are so holy and so mysterious that one hesitates before discussing them. It presupposes a joining together of two terms—God and the soul. In this union, God is not primarily the creator and the one whose perfection is partly reflected in visible aspects of his creation. He is the God who exists in the hidden depths of his divinity and in the living, active interchange and the tranquillity of his life as Father, Son and Holy Spirit.

Although he is not the unknown God whose altar Paul noticed

at Athens, this God is nonetheless the hidden God of the prophet Isaiah (Isa. 45. 15). He is hidden in his ways and even more completely hidden in his essence, because he is inaccessible and beyond all things. He is the one whose name the Israelites did not dare to speak aloud, believing as they did that only God knew God. Only the Spirit, uncreated and substantial love, can penetrate to the depths of this bottomless abyss where, in light and tenderness, the Father begets a Son who receives from him the whole of the divine nature.

There is also the finite reality of our soul. This is also a mystery, since we know it in this world only by its effects. It has only to be separated once from its body and deprived of any point of contact with the world of the senses for it to be revealed to us in its naked truth. The human soul is a world that is greater than all the worlds of heaven and earth that we can perceive with our senses. Those worlds do not produce a single thought and our thoughts are there to grasp them. Julian of Norwich described how the Lord opened her spiritual eyes and showed her her soul in the midst of her heart. When she saw it, it was so big that it seemed to her to be an immense world and a blessed kingdom. Léon Bloy wrote in a letter to Elisabeth Joly that there was in every soul an abyss of mystery and that the hidden things that are revealed to us there may cause us inconceivable astonishment.

God takes our soul out of nothingness and gives it his breath, thus creating it in his own image and likeness (Gen. 2. 7). It is as though he wanted to make it emerge from the most intimate part of his being. Jan van Ruysbroeck called it such a noble reality that no creature could have any influence on its essence. Only God was, in his opinion, capable of influencing the soul, because he was "the essence of essence, the life of life and the principle and the support of all creatures."

Is it surprising, then, in view of this, that the soul should have very special reserves of nobility and greatness, despite the injury and imbalance caused by original sin and the propensity to evil that goes counter to its fundamental orientation toward God, its creator? Is it true that God so loved the world, which was made for souls and in which souls ruled, that he gave his only Son for it? Did he in fact give souls the power to obey, by which they would be able to share in his divinity and thus in his grace? Is it possible for us to love God as he loves himself and to know him as he knows himself, by means of a supernatural organism formed by the theological virtues, the gifts of the Spirit and the infused moral virtues?

It is, unfortunately, true that the deepest realities of our spiritual life are often those that we examine the least. We are all too ignorant of the treasures deposited in us by God and his Church when we were baptized, and we are not aware of the way in which they make us open to the infinite nature of God.

God and the soul are two mysterious realities, but their union is equally a mystery that only the Spirit of God, the bond between them, can reveal to the eyes of the heart. It is quite certain that we can gain no idea at all from the strength, intimacy and sweetness of earthly love of the interpenetration of the spirit and the Spirit (1 Cor. 6. 17) with the one who is already, at the deepest level of our being, more ourselves than we are simply because of his presence that creates us and keeps us alive.

If we are to understand this mystery of God's presence and love, we must situate it, so to speak, within its context. We have, in other words, to look at it in the light of God's universal providence and within the framework of that great order which Augustine loved so much to contemplate and which reveals to us the whole complex of beings and their perfections directed toward a single end in accordance with a single, eternal decree.

That single end is God himself. Everything that receives its being from him is created to return to him. God therefore gives each creature, whether it is animate or inanimate, an irresistible inclination to reach its end. Left to itself, a stone falls to the ground. As it is fed more and more by everything that it consumes, fire rises upward. Because he is both flesh and spirit, man, on the other hand, is divided and obeys a double weight, downward and upward. When, however, he is open to the action of God's grace, he inevitably rises up, like a flame, to join his God. When this happens, he says with Augustine: "My love is my weight," and it is true that God is the weight which is without weight that draws everything to him. When he comes in our flesh to this earth, raised above it by his redeeming cross, he will draw all men to himself (John 12. 32).

It is not difficult to understand, with this in mind, how the universe seemed to Dionysius the Areopagite and other Church Fathers in a great vision of unity to be a harmonious symphony of different loves, all with an irresistible inclination to return to the divine principle from which they had originally emanated. Thomas Aquinas, who developed this teaching, said that "when they proceed from their first principle, the creatures move, as it were, in a spiral or a circuit, going back, as though to their end, to the cause that produced them" (I Sent. 14, q. 2, a. 2).

God is everywhere in this immense circular movement. Even before his act of creation, he is in the eternal model of each one of us that he has in his Word and in accordance with which he creates in time. Then, carrying out our call to existence, he is also in us, in the immense creative presence, according to which "it is in him that we live and move and exist" (Acts 17. 28). He is in us too in the presence that we call the state of grace. Because of this presence, we finite beings are able to seize hold of him in this world and to recover the purity of our original image. Finally, he is at the end, when grace, which is at the beginning of glory, has been fully and definitively opened up and we see him as he is and are like him and totally deified.

When we have made the vow that Ambrose made when he was mourning his brother's death: "We all have to return to the place from which we came," and when we have been tossed about for a time on the changing waves of human life, we shall go back to our point of departure and be finally and forever at rest.

Rest. Surely it is no more than the affirmation and the enjoyment of a presence that supports us and with which we have everything that we can want and love.

God so loves man created in his image and recreated in Christ that he does not want to give him any other end than the one that he so tirelessly seeks for himself. That end is rest. Divine Wisdom, which is God himself, revealed this long ago to Ben Sirach: "Among all these I searched for rest" (Sir. 24:7).

With what great pleasure God tastes this rest in his blessed life in the Trinity! The Father contemplates himself in his Son in whom all his satisfaction rests. Between them, there is a constant flow backward and forward, a vital circulation of infinite intensity—circumincession—and there is also a circuminsession in which the Father and the Son live in each other in a similarly infinitely unchangeable state. The Holy Spirit is this tranquillity, this rest in the unity of essence and life, as the frontier without frontier of the divine ocean.

This inexpressible rest, God, in the gift of himself that he gives to us, wants to be ours and wants to extend itself in us, as it were, by the rest that it will find in us and the rest that we shall find in it. Our rest, then, is the fruit of God's presence experienced beyond everything, and the greatest glory that we can give him is to consent to his eternal intention to love us and to be fully aware of his presence in us and in the whole of the universe. We can also give him glory by continuing to be astonished by the fullness of his being and his presence. This fullness makes him what is furthest from us by his transcendence and inviolable holiness and what is also closest by his immanence, his creative influence and his infinite love. He is the only one in whom we can trust, and his faithfulness is as perfect as his truth and the reality of his presence.

Rock, bulwark, shield, fortress—these are the Old Testament titles given to God. The Israelites knew him as the one who never yielded to the attacks made by enemy powers and whose support and protection could never fail. He was and is the one in whom we can trust and rest, as John rested on the heart of the God-man at the Last Supper, listening to the beating of that heart in order to make it pass into his heart.

In seeking the rest, we are bound to avoid not only feverish activity and noise, but also inertia, idleness and passivity. We should be healthily active and carry out our duties conscientiously.

The true Christian will always try to preserve inviolate a place of silent retreat in the depths of his being where he can seek refuge, if only as an expression of the most intimate intention of his heart and will. He will always be at rest in that part of his being, like God and with God, and will therefore be able to say with Christ: "My Father goes on working and so do I" (John 5. 17).

Man can imitate the God who rules the universe of his creatures that he brought out of nothingness by speaking a single word, whether he is in the silence of a monk's cell or a hermitage or whether he is in the midst of other people, by working for his fellow-men. He can, moreover, serve others in this way without ever leaving this place of rest where God is in him and he is in God.

The more deeply man sinks down into rest with his beloved, the rest of the life of the Trinity, the more completely God will remove all obstacles to that rest, extending it in him until it becomes, as it did for Gertrude the Great, a place of inexhaustible interchange of tenderness and satisfaction. The more man descends into that rest too, the more fully his soul will respond to the call of that grace which invites all men—and has always invited them—to be gods by sharing God's divinity, true children of God and always conscious of his presence.

The author of the book of Revelation invites us to enter this rest when he speaks of God's great sabbath that followed his creation of man and calls on us to observe the rest of the seventh day. It is true, of course, that it is a holy law for Christians to rest on Sunday and to remember the passover of Jesus Christ who died and was raised to the right hand of the Father. God's true rest in us and our rest in God, however, are outside time. It is eternity that has already begun here on earth, thanks to the indestructible presence of the one who is eternal.

Now, in the twentieth century, we need this rest even more than in the past. Living in an age of rapid scientific and technical progress, increasing productivity and growing emphasis on personal ambition, man is in urgent need of a powerful counterbalance if he is to remain worthy of his calling as man. The more he is forced to turn outward, the more conscious he ought to be made, by that counterweight, of inner values. How is he to avoid being completely engulfed by the material world if the life of his soul does not demand more urgently to penetrate to its real depths and those of God? He needs what Henri Bergson called, many years ago, before the invention of the atomic bomb and of spacecraft, the "soul supplement."

Man is anxious to discover the secrets of the universe, both in the depths of the sea and in the starry skies that God entrusted to man in his earthly paradise. He is encouraged by his conquests and tempted by the false promises of the prince of this world. He aspires to immortality but wants to forget God and eternity. He wants to escape suffering and to find here on this earth his place of rest and blessedness. "What will a man gain if he wins the whole world and ruins his life?" These words of Jesus (Matt. 16. 26) have an even greater force and poignancy in man's present situation.

Who, then, will save us from this destructive ambition to inhabit a false Eden and to become supermen, the worst possible caricatures of God and a mockery and negation of his plan for us when he created us, in the words of the psalmist (Ps. 8. 5), "a little less" than himself, and recreated us in his Christ?

Humility and greatness—these are what we gain from contact with his presence. The universe has its heights and its depths and man's task is to explore them. Through this contact, however, he can discover that the human spirit is even vaster than the earth and more unfathomable than the oceans, and that these inner heights and depths are merged with those of the God who lives in him. He can fly into spaces without spaces and these are even more fit than the visible spaces of the universe to be the object of a loving and careful search. It is, however, only in the light of the divine and universal presence of the one who is light itself that man can venture to search in the true homeland of his soul where he will one day reach his end and will never leave again, even though everything on earth will pass away. If man directs all his activity and the whole of his life toward this end, living in the friendship of the God who gives him light and strength, he will possess the earth, the earth that God promised to the meek of whom the Lord spoke on the Mount of the Beatitudes. And these meek ones are the strong who have conquered the world of human passions.

What, one wonders, would our world be like if we really set about conquering this inner universe, fully conscious of God's presence and becoming more and more immersed in the rest of that presence? Surely, we would be on the way toward a realization of the kingdom of God in a world that was fragile, but becoming more and more holy.

Our conquest of that world would be exclusively at the service of love and universal happiness. It would be a great symphony of thanks and praise offered to God as creator and savior. Everything would be redeemed by man who had become one with the second Adam, Christ. The great hope of all inanimate beings, whose mysterious groaning was heard by Paul (Rom. 8. 19–21), would be fulfilled in the revelation of the children of God. Creation would no longer be the object of man's purely physical enjoyment, selfishness and pride. On the contrary, all things would be there for the triumph of God's love, which is based not on poverty or need but on knowledge of the Father's inexpressible gift to his children.

It is clear, however, that even if there have been, in the past, certain times in the history of mankind when holiness has flourished, and even though we may still hope for this to happen in our own time, this will not be—and has never been—a universal experience. Man's old sin will always make its presence felt and men will continue to listen in fascination to the promptings of the devil, the father of lies: "When the Son of man comes, will he find any faith on earth?" (Luke 18. 8). There will only be a handful of believers ready at the end of time to come face to face with the terrible and glorious manifestation of Christ's presence, when he comes in majesty to look for his own and to judge the living and the dead. Those Christians will be a point of intense light forming the Church.

Here on earth, God has always adapted his presence to man because he is also our Father. In the Old Testament, his presence often takes the form of striking miracles and wonders. He did not hesitate to manifest himself in a burning bush, to divide the waters of the

Red Sea and to give his law in thunder and lightning on Mount Sinai in order to unite a group of roughly-fashioned tribes as a single, chosen nation.

Later, when the two visible missions of the incarnation and Pentecost had been completed, these continued to be carried out invisibly in the depths of men's souls. There have been a few exceptions, such as the conversion of Saint Paul, but for the most part God has revealed his presence in the silence and recollection of the heart. Elijah knew this on Horeb and Jeremiah, the prophet with such an admirable inner life, was also aware of it long ago. It will also probably take this form until the Lord returns.

Then at the parousia the explosive and triumphant aspect of God's presence will appear, and the world, reduced to nothing by the omnipotence of this presence, will be transfigured and made new, becoming the heavenly Jerusalem that was glimpsed by the visionary of Patmos. We, who will if necessary have been purified since our death and already be in possession of the light of glory, will enjoy the beatific presence of God in unveiled contemplation. We shall not see him totally then, because he will remain inexpressible even to his angels, but we shall see him *totus*, entirely.

One further question has to be considered before this introduction is concluded. I sometimes speak in this book of the Lord's "passing." How can this be, if God is everywhere and always present?

This is God's wonderful prerogative. We can only go to the place where we are not yet. God only comes or goes to where he is already. How is it possible for him to go to where he is not, since that is the place of sin, which is a negation of himself? He can only go there to save the sinner.

The Lord is not present passively or statically. His is a living, active and dynamic presence. He is eternal, but his providence, his grace and the slightest signs of his holy will follow the slightest outlines of time and space to make, with man's collaboration and in and through his consent and opposition, what we call history.

Since the events of the incarnation and Pentecost, we cannot expect God to do anything new until the Lord's second coming. There is, however, a history which is that of God's passing among men and the passing of men into God.

We say, for example, that God has passed by when he strikes the world, a group or an individual with such powerful blows that everyone can hear. In such cases, is it not true to say that he wants to draw us out of our spiritual torpor or our false and all too human security? These blows take the form of a worldwide catastrophe, a great national disaster or a tragic event in the life of a public figure on the one hand or the death of a person who is especially dear to us, the conversion of a sinner or an event of great joy in the life of a friend on the other.

God is in fact always passing into the everyday and often colorless fabric of the life of each one of us. This everyday experience may even be the sphere into which he prefers to introduce his grace. The slightest event in our lives and the least discernible movement of his grace point to the passing of his justice and mercy into our lives and to his desire to appeal to our faithfulness and to draw us toward him.

He passes in this way among us in order to fashion us into his form and likeness and to perfect us in his love. Sometimes he does this slowly and silently, acting like the drops of water that take so many years to hollow out the rock, and with so much discretion that we are hardly aware of it. At other times, he acts so quickly that he takes us by surprise, as he does through his priest at Mass, when, in a few words, he changes the bread into his body and the wine into his blood. This passing of the Lord becomes our own rhythm when we pass from death to life or from a life that is dying to a death which gives life. Newman was deeply impressed by this "passing" of the words of consecration and described what they meant for him at the time of his conversion in *Loss and Gain*. They passed by quickly, he said, because they were the formidable words of sacrifice, and the Lord Jesus himself passed with them as he had passed along the shores of the lake when he was still in the flesh, calling first one man, then another. They passed quickly too, because they were like Moses' words when he called on the Lord as he came down in the cloud. Like Moses on the mountain, he concluded, we also pass.

We are also, like the bread and the wine, not purely passive substances and God does not pass by in order to change us suddenly into his body and blood. He passes rather in order to transform us gradually, to deify us slowly, to integrate us into his person and to make us, with the passage of the centuries, his mystical body and his total body. This means that, whether the Lord passes rapidly or whether he passes gently and imperceptibly, we should not stop. In the unchanging presence of God who builds us on the rock, we should be continuously passing into him and with him. If we are to perceive the Lord's passing and be aware of its significance every time it happens, we must become very sensitive and intuitive and be quietly open to his presence and faithful to it. If we are really listening, we shall know that the one who is eternally young never passes in the same way more than once. He is inexhaustibly inventive.

The soul that is able to hear the slightest inflections of his voice also knows that its echoes, both in the most intimate part of man's being and in the things and events outside him, are very vague. The soul that is sensitive to the light of God's presence knows too that the light that illuminates the step that it is about to take—"your word is a lamp to my feet and a light on my path" (Ps. 119. 105)—is not the same as the light that will illuminate the next step. But the soul always recognizes the voice and the light of the one who is always passing, because he is the eternal present and eternal love.

1

God's Life in Us
and Our Life in God
Through Our Eternal Model

It was Lautréamont, I think, who was surprised to learn that he had begun life by being born the son of his father and mother. The half-made poet was not, however, completely wrong in believing that he had come from further back. We do come from very far back, because we are eternal. We are eternal because of the grace that flows into us from the heights of the eternal God. We are eternal too because of our destiny as children of God and co-heirs of Christ, called to be eternally face to face with God. Finally, we are eternal because of our origin, which is eternally present in the thought and will of our eternal creator.

It is true, of course, that it is not our eternal preexistence that makes itself known to us in the first place. Like God himself, of which it is, so to speak, the place, that preexistence is a mystery. No, we are first of all aware of our existence on this earth. The little child who is brought to life knows that he exists. He understands that good and harmful things exist quite close to him. He does not think this or formulate it, but he knows it.

This existence of beings and things presupposes the reality of the only one who exists. He is the cause of every created being, in both the effective and the exemplary sense, because it is true that the temporal things were called into being since they were eternal things and, before all creation, God had in himself the creative ideas of everything that was to appear in time and space. It is therefore in God himself that we should try to discern, beyond time and space, a first great, mysterious and hidden modality of his presence in us and our presence in him.

Entering the life of the only one who exists is penetrating into the abyss of his life in the Trinity, his inaccessible life that is the object of our faith and of which we receive everything. There are myriads of possible creations there which the Father begets when he begets his Word and which are contained within the embrace of the one Spirit of truth and love.

This doctrine of an intelligible world living from eternity as an ideal in God is quite traditional. It originated in the religious genius of Plato, and there can be no doubt that many pagan souls who were thirsting for truth were raised by this teaching above the world of the senses to God. Through neo-Platonism and especially Plotinus and Porphyry, it became Christian and was given prominence by Origen, Augustine and other Fathers of the Church. It was taken up again by the great theologians of the Middle Ages and emphasized in both of the major schools, that of Saint Bonaventure and that of Thomas Aquinas. Jan van Ruysbroeck, Louis de Blois and Jean-Pierre de Caussade were all influenced by this doctrine, and no great spiritual writer has ever dreamt of denying its importance.

Has the full significance of this teaching been sufficiently stressed in the life of the Christian who is really seeking God and wants to base his faith on the most solid of foundations? It is certainly a sphere that goes far beyond anything that we can imagine or grasp with our senses. It is, however, a sphere that we should contemplate and admire, and it should be the object of all our thoughts and all our thanksgiving.

God is, God lives and God knows himself in his Word, the Word who is his Son, radiating his glory and bearing the impression of his substance (Heb. 1. 3). In this Word who is consubstantial with him and is at the same time his thought, his word, his reason, his wisdom and his art, the Father contemplates everything that he causes, in the superabundance of his too great love, to emerge from nothingness. There is infinite satisfaction in this contemplation, a satisfaction that spreads to the third person of the Trinity, the single, burning breath of the first two—the Holy Spirit.

The Father begets all the possible ways of participating in his divine essence in the Word who is his only model and with him. There is an almost unlimited number of forms of participation and these have, in the Word, their archetypes, their ideal forms, their species, their order, their place in the hierarchy of values, their harmony, their beauty, their variety and their unity. These qualities have been present in the Word from the time of primeval chaos and the first light of creation, and will be there until the end of time and the consummation of the Church of those who have been redeemed by the blood of the Lamb. They have been there since the creation of the immense starry sky that human eyes will never penetrate and the single grain of sand that I crunch beneath my feet. The splendor of this intelligible world is the beauty of God who embraces it. It is a world that is destined to radiate his glory in the unlimited dispersal of created things and beings.

All beings are rooted in the Word. The Word is the source of the fulfillment of their existence and the origin of all that is most noble and true in that existence. They are both unchanging and eternal in the Word.[1] All things and beings are life there, a life that cannot deteriorate because it is God's life. In the Word, everything is God because in God there is only God.

Only sin is excluded from this ideally pure and true zone because sin is negation and lying. If it is true that everything that can be created is engraved in God and is part of his infinitely simple being, then, as Tauler said, it would be as impossible to take these creatures away from God as it would be to separate God from himself.

We should therefore not be surprised to learn that Plotinus thought of God as an architect who had even the smallest details of every part of the city that he intended to build firmly imprinted in his mind long before his act of creation. We can see, then, that an intelligible city is present in the Word as the Idea of ideas and the eternal model. We can also understand Boethius, that great early spiritual writer who formed the link between Platonic and Scholastic thought, when he declared: "O God, you draw everything from a supreme model, you who are the most beautiful of all beings! You have the beauties of the world in you and you made that world in your own image."[2]

We must know why God creates if we are to understand all these creative ideas that have been present from eternity in the Word. We have to consider the propensity of the one who is infinitely good to express freely, and with a generosity that is worthy of his unlimited richness, the effects of his sovereign goodness. In this creative process, one single creature would clearly not be enough. In the one Word, the one God spreads himself out in a great fan, because he needs an endless number of beings in order to express himself, just as many different words and syllables are required in a speech to express what cannot be articulated by one word. As a result of this, the failure of one creature to express God is made good by another or by all the other creatures. That is why God, confronted with this infinite variety of the creatures that constitute his universe, declared that they were very good (Gen. 1. 31). Taking them as a whole, they constitute the perfection that has always been sought by God and a translucent vision of his wisdom. These created things, which have a transitory and fleeting existence here on earth because their essence is in God himself, are of unspeakable value. As far as it is possible to do so here on earth, to see all these things in the root and cause of their being is to penetrate the divine secret and to regard them as a revelation made by the hidden God who gives himself to us. Because of this, despite the weakness and emptiness of so many of these beings, they are very good and valuable.

When we consider not the mere traces of God in frail, broken-down beings, but immortal creatures made in his image, we can begin to sense the deep meaning of this traditional teaching. Such creatures are not blindly drawn into the great stream of God's providence as more or less perfect likenesses of his goodness. They are rather involved as free agents that are capable of joining God through their intelligence and love—the God who has always, from eternity, kept them in his intelligence and love.

By giving full consent, then, man can return to the full idea that decreed his existence, in the same way that a painter's masterpiece can once again penetrate into the mind that conceived it and thus join its own model. Bossuet expressed this truth magnificently in a letter to Sister Cornuau:

Let yourself flow into that great everything that is God, so that you become nothing but in him alone. You were in him before all time in his eternal decree and you were taken out of that decree by his love which drew you out of nothingness. Return to that idea, to that decree, to that principle and to that love.

Does this not point to the supreme significance of life? In the light of this understanding, what is living but ascending toward oneself and becoming oneself, a self in whom God has been satisfied from eternity, as he is satisfied in his Son, the beloved, whom he begets in begetting me with him? Living is surely feeling that I am both embraced and penetrated by the tenacious will, the *tenax vigor*, of this God who cannot change, *immotus*, and whose tenderness, expectations and call are permanent.[3]

Here on earth, I feel weak and lost, a mere nothing in a world in which everything is tending toward death. My substance seems to be nothing to God, yet I am conscious of a hope, an expectation. That hope is the Lord himself. It is so deep and so alive in me that it has become my very being, a gift in which my whole being is in you. In its most original, pure and permanent form, corresponding to that new and secret name that no one knows except God and the one who receives it (Apoc. 2. 17), my soul is there. That name is a victorious name, given for the conquest for which God has created us and recreated us in his Christ.

In his Christ. This is the point to which the apostle Paul, going further than Plato, leads us, taking us to a deeper level that could be reached only by divine revelation, in his hymn of thanksgiving, joy and adoration in the introduction to his letter to the Ephesians.

In his providence, God has seized hold of that part of the human mind that is most noble and most closely in accordance with the truth and had, moreover, been working for centuries to bring men to an insight into the eternal Logos, the Idea of ideas and the archetype of everything that can be created. A seed of the Word germinated at a given moment in the pagan world and enabled Greek thinkers and Hebrew theologians, who were very near to thinking of wisdom as a hypostasis, to recognize each others' notions as being as closely related as two sisters. Both were therefore ready from then onward to welcome the message of the God-man with the same clarity of a divine hereafter.

It was, however, Paul, the pharisee who had been completely upset, overwhelmed and blinded by the light of the risen Christ on the way to Damascus, who went even further. Dazzled by his vision, the apostle did not separate Christ's human from his divine nature, his temporal from his eternal nature. Paul was both a mystic and a realist. All his thought was concrete. In the Christ who appeared to him, he saw nothing but the only one who exists, the God whose lordship was universal even before he entered time.

There are certain places in Paul's writings that should be read and reread in the light of this heavenly clarity. In the first chapter of his epistle to the Ephesians, the form is breaking under the weight of the all-too-dense thought. In the first chapter of Colossians, the eternal and cosmic Christ, the first-born of all creation in whom are contained all the visible and all the invisible worlds, rises up like a giant.[4]

In God, Jesus' human nature, then, is inseparable from the person of the word who assumed it in time. It is, among the myriads of possible creations, the object of a singular predestination. It is blessed among all human natures and in it we too are blessed, predestined, called and saved. The good shepherd revealed to us in the fourth gospel is already present in God, knowing the sheep whom the Father has entrusted to him by their names in order to lead them to divine pastures. The Father loves us in him, in his own beauty, and before all creation let his glance fall on us in satisfaction and infinite love, without any merit on our part.

Our first cradle, then, is in Christ, who was blessed before all ages, and in the mystery of the Father who created, recapitulated and brought everything back to him, at the cost of a sacrifice already accepted in advance by Christ, for a wedding feast and a blessedness without end. Even before we are born, we are his brothers, his betrothed. This living source of his being and of our being that is inseparable from his must be our point of departure if we are to understand this mystery of love that goes ahead of us and is quite gratuitous. What a great vision there is and what a deep mystery in Christ, for the praise and glory of the Father! It is a mystery in both senses of the word, because it is a reality that is inaccessible to the human mind, but at the same time a reality that is open to our knowledge and our love. It is revealed to us so that we should live from it. As Romano Guardini said, this reality enables us to sense that man and human nature are not face to face with God in the way that we think they are.

All the forms and values that exist in the universe, everything that enters both the depths of man's mind and the cosmic spaces, all human destinies, all the events that help those who love God to love him more, all the grace of salvation, everything that is able to transfigure, deify or glorify man and everything that enables souls to penetrate into the life of the three persons who are consubstantial in the Trinity—all these are contained in the power of Jesus, the only Son in whom the great number of adopted children live. This Jesus is the way, the truth and the life of those who are called to be holy and immaculate in and through him. He is the measure without measure, the norm and the law of everything that is and will be created.

It is certainly inexhaustibly good to follow Jesus step by step, from his birth to his ascension, along the roads of Judea and Galilee. But we should never forget the eternal Jesus, the one who lived before creation and who made his eternal consciousness known when he declared: "I tell you most solemnly, before Abraham ever was, I am" (John 8. 58). It is this Jesus, who is before Abraham was, whom we must embrace. We are present in this "I am" just as he is perfectly present with us and has always been from eternity.

At this point, we should ask this question from a subjective or psychological point of view and ask whether it is possible to experience eternal life in God here and now in this world. Can we, in other words, have any intuition of the preexistent life that precedes our existence in time? I am bound to answer that this intuition can exist in the order of nature and the order of grace, but that it only rarely happens and, when it does, the grace is fleeting.

In the natural order, it can be described as the sudden emergence of a thought that is looking for itself and becoming conscious of itself.[5] It is possible to describe its essential aspects in the following way. I am reflecting. My thought, which is seeking some sublime truth, is also as clear of every image as it is possible to be in the case of a rational creature, whose knowledge usually reaches him through the windows of his soul, his senses. It continues slowly along its pure path, when I am suddenly seized by a kind of evidence. How did I, who am thinking in this way, begin to exist on this earth?

I know that I was born at a given moment in time and at a given place in space. I know too that my existence had for a long time been prepared by a whole network of contingencies that resulted in the coming together of the man and the woman who were my parents. But this is not the question with which we are concerned here. The real question is: how is it that, before being born, I was simply a nothing? This knowledge is not the result of a logical deduction. It is a flash of intuition that crosses my mind and a kind of certainty that strikes me. I do, however, begin to reflect at this point and I deduce therefore that, if I have always had a preexistence, it must have been somewhere. Where, then, was I?

It is clear that this preexistence could not have been in myself, within the limits of my personality that was at first confused and uncertain, but which has become firmer and more clearly defined with the passage of the years. It must therefore have been in the life of a being who is beyond all created being and from whom all created being emanates. It was in the life of a transcendent and eternal being from whom I have never been separated and who has left his indelible impression on me. It was in the life of someone who is more myself than I am in receiving the being of his being. I have therefore to make a distinction between this life on earth and that existence outside time which I have in God.

This is an important experience and we do not know exactly what part is played by actual grace in the fact that, if only for a moment, the soul has broken through the limitations of time and its own personality and has breathed the atmosphere of the mystery beyond this life. This intuition may even play an important part in our search for God.

There is, however, also another experience that is less fleeting and much more delectable. Sometimes this other experience is obscure and at others it is shot through with a light that may even dazzle us. It is the experience of a soul that has been made more interior by love and renunciation and especially favored with the gift of contemplation by the one to whose will it is completely abandoned. In this experience, the soul is brought by grace back to its center, its most intimate depths and the root of its powers, the place where it is nothing but an impulse toward God and where the eternal image that presided at its creation is inscribed.

It would, after all, be naive and even wrong to think of the eternal model according to which we were created as a kind of ideal reality hanging above our head and with no more than slight contact with this poor being fashioned from clay who struggles as well as he can within the limits of his finite personality. We can distinguish between our eternal being carried along in the generation of the God who is three times holy, the age without a beginning or an end, and our being that has been created in time and space, but we can never separate the two. This ideal being, which is divine and which cannot be touched by sin, shines in the deepest center of our life and lives there in the inviolable purity of the image of our creator.

The depths of our soul reflect the Trinity as a mirror so closely united to the image it reflects that it is inseparable from it. The contemplatives are those who, thanks to the virtues that make them resemble God himself, have found the purity of this image that is unfortunately hidden in the most intimate sanctuary of our being beneath the rust of imperfection and sin. With God and in God, they discover themselves in the intimacy of their true selves, both beyond their own personality and also in the most intimate part of that personality and both beyond their created selves, where they have always been and will always be, and within their created selves. They therefore find their point of departure and their place of origin at the point where they arrive.

Their faith is stripped of all excrescences and is quite translucent, and in it they are able to some extent to perceive the life of the Trinity of which they are themselves the image. According to Jan van Ruysbroeck, they live "in the fertile nature of the heavenly Father without being either manifested or begotten. They are begotten as the chosen of the Father in the Son and are eternally loved in the Spirit."[6] The man who has been led to the point where he is blessed by this experience will therefore know, as his eternal dwelling place, the place to which he returns thanks to his existence here on earth and in the full freedom of a soul transfigured by God's gifts and virtues.

The life that he has found in this experience is a "living life"— it was Ruysbroeck who called it this, borrowing the term perhaps from Saint Bernard—a life beyond all ages, a life that will never die, a life that is always alert, even if our body is sleeping and renewing its strength in an apparently unconscious state, a life that will survive beyond our sins and a life to which we can always be connected whatever our situation may be.

This doctrine of a higher and eternal life may seem to those who have not had this experience, or who are too far removed from it to be able to understand because they are too closely involved in creation, to be so sublime that it is almost valueless. They may also think that it is a truth that is so remote from the contingencies of our everyday existence that it should be relegated to the sphere of those ideals that have hardly any effect on our moral life. This is, however, not the case at all, since the most sublime truths are almost always the most practical.

When we try to grasp the reality of a higher form of life in the most intimate part of our being, which is at the same time the root of our existence and God's gaze directed toward us, we see ourselves and all things in the perspective of their eternal truth. In the depths of this pure blue on which we rest—"I will set your foundations on sapphires" (Isa. 54. 11)—we are no longer tempted to say that we were created at a given moment, something that satisfies our imagination more than our reason enlightened by faith and makes us believe that at that given moment God acted within time. This too is a misunderstanding of his unchanging sovereignty and his eternity, which has no moments, but is a duration that does not last and which should be thought of not as an endless line, but as a dot.

If we hope to sink to these depths of our soul where our true life is to be found, we must know that this can only be done if we are truly recollected. This recollection is much more than simply overcoming external distractions so that we can devote our heart and mind to the things of God. In the unity of all being, it is a descent into the most austere and authentic part of our being, where we are ultimately united with our uncreated source. A kind of flowing back then takes place in us. Our sensory powers are taken back to our higher faculties and these are plunged into the divine depths in which the bond between Spirit and spirit is effective and becomes a supratemporal unity between the transcendent God and us, who are the place where he is immanent.

Louis de Blois, who was one of Ruysbroeck's most fervent disciples and who followed the same patristic tradition as his master, used the most persuasive language to impress on us the need to discover the most noble element of our being. This is apparent from the conclusion of his *Institution spirituelle:*

O noble center! O divine temple which the Lord never leaves! Excellent retreat! Dwelling of the holy Trinity! Source here on earth of eternal pleasures! To return once to this center, to God himself, is a thousand times better than anything that we can do in this world. If you have been wasting your time for ten years or more, everything can be redeemed by this simple movement. A source of living water springs from this center of the soul. It is for eternity and it is so fresh and so effective that it can never be opposed by the bitterness of vice. In its presence, nature soon ceases to resist. It is a refreshing drink that spreads an excellent purity and a wonderful fertility in the soul and the body. We should never tire of going to this fountain. We only have to taste its waters to forget at once the thirst of vanities and corruptible creatures and to have one single desire: God and his love.[7]

Another blessing that is derived from returning to this center of the soul is that we can enjoy there a kind of solidarity consisting of harmony and peace with the whole of creation living with us in the Father's Word. In this solidarity, the Father contemplates his creation in his Son.

There, we are conscious of and in touch with a relationship in God between ourselves and all things. One of the undoubted effects of the gift of divine wisdom is not to make us ascend from God's creatures to God himself—the gift of knowledge does this—but to make us see God first and all his creatures as eternally born in him and coming from him through the inexpressible gratuity of his creative love. Chesterton believed that, for the just man, everything that existed illustrated and threw light on God, whereas for the true contemplative, it was God who illustrated and threw light on everything that existed. In his soul, then, the contemplative lives in a mysterious but very real brotherhood with everything that has ever been created and derives a pure, holy joy from that communion.

This teaching applies particularly to our life with our fellow human beings, since it is the very basis of our love for them. As Ruysbroeck pointed out:

> If we continue to be united with each other by charity and by the community of human nature, we shall certainly be united by the superior life in which we are united to God in a union which goes beyond sense and reason and which makes us one spirit and life with God.[8]

Ruysbroeck also stressed that the image in which we were created was both essential and personal to all men:

> Each one of us has this image entirely and undivided and all men together do not have any more of it than any one of them. In this way, we are all one. We are intimately united in our image which is the eternal image of God and the source in us of our life and our claim to existence.

We are therefore all called to find this image by likeness and blessed in Christ before all creation. We are united and included within the same creative and redemptive thought and the same plan of love for the execution of this symphony of countless voices, this voice of the great waters that the visionary of Patmos heard, the voice expressing the collective name and the individual name of each one.

In this symphony that is completely one, each one is a single note because, as we have seen, each one is an inimitable sharing in the divine essence that is quite simple, but at the same time infinitely imitable. If, then, this truth of our eternal life in God is the deepest reason for our communion with everything that is created and for our love of our fellow human beings, it is also the deepest cause of our faithfulness to our own way and our respect for the way followed by others.

There are many paths within this one, immense and universal way which is Christ himself and along which he goes ahead of us as the good shepherd. Each one of us has his own path that has been destined for him from eternity. If we explore within these limits and at the same time are in communication with our fellow-men in charity, we shall reach the infinity of God.

Christian wisdom is achieved in discovering our own path, responding to the eternal formula provided by God about himself, removing what is useless and only distracts our attention by appealing to our empty curiosity, abandoning ourselves to God's will as manifested in the many different works of divine providence, which can be found in a hidden form in what we call life's contingencies, and bringing all this into harmony with the inner movements of divine grace. The way of Christian wisdom is a humble, but nonetheless great way. The Father of light, from whom every perfect gift comes and who, according to Thomas Aquinas, was the "ultimate reality toward which everything moves," invites us to follow that way in his only Son.

Now the Father, who bears in himself everything that we are to become, has given us existence. This is his first gift. Because of this, we must now place ourselves before him, our creator, and try to examine his presence of immensity, from which nothing that exists can escape.

NOTES

1. Augustine, *De Gen. ad lit.*, 5. 23, 45.
2. *De consolatione*, 3; *PG* 63. 58, 59.
3. *Rerum Deus tenax vigor, / Immotus in te permanens.* ("God, steadfast power of things, motionless and enduring in yourself.") Hymn sung at None.
4. See Jean Mouroux, *Le Mystère du temps*, p. 81, on "the Word and time." In this context, I would recommend one of the best chapters in Romano Guardini's book *The Lord*—the chapter dealing with "the first-born before all creation."
5. This experience was analyzed by Jacques Maritain in his *Approche de Dieu*, pp. 81ff. Those who have undergone it know that it contains real

evidence of God's existence and that it is neither too subtle nor too hypothetical to form a "sixth way."

6. Ruysbroeck, *The Seven Bolts*, 15.

7. *Oeuvres spirituelles*, II, p. 103.

8. *A Mirror of Blessedness*, 8.

2

The Creative Presence of Immensity

God the creator—everything that is eternally life in his Word is what God, as it were, throws out of himself, holding it up over the abyss of nothingness by the all-powerful word of his Word and the all-powerful will of his Spirit of love. Irenaeus called the Word and the Spirit the two creative hands of God.[1]

The Word, the Wisdom of the Father, was already revealed in the book of Genesis, in that divisive word, which the author of the letter to the Hebrews compared to a two-edged sword (Heb. 4. 12). With every "let there be" pronounced by God, each of the elements of primeval chaos is separated and given its place in creation. The Spirit of God is there, hovering over the waters, unchanging, like a great bird brooding over its eggs and beating its wings to fan into being sometimes a powerful wind and at others a gentle breeze so that they will hatch and reach maturity.

As the creatures pass slowly and in silence, everything moves, on the Father's initiative, toward its end, to what it will become. Animate and inanimate creatures—everything finds its completion in man, in whose soul God wants above all to dwell. Then man himself, descending from the first Adam, moves toward the God-man, the second Adam, Jesus. An unutterable impression of majesty, order and harmony and of great wealth and abundance emerges from the biblical story of creation.

How special for us is this appearance of being, this great spectrum of beauty spread out to receive us, this first sun of the first morning! Having appeared on earth, we poor little human creatures were taught by God to look at the infinitely varied splendors of his natural creation around us. The gentle plain, the great expanse of the seas, the high mountains, exciting rather than crushing the human spirit in their ascent to heaven, and the blade of grass sparkling with drops of dew—all these speak to us of the greatness and goodness of God.

When we consider creation, as presented to us in the Bible, we are a very long way from the conception of the ancient Greek philosophers. They thought of creation in its ideal state as the Idea of ideas that was the divine Logos, and regarded the natural world as a descent or fall of that one ideal form into matter. The one had been reduced, like dust, to many particles.

In Scripture, on the other hand, everything coming from God's creative activity is very good. Despite man's sin—a terrible accident, but after all one that can be overcome—God achieves his purpose and everything is remade admirably for his glory. God himself created matter as well as souls and, far from serving as a prison for the soul, it is saturated with spirit and is its channel. Everything that we meet on our long journey throughout history points to God's intense concern with this reality of creation that his entirely gratuitous love has brought into being.

Creation, then, is far from being a loss or a fall. On the contrary, it is a beginning. It is the beginning of an eternal plan of mercy and glory that is carried out in a series of interventions, promises and covenants in which the spring of goodness that pours from the heart of the transcendent God overflows and never dries up.

The first appearance of each one of us in time and space is clearly of utmost importance for us. What use would it have been for God to have thought of us from eternity if he had not created us? This point at which our existence began dominates our life and our entire destiny. It is the foundation stone of the great virtue of hope that forms the motivation, the nourishment and the impetus which drive man forward on his way toward the conquest of himself that is the fruit of collaboration between his creator and himself.

In God, in his eternal thought, we were God, but now we are no longer God. We are, however, called to become gods: "I say, 'You are gods' " (Ps. 82. 6). Not miserable little idols standing on an imaginary pedestal, but real images of God, with thoughts and wills— gods by participation as adopted sons. The world is, man exists, a lit-

tle lower than the angles (Ps. 8) and God is good with a totally gratuitous goodness. This opens up an immense perspective of
inexhaustible richness and fruitfulness. We enter a future wrapped
in a mystery that we can only sense and which only God can pierce,
a future that is destined to be lost in God's infinity.

Everything flows from this first act of existence—the pouring
out of grace that fills the abyss between what is created and what
is uncreated and raises us up to God. Then, after the fall, the sad
consequence of our freedom, there is the redeeming act of the incarnation. Then there is, after mankind has at length been gradually
saved and deified, consummation in the splendor of unity and in
glory.

God, who called us into existence, is always unchangeably present with his creature. If he were not, we should return to nothingness. But our very creation implies a dramatic and mysterious contrast—we are separated from God, yet are at the same time totally
dependent on him forever.

We are separated from God. Since every creature dwells in
God's thought before receiving its existence from him, it begins, at
creation, to move away from its principle. "The creature begins by
moving away," Saint Bonaventure declared. Theologians claim that
there is a separation of the being of the effect from the being of the
divine cause, because the effect is thrown out of its divine cause in
order to live its own life in autonomy. It is clear that we are in fact
self-sufficient and able to manage on our own resources and become
the efficient cause of our own actions.

We are totally and permanently dependent on God. Preaching
to the people of Athens, the apostle Paul said: "In God we live and
move and exist" (Acts 17. 28). We cannot exist for a single moment
without the support of this creative act that continues so that we
can go on living in time and in this way becomes an act of preser-
vation. We cannot go on living without this constant flow that
springs from the depths of our being and makes God poured into us
rather than simply near us.

We have the task of reflecting about this creative presence of
immensity and it should be the object of our faith and loving adoration, but we should not attempt to portray it. It is, after all, impossible to portray the presence of a pure spirit. How could we in-
vest with any image or combine with any matter such a subtle and
airy presence? How could we subject this divine essence, which is

absolutely pure, simple and indivisible, to the laws of space? While he was still under the influence of Manichaean thought, Augustine did not avoid this danger.[2] He later warned Christians against this serious error in a long letter to Dardanus, which is almost a complete treatise on the presence of God.

To give us an idea of this mysterious presence, Augustine discusses such intellectual, moral and even physical qualities as wisdom, justice, health and purity and shows that they are indivisibly the same both in a small body and in a large body and also in the whole body as well as in any one of its parts.

"God," he declares, "is present because he is not absent from anything and because he is entirely present everywhere."[3] These qualities are present in a substance which upholds them. Why, then, Augustine reasoned, should the substance of God the creator, who is complete in himself, whether or not he finds another substance that is capable of receiving him, not be able to do what the quality of the created body can do in a body?[4]

It is this absolute spirituality of God that enables us to understand that it is also true that God is in us and that we are in him. It is not difficult to grasp that, unlike corporeal realities, the spiritual qualities are able to contain that in which they find themselves, since they are gifted with a power to penetrate and enclose, so that nothing can escape from their grip. It is probably this very power to possess us, either by penetrating or enclosing, which God has as an integral aspect of his divine essence, that inspired Ben Sirach to say that "in a word, God is all things." This is undoubtedly the real meaning of the Greek version of Ecclesiastes 43. 29, which has been toned down in the Vulgate translation.

We are surrounded by God and full of him. He dwells in the most intimate parts of our being. He is in us and we are in him. As Saint Gregory, following Saint Hilary, said: "God dwells in us entirely. He is outside us, above us and below us. He penetrates beings by dwelling near them and he dwells beside them by penetrating them. His energy, greatness, power and subtlety shine out."[6] It is because he transcends us that nothing can escape his immanence, and in us he is more ourselves than we are.

A very striking word that the Fathers of the Church and even later theologians used to express the intimate nature of God's creative virtue was "touch" or "contact." Clearly, in using it, they were not thinking of touching in the purely human sense. It is worth recalling, however, in this context that there are degrees in human touching. There is, for example, on the one hand, a light, superficial and passing touch and, on the other, a deep and penetrating touch, like that of the artist shaping a statue, giving the clay the form that he has in his mind by the skillful and intelligent pressure of his fingers and illuminating the whole shape with the living light of his soul.

This second kind of touching is intimate, but it is still infinitely far from the touch of God, because what is touched by human hands in this way is a preexistant matter that was not created by man. God's touch presupposes nothing, but it brings about what suddenly springs from the hand that acts according to the eternal model. It is a touch that is so spiritual, pure and virginal that it calls quite spontaneously into being the one who is, the life of the one who is life and the movement of the one who is motionless because of an excess of vital movement. It does this with such abundance that it is for us an inexhaustible source of astonishment and thanksgiving. This touch of God was described by a commentator on the work of Thomas Aquinas[7] as *perfectissimus*—absolutely perfect— *summe intimus*—supremely intimate—and *illapsivus*—penetrating. The end of this divine touch is the fruit of its action and it leaves an indelible impression on the being that is brought into existence by its impulse. It enables that being to turn back to the one who created it and is its weight, its attractive power and its entire good.

We must pause for a little while and consider the reality of that being. God has the key to the mystery of that reality and we can see only its appearance, its qualities and the ways in which it manifests itself. Can we ever do more than simply guess at the energies that are hidden in this being? Those forests of oak trees that can grow from a single acorn? The one huge tree from which so many others come—from a single grain of mustard seed? That embryo that will become a child—can it contain all those material and spiritual promises? This being is the deepest and most intimate aspect each reality that exists contains. It is from this being that each subject receives its presence with itself.

God is in his creatures by the gift of this being more completely than the soul is in the body, since he is much more than the principle of life. He is the root of the whole of his creation by his work. This is what we have to bear firmly in mind when we consider Claudel's statement: "O God, you are in me more myself than I am!"

It is impossible to overemphasize the enormous power of this creative influence that transforms us into the living work of the one who is alive and makes us totally dependent on him. The saints who have suffered and have undergone this change have experienced lasting happiness in it. Every Christian can be greatly strengthened by an insight into God's creative power. In this power, he can be sure that his faith is protected against loss. It is not only the source of great joy—it also makes us want to penetrate the mystery of the nature of the God who bears us up and surrounds us always.

Yet, in spite of God's constant presence, his sovereign goodness and his holiness remain hidden even from the angels. Isaiah tells us that the most exalted of these pure spirits, proclaiming God's holiness three times, cover their faces with their wings (Isa. 6. 2–3). In his commentary on the prophet Ezekiel, Gregory the Great said:

> Let us place before the eyes of our spirit the reality of this divine nature which embraces, fills and upholds us. It does not simply partly embrace us. It fills us as it embraces us and embraces us as it fills us. It rules us as it upholds us and upholds us as it rules us. When, with our limited intelligence, we think of the power of this nature, a voice is heard above the firmament, according to the prophet's words, because the spirit thinks in this way of the intelligence of the one who, because he is incomprehensible, goes beyond the intelligence of the angels.[8]

Saint Gregory also said that God's creative touch is filled not only with his power and gratuitous love, but also with his generosity and riches. God is one in his essence, but he is also infinitely diverse. This is because, as we have seen, he touches beings following countless ideas, models and types, all of which are contained eternally in the Word, from whom, as Augustine declared, "all beauty and order come and the seeds of forms and the forms of seeds are derived."[9]

"God touches what he creates, but he does not touch all equally," Saint Gregory claimed, going on to point out how there are contacts conferring being without life or feeling, others which bestow being, life and feeling and yet others which give being, life, feeling and intelligence. It was with this last touch that God created angels and men. In this way, although he is always the same, God touches different beings in a different way.[10]

What, then, is the full implication of this touching by God for man? God touched man with particular pleasure because he wanted to bring about in him his eternal plan of salvation and glory. He wanted to make each one of us a privileged being at the heart of his created universe. He wanted each one of us to be intelligent, free and with a soul made in his image and called to join him. He touched us and continues to touch us by creating us and to create us by touching us.

For man, then, God's creative touch is an illuminating touch. We have been created as reasonable beings and it is possible for grace to raise us higher than nature and adapt us to God's being. This is because the Word of God, who is the knowledge that the Father has of himself and the infinity of his understanding and contemplation, puts us continually in contact with himself, the light that never sets.

In the prologue to his gospel, Saint John calls him the light that enlightens all men (1. 9), and Cyril of Alexandria wrote: "The essential light is the Son of God and every being gifted with reason is like a beautiful vase shaped by the great artist of the universe so that it can be filled with this divine light. The eternal Word leaves in our souls emanations of his own substance."[11]

The Scholastic theologians knew that, before giving man supernatural light, the Word continues to speak to him through the brightness of the great rational and moral principles that are the luminous stamp that God leaves on the soul. God directs this natural light that he pours into the soul in such a way that the human spirit cannot act without the operation of the first cause, God himself. Saint Thomas goes on to say: "The natural light that is in us is a participation by likeness in the uncreated light which contains in itself the eternal reasons."[12]

This helps us to understand the enthusiasm that the Fathers of the Church felt in the presence of God's masterpiece, man. Reason, wisdom, order, speech and knowledge—God sees all these realities in his Word, contemplates them with love and knows that the name "Word" points to all these noble qualities that shine in man and, as Saint Athanasius said, make him the "shadow of the Word." Saint Ambrose declared: "To do all things with the Word, all things must be done with reason, for, O Man, you are a reasonable being."[13] And because Christ is, according to Origen, "the crown of rational nature," there are points of contact, even natural ones, between the soul of man and the incarnate Word. It is because of this that Tertullian was able to say that man's soul is naturally Christian.[14]

But, among these countless human beings who come into being

each moment at the touch of God, there are no two that are absolutely similar. Each is unique. Each is called into existence at a certain point in time and space with the freshness and newness that mark everything that comes from God, who is both the Ancient of Days and the eternal Today. God creates us without cause. He never ceases to create us, in such a way that he is there, at the root of our being, now for the first time and has also always been there from eternity.

Some souls may, for a very brief space of time, be able to see in quite a natural way the emergence of all created beings, including themselves, from God who is present at the very source of their beings, the suspension of everything that belongs to the highest one in existence. When this happens, we are made aware of God's presence with extraordinary certainty. The evidence exists beyond all doubt. We become conscious of his presence in a peaceful flash, as it were, of intuition that goes beyond reason.

We do not know precisely what part is played by actual grace, secretly working within this experience, but we do know that we must thank God, who is so great and inaccessible to us, for letting us undergo the experience. However mysterious our contact with him is, it certainly exists. We do not know what he is, but we do know that he is and, what is more, that he is there.[15] The intuition is so powerful that anyone who experiences it is bound to regard it as an authentic proof of the existence of God. The sight of this being with nothing calls for the necessity of the Being with nothing. It is a real illumination that moves from one imperative certainty to another.

This experience is, of course, unusual and only rarely happens. Far more common is a movement of rational thought motivated by goodwill that begins with the knowable effects of creation and ends with their invisible first cause. Saint Paul was speaking of this process in Romans 1. 20, when he said that the pagans could not be excused for failing to find the one God behind his creation, which is, after all, no more than the reflection of his invisible perfections.

It is, however, even more delightful to discover God's creative presence of immensity in those in whom he lives through faith and in whom the God who lives in the soul joins the God who both reveals and conceals himself behind the veil of created things. This process can be followed from error to truth in the confessions of Augustine, that great expert in the psychology of conversion. For a very long time, he remained captivated by the charm of creatures and did not let himself be raised up from them to their creator. He, who was so sensitive, continued to be seduced by them, instead of looking for God first of all in himself. Later, this caused him infinite regret: "Too late have I come to love you, O beauty so old and so new, too late have I come to love you. And yet you were within me and I was outside myself!" Then he adds these words, pregnant with meaning, to which we will return: "You were with me, but I was not with you. And they kept me far from you, those things which would not be if they were not in you." He concludes with the moving and concise description of the overwhelming effects of grace: "You called me and your cry broke through my deafness . . . You breathed out your fragrance and I breathed it in and yet it is for you that I sigh. I have tasted you and yet I am still hungry for you. You touched me and I am burning with love for the peace that you give me."[16]

Augustine, then, and all who have been transfigured by grace believe that the world has been transformed by the radiation of God's presence in the love that spreads in light and the light that is disseminated in love. It is much more than a concealing appearance. It is a revealing and transparent reality. There would undoubtedly be one single answer from all creatures if they were questioned about their identity. They would say that they were not God and that they had not created themselves. They had come from the creator, they would insist, and were a radiation of his beauty and signs of his presence.

Augustine had loved too much as a sensual man, but he found all this in God living in his soul, transformed and offered for the delight of the new man. In loving God, he loved "a light, a voice, a fragrance, a food, an embrace." He described this love as

the light, the voice, the fragrance, the food, the embrace of the inner man in me. What shines into my soul is a light that is limited by no space, a voice that sings melodies that are not taken away by time, a fragrance that is not dispelled by a breath of wind, a food with a taste that is not destroyed by eating and an embrace that is not broken by satiety. This is what I love when I love my God.[17]

Those, then, whose "eyes are enlightened by their heart" find in their experience the truth of the beatitude: "Happy are the pure in heart: they shall see God." We know, of course, that the obvious meaning of this promise points to what life would be like if the kingdom of God were suddenly revealed in its fullness. This promise also indicates what attitude is needed by man who is renewed by the light of life and blessed with a vision of God whom he can see beyond all created things. God's invisibility is pierced by man's intelligence through the created world that can be seen. This means that everything, even what is most insignificant and humble, is an object of wonder.

What are these everyday things that remind us of God? The little flower that has just enough space between two stones in an old wall to press its stem and open its leaves and blossom, the thick shadow of night, that great black-eyed girl surrounding our sleep—these reveal God's infinite gentleness and love as much as the great ocean, the dark forest or the vault of heaven studded with stars. Everything expresses God's generosity, beauty, order and wisdom. Everything in creation is an apocalypse of the Word in whom, Saint Athanasius declared, was disclosed eternal reason, the conceiver and creator of all things and the one who has left in the world a trace of his constant movement in it.[18]

There are several saints—Francis of Assisi, for example, or Paul of the Cross—whose hearts were wounded by God's love, a wound that Origen, in the Prologue to his Commentary on the Song of Songs, described as the result of contemplating nature adorned with beauty: "Struck by the beauty of things and pierced by the magnificence of their splendour as by an electron dart, he will, according to the prophet, receive salvation and burn with the blessed fire of his love."[19]

How could this contemplation result in anything else but burning love, when God's Word is both the art and the artist is almighty God himself. The Word contains within himself all the shapes, forms, colors and voices of nature, because he is always there, working with the Father and the Spirit to unfurl before the gaze of us men the marvelous flag that probably belonged to the world of angels before it came to us like the white light of a prism.

Like the bridegroom in the Song of Songs seen through the latticework of the window, God is there, behind his creation and, if we listen attentively to the voice of his silence, he will teach us to look—to look at him behind the veil of his things. It is, after all, true to say that "to know God through the world is in itself a kind of revelation. My spirit does not rise from the world up to God—on the contrary, it is God who descends, through the world, to my spirit. God gives me a sign and I must be alert to it. The initiative, however, does not come from me."[20]

The prophets and the authors of the Wisdom literature in the Old Testament proclaimed again and again the creative presence of immensity. Jeremiah asked: "Can anyone hide in a dark corner without my seeing him? It is Yahweh who speaks. Do I not fill heaven and earth? It is Yahweh who speaks" (23. 24). The author of the book of Wisdom said that the Spirit of the Lord filled the universe and described Wisdom as being so pure that she pervaded and permeated all things. "She is the breath of the power of God," spreading "her strength from one end of the earth to the other, ordering all things for good" (7. 24, 25; 8. 1).

How many more texts from the Old Testament could be quoted to illustrate this theme! Some of the psalms especially are full of a tender and spirited lyricism in their expression of the beauty, order and infinite variety of the created universe.[21] One of them is perhaps more worthy of our attention than the rest, because it expresses so eloquently the presence of God in the universe from the vantage point of his omniscience and because its author seems to be almost outside himself in his deep consciousness of God's presence:

Lord, you examine me and know me,
you know if I am standing or sitting,
you read my thoughts from far away,
whether I walk or lie down, you are watching,
you know every detail of my conduct.

The word is not even on my tongue,
Lord, before you know all about it;
close behind me and close in front you fence me round,
shielding me with your hand.
Such knowledge is beyond my understanding,
a height to which my mind cannot attain.

Where could I go to escape your spirit?
Where could I flee from your presence?
If I climb the heavens, you are there,
there too, if I lie in Sheol.

If I flew to the point of sunrise,
or westward across the sea,

your hand would still be guiding me,
your right hand holding me.

If I asked darkness to cover me,
and light to become night around me,
that darkness would not be dark to you,
night would be as light as day.

It was you who created my inmost self.
and put me together in my mother's womb;
for all these mysteries I thank you:
for the wonder of myself, for the wonder of your works.

You know me through and through,
from having watched my bones take shape
when I was being formed in secret,
knitted together in the limbo of the womb.[22]

This awareness of God's presence has been no less important for Christians than it was for the psalmist. It made Gertrude the Great, for example, tremble with joy, feeling herself pierced by God's gaze. All Israel's consciousness and expression of the eternal truth, then, was experienced later by the Church. Christians throughout the ages have been carried away by love of God's creation and have seen that creation in the Word who assumed our humanity by taking a body—that creation which reflects the presence of God the creator.

Moses and the people of Israel recognized God's creative presence in the desert, but Christians have always been even more vividly reminded of the abundance of creation. The two basic elements of the earth that provide food and drink for man—wheat and the vine—have for them also become the elements of salvation—the body and blood of Christ. In the knowledge of what is hidden in these signs and symbols, the Church happily recalls, in the liturgy, the wonderful events in the history of Israel and calls on elements that break the ordinary laws of creation in an act of obedience to the God who came among his people with the purpose of saving them. The sea suddenly took flight, the Jordan ceased to flow, the mountains skipped like rams and the hills like lambs. The rock split open and water flowed out and the desert began to flower.

The Israelites were aware of God's presence, but the Christian should be even more aware that he is behind his creation like a mother smiling over her child. The sun, bright gold tinged with purple, goes to rest and becomes gradually blurred above the heavy grey-blue clouds. This is not simply a grand, majestic spectacle. It is also a revelation of the mystery of God and his creation.

God did not just let his presence be affirmed by the inspired words of the Old Testament authors. Under the old covenant, he also made it known by those mysterious interventions that we call theophanies. Several of these are recorded in the Bible. His great plan of love and salvation could not have been achieved without them. He wanted the people whom he chose for himself and whom he called to be a torch illuminated for the world—the messianic race—even before they became a nation to know that he was present, and he wanted them to take part in his plan of salvation. To ensure their collaboration, he revealed himself again and again in different ways. Sometimes he came as a voice, an angel or a man. Sometimes he showed himself in the form of fire, a storm or a gentle breeze. He came to man sometimes when he was awake, at others in his sleep. He often appeared to men when he gave them a task— Noah, Abraham, Isaac, Jacob, the parents of the judge, Samson, Moses, Elijah, Isaiah, Ezekiel and Daniel. He even appeared to the twelve tribes together and to Solomon and the people praying in the temple. Such appearances were always deeply impressive and those who experienced them received the grace of reverence, power and confidence in God's providence.

What is the meaning of this way of acting? Would it not be right to say that God became human and, despite the distance that separated him as uncreated from what was created and the gulf between time and eternity and the finite and the infinite, came into contact with men? He spoke to men, after all, showed them their way, confided his secrets to them and appeared to them when he made promises or a covenant with them. In one of his interventions into human history, he struggled with his creature Jacob and pretended to be defeated, as he does when we pray to him.

The Fathers of the Church boldly claimed that he was foreshadowing his incarnation in these actions, trying out his ultimate revelation of himself in the Word, because he delighted to be with the children of men. In the fullness of time, he would be the Emmanuel, God-with-us. For more than thirty years, the virginal Word, as Saint Ambrose called the Son who was born in the womb of the Virgin Mary after being conceived by the breath of the Spirit, was present in the flesh of a man who was to draw all men to himself (John 12.

32), in a sacrificial act of perfect love. Cajetan called the redeeming incarnation the assumption of the universe by the Son of God.[23]

In Christ, God's presence pours grace over all men, whose destiny is to become the body of Christ. Beyond this presence, there is only one Christ who loves himself in the clear view of heaven, but even before this end is reached, when glory and unity will be achieved in a triumphant love, Jesus, the God-man and mediator, has already fulfilled in his own person what was foreshadowed in the Old Testament theophanies.

Jesus, then, is the fulfillment of the ladder seen in a dream by Jacob, with angels going up and coming down, the angel with whom, like Jacob, we fight to beat God and to be beaten by him, the burning bush burnt without being consumed by God's fire, and the true temple where God manifests his glory and men pray in spirit and truth. He is already eternally present in the world and in his Church. He is the same today, yesterday and forever (Heb. 13. 8). Then, in our ultimate home, he is the Lamb who enlightens the heavenly city and the one who is unchangeably present and who will receive us.

NOTES

1. "God did not lack hands to do what he had decided in himself to do. He always had close to him the Word and Wisdom, the Son and the Spirit, through whom and in whom he did everything freely and of his own accord and to whom he also said: ' "Let us make man . . .' " (*Adv. haer.*, 4. 20, 1). This passage may perhaps recall Job 11. 8 and Psalm 119. 73.

2. *Confessions*, 5. 10.

3. *Ep.* 137. 5, 17.

4. *Ibid.*, 4, 10.

5. Dom Hilaire Duesberg has provided the following commentary on these words of Ben Sirach: "Was the author making an offering on the altar of pantheism? A lapse of this kind would be very surprising in one who never ceased to celebrate the one God again and again in powerful language. No, Yahweh, Ben Sirach is saying, is all things in the world in that he is the only explanation of those things. The existence of these things cannot be justified in itself, nor can their finality. All things, even the most lowly, come from God in order to return to him. They participate in the perfections of the one who made them and whom, in return, they proclaim" ("Il est le Tout," *Bible et Vie chrétienne*, 54, p. 31). My development of the theme is, I think, in accordance with Dom Hilaire's commentary.

6. "He dwells in all things. He dwells outside all things. He dwells below all things, higher by his power, lower by his position and inside by his subtlety, ruling from above, supporting from below, encircling from out-

side, penetrating inside ... Unique and the same, entirely present, he supports by ruling and rules by supporting, he penetrates by encircling and encircles by penetrating" (*Moral.*, 1. 12).

7. John of Saint Thomas, *Quaest.* 1 *pars, dist.* 8, ad 3.

8. *In Ez.*, hom. 8, note 16.

9. Augustine, *City of God*, 4. 2.

10. *In Ez.*, hom. 8, note 16.

11. *In Joh.*, 3. 1.

12. *Summa Theologiae*, 1a, q. 84, a. 5.

13. *In Ps. CXVIII*, Sermo 14. Hamlet's lines from Shakespeare's play (II, ii) are very much in accordance with the ideas of the Fathers of the Church: "What a piece of work is man, how noble in reason, how infinite in faculties, in form and moving how express, and admirable, in action how like an angel, in apprehension how like a god: the beauty of the world, the paragon of animals."

14. Apol., 17.

15. This experience can assume many forms. Raissa Maritain has described one that is interesting because it shows how deep and sensitive her soul was, even before her conversion: "Once, on a train journey, looking out of the window at the forests going past, I felt the presence of God for the second time in my life. (I had this powerful but fleeting emotion the first time when I was reading Plotinus.) I was looking out and thinking of nothing in particular. Suddenly, a deep change took place in me. It was as though I had passed from sense perception to an entirely inner perception. The trees moving past had suddenly become bigger than themselves. They had become immensely deep. The whole forest seemed to be speaking and speaking of Another. It had become a forest of symbols and seemed to have no other function than that of pointing to the creator ... Before I gained the certainty of faith, it often occurred to me to test, by means of a sudden intuition, the reality of my being, of the deep first principle which places me outside the void. This intuition was sometimes so violent that it frightened me. It also gave me my first insight into a metaphysical absolute" (*Les grandes amitiés*, IV, p. 155).

16. *Confessions*, 10. 27.

17. *Ibid.*, 10. 6.

18. *Contra Gentes*, 47; *PG* 25. 94.

19. Prologue to the Commentary on the Canticle, *PG* 13. 67.

20. Henri de Lubac, *Cité nouvelle*, 23 February 1942: "Reflections on the Idea of God."

21. See especially Psalm 104. Chapters 42 and 43 of the book of Ecclesiasticus also bear witness to this admiration that is unending as a source of joy. These feelings are summed up in Psalm 92. 4–5: "I am happy, Lord, at what you have done; at your achievements I joyfully exclaim: 'Great are your achievements, Lord, immensely deep are your thoughts!' "

22. Psalm 139.

23. IIIa, q. 1, 8.

3

Grace: Preliminaries

There are so many wonders contained within the mystery of grace that, however fervently we may long for the infinite goodness of God, it always lies outside our reach. It is indeed so far beyond us that we are seldom able to be fully conscious of the magnitude and depth of this inexpressible gift. According to Catherine of Siena, the gift of grace is so powerful that, if we were able to see a soul in a state of grace, we would surely die.

"He spoke as he was able to speak," Saint Augustine declared in one of his sermons on the words of the beloved apostle. It is, after all, hardly surprising that it should be so difficult to speak about the mystery of grace. Grace, which comes directly from the depths of the Trinity itself, is the gift of God, who is love and whose plan is for beings to love, contemplate and glorify him on earth and in heaven. It is the gift of the one whose wish it is that the ardent yet serene life of the three who are consubstantial with him should be extended beyond himself.

It is true that grace, this treasure that is hidden in the most intimate part of our souls and radiates its power throughout our being, is contained in earthenware vessels (2 Cor. 4. 7). These vessels are imperfect and easily broken, but this should not make us reluctant to plumb the depths of the greatness and richness of God's gift.

"Grace is the mystery not only of man's salvation, but also of his deification. Eternal life begins in us with grace," Thomas Aquinas wrote.[1] It is a reality that must either die forever in us or else must spread within us, enabling us to see God face to face in his glo-

45

ry. It is a reality that is invisible in itself, like the God from whom
it comes. It is also so modest and adaptable that it never goes beyond
the limits of the nature that it perfects. It is finally so powerful and
effective that it allows us to perform actions that are both human
and divine and transfigures us to such a degree that we become gods
by participation, sons of God in the one Son and the fullness of the
Spirit.

Although God is the author of both and although everything is
in a sense gratuitous and therefore grace, there is a great gulf between the natural and the supernatural orders, in other words, between what Augustine called "being in God" and "being with
God." In his treatise on the Trinity, he wrote:

> What is not in God, of whom it is written: "All things are from
> him, in him and through him" (Rom. 11. 36)? And yet not ev-
> eryone is with him in the way in which the psalmist said to the
> soul: "I am always with you" (Ps. 73. 23). And he is not with
> everyone in the way in which we say: "The Lord be with you."
> How great is the misery of the man who is not with the one
> without whom he cannot exist. If he is in him, he is certainly
> not without him. Yet, if he does not remember him, understand
> him and love him, he is not with God.[2]

According to Augustine, then, being in God and being with
God are two ways in which God communicates with his creatures
and two ways in which we can be in relation to God.

Being in God is being face to face with him as the cause—the
first cause—of our being. Being with him is being able, because of
his goodness as our Father, to enter the secret of his intimate life and
to share in the joy, rest and intercommunication of his relationship
between the Father, the Son and the Holy Spirit.[3]

Being in God is being held, together with everything that exists,
above the abyss of nothingness by God the creator. It is being totally
dependent on God and existing as a reflection of his infinite perfections and as the fringe of his royal garment. Being with God is turning of our own free will, but nonetheless driven by his divine power,
toward the God who lives like a guest and a friend in the most intimate part of our being. When we are with God, we can know him
with the knowledge that he has of himself and love him with the
love that he has for himself.

Being in God is being face to face with the unknown, transcendent one, the *Tremendum,* an enigma that can easily become an agony or can be forgotten if we let ourselves be drawn into material preoccupations. Being with God is being more with God as the *Fascinans* than with God as the *Tremendum.* It is believing not only in his infinite transcendence, but also in his infinite condescendence. It is clinging with the whole of one's soul to the mystery that he has revealed to men and taking part with him in a dialogue that is both personal and silent and at the same time never ending, both on earth and in heaven.

This transition from "in" God to "with" God is a mystery that is well worth looking at more closely. It is the realization of the eternal plan of love of the God of whom the psalmist said: "He does what he pleases" (Ps. 115.3). It is enough for God to desire it for man to be raised up to him and for the immeasurable gap that separates what is created from what is uncreated, what is finite from what is infinite, to be filled. Man, in response to God's plan and infinite goodness, is therefore able to reach the supernatural order. This order is so perfect that it goes far beyond anything that can be expected by any nature, either created or uncreated, whatever its resources may be.

God, however, is also infinite wisdom. Despite his acts of foolishness that he performs in love for the salvation of the world—a foolishness that is, according to Saint Paul (1 Cor. 1. 25), wiser than all human wisdom—and despite the law that his love obeys with sovereign freedom, God never comes into conflict with what is contradictory or absurd. He arranges everything with perfect harmony and continuity. There is nothing missing from the chain of his blessings. The early Fathers of the Church—Irenaeus, Clement of Alexandria and Tertullian, for example—saw God and the God of order, the God of agreement, the God of adaptation, the God of transition, the God of immanence and distance, the visible and dynamic God and the underground God who hollows out openings that he himself fills. One question calls for an answer, in the light of God's desire to fill man to overflowing with happiness and glory. It is this: What has God done to prepare man to receive his grace and to become the temple of his Trinity?

When he created the world, God also created time. For countless millennia he prepared for man's appearance by creating the universe on the five first days presented in the great vision of the first chapter of Genesis. This universe was without a soul, but it was on the way to finding one in man, who was created on the sixth day and was the reason for the existence of that universe, its crown and its king. The Russian thinker Vladimir Soloviev called man the ideal peak by means of which created nature, separated from God by its real basis, earth, is united to its creator.[4]

Man appeared as the last of God's creatures in this world of bodies and spirits in which the heavenly hierarchies were already present, glorious and bathed in supernatural light. This man is both a microcosm, a little world in the great world, because he sums up in himself all the realms of creation, and a macrocosm, a great world in a little world, because he transcends, by virtue of his immortal soul, the rest of creation, which was to be the framework within which he worked out his fate.

What is very important in this context is that man is, because of his immortal soul, not only a reflection of God, but also an image of the creator who, in his unfathomable mystery, has created the thought of his thought and inspired it with the one Spirit of love. We should therefore not be surprised if the Bible presents us with the idea of God retiring into his life of the Trinity to fashion man with his own life-giving breath (Gen. 1. 26; 2. 7). A being who remembers, thinks and loves and who is open to what is universal and infinite therefore comes into being from God the Father, the Word and the Holy Spirit.

The human trinity, which is both static and dynamic, and the divine Trinity—this is the possible wedding that is announced and for which preparations have been made. God is the bridegroom, as the Son, the Word, the second Adam, whose face, which was to appear to men in the fullness of time, the Father contemplates in his act of creation via the first Adam.[5]

Thus, despite the gulf that separates God from man, they are indissolubly related. Artists have represented this deep mystery, and a striking example of this is the impressive fresco made by Michelangelo in the Sistine Chapel in Rome showing the creation of Adam. Adam is shown lying facing God. His body is heavy and fleshy, indicating his terrestrial origin, but what a contrast there is in his face! It is thin and emaciated and his eyes are fixed on God. Adam is clearly expecting everything from his creator. His soul is lit up by a pure flame of passionate expectation. Adam is, in other words, totally orientated toward the one whose image he bears. God's right arm and Adam's left are stretched out toward each other and their first fingers are almost touching. What spark, one asks, would spring from their fingertips as they touched?

The next fresco shows the creation of Eve. What a wonderful expression the artist has depicted on the face of the first man! Yet it is quite different from that of the previous representation. Adam is shown asleep, but his closed eyes still light up the face, which shines with a serene peacefulness and an unutterable melancholy. Here is man completely given over to God's action, with great gentleness and total abandon. The divine artist is seen continuing his work of creation. He continues to give form and beauty to this man whom he has moulded with his hands, doing so by sending the Word and the Holy Spirit both visibly and invisibly at the wedding here on earth between the Word and his Church, symbolized by the creation of Eve.

In the book of the prophet Jeremiah, Scripture appears to refer to this action by God and this docile passivity on the part of man in God's hands. The prophet compares God to a potter and says that he "went down to the potter's house and there he was, working at the wheel . . . And the word of the Lord was addressed to me, 'House of Israel, can I not do to you what this potter does? As the clay is in the potter's hand, so you are in mine, House of Israel' " (Jer. 18. 4–6).

We are all of us together this House of Israel and each one of us is also the House of Israel. We have been created man, that is, we have been born into openness, receptivity and readiness in order to be easily moulded as clay in the hands of the divine potter, as long as we, in our terrible and sublime freedom, do not say no. This constitutes what the classical theologians of the Church call obediential power. Even before God revealed himself to us, this power was there as a predisposition, an acceptance of God's grace. It is, as it were, a point of departure for the development of our supernatural life.

Our hearts have to become deep and childlike if we are to be ready to be moulded in this way by God who created us in his own image, making us, as Meister Eckehart commented, most unlike and yet at the same time most like himself, the creator. Children never cease asking questions, and it may be because they are so close to the source of their life that they constantly feel the need to go back to this again and again. When they ask: "Why?" our reply is all too often: "That's why!" or perhaps more fully: "That is the inevitable consequence."

But it does not happen inevitably. At the basis of every action is God's tenderness, a tenderness that is inexplicable because it is its own explanation. It is not simply inevitable that God created us in his own image, open and receptive, destined to know, love, serve, praise and contemplate him forever and be happy in his blessing. It is not inevitable that he created us man and not, for example, a stone that cannot move or a tree that raises its trunk to heaven and spreads its branches out to receive the light or a dog that frisks about close to its master.

It is not simply inevitable that, as the Angelic Doctor has pointed out in his calm, serene way, inferior natures should receive their perfection from natures that are superior to themselves, but man's nature is only perfected by God and his grace. Children are often spontaneously surprised and adults, who are more mature and reflective, can also be astonished. What is more, in the evening of his life, an adult often feels the need to return to the source, responding, in the childhood of wisdom, to a wave of thankfulness welling up in his heart and carrying him toward the God who created him man. He was, after all, created man in Jesus Christ, who was, as Paul has pointed out in his letter to the Colossians,[6] already present at the moment of his creation. Because of his creation in Jesus Christ, he has been given a greatness that not even sin can take away.

Grace, we may conclude, has the effect of redeeming, purifying and deifying man. Thanks to the obediential power that makes him open at birth to God's gift, man is always going beyond himself in a movement of self-fulfillment in which he becomes himself in the Christ who "lives in his heart through faith" (Eph. 3. 17) and who, from the cross, draws all men to himself (John 12. 32). "Sharing in the divine nature," as Saint Peter says (2 Pet. 1. 4), man goes from grace to grace toward the end where there will be nothing but glory and a "God who is revealed to and united with gods."[7]

NOTES

1. *Summa Theologiae*, IIa, IIae, q. 124, a. 3.
2. *De Trinitate*, 14. 12.
3. "When God has communicated to a thing in order to be the whole being inside the thing, he can communicate by the whole being that is inside himself," E. Mersch, *Théologie du corps mystique du Christ*, II, p. 171.
4. *Russia and the Universal Church*, p. 230.
5. Tertullian, *De res, carnis*, 6: "Recogita totum illi Deum occupatum se deditum, manu, sensu, opere, consilio, sapientia, providentia, et ipsa in primis affectione, quae lineamenta ducebat. Quodcumque enim limus exprimabatur. Christus cogitabatur homo futurus, quod et limus at caro sermo, quod et terra tunc. Sic enim praefatio Patris ad Filium: Faciamus hominem ad imaginem et similitudinem nostram. Et fecit hominem Deus. Id utique quod finxit, ad imaginem fecit illum, scilicet Christi."
6. Colossians 1. 15, 18.
7. Gregory Nazianzen, *Oratio in sanctum Pascha*, PG 36. 627.

4

Grace and the Presence of God in Christ and in Us

Pope Paul VI once said: "What carries us away and what we love passionately is our Lord Jesus Christ, his truth, the gospel and grace."[1] Grace—it is certainly true to say that this mysterious reality cannot be separated from the other realities mentioned by the pope. Grace comes to us from the person of our Lord Jesus Christ, the eternal truth sent by the Father to men to announce the good news to them and to save the world. In its widest and most usual sense, grace points to God giving himself in and through his beloved Son to his human creatures to redeem them, deify them and make them his children and lead them back to him.

This grace can be seen as an immense river springing from the inexhaustible source of God's eternal glory and flowing through the centuries to lose itself finally in the great ocean of glory to which Christ himself, on the eve of his passion, asked the Father to introduce him (John 17. 5). Grace is immense because it is one and it is one because it is immense. It is a mystery of infinite love that follows God's unyielding plan. It is a height without a summit, a bottomless depth and a length and breadth without limits (Eph. 3. 18). In the synoptic gospels, Jesus used an image that appealed strongly to the Jews and called it a kingdom. But it is a kingdom without frontiers, a universal, triumphant, rich and peaceful kingdom, well ordered by an all-powerful and all-loving king. In the gospel of John, Jesus presents it as life. But it is a life of which we can only catch

51

a glimpse, since all that we can see of it are its external signs in acts of charity. It is such an inner life that it is of necessity secret, like the sap rising in the tree or the fruitful juice of the vine in the plant and the branches. It is also a life of such dynamism that without it we can do nothing (John 15. 5) and with it we can do everything (Phil. 4. 14).

Paul, who experienced more of the weight and the wonder of grace than perhaps anyone else, called it a mystery. As such it is a reality within which we can sense the great depths of God who sees us and predestines us in his beloved Son and the depths of our own souls, which he wants to be holy and spotless in his presence (Eph. 1. 4). The same Paul shows us, in a hymn overflowing with enthusiasm and at the same time reflecting a deep recollectedness, that God made, recreated and recapitulated us and all things in his Christ, who was eternal and who had existed before all creation, "to make us praise the glory of his grace" (Eph. 1. 6).

It is not my intention to write a treatise on grace. All that I want to do is to make it possible for the transcendence of God's gift to be sensed, and for the gift of intimacy and nearness between God and ourselves that comes about if we welcome God's presence. This presence goes beyond all our hopes and, if we are to become fully aware of it, it calls for abandoned trust and a freedom of heart and spirit that is in itself, as Paul tells us, a grace. It invites us to cling to the supernatural realism of the Word, the promises of Christ who has revealed the Father to us and the eternal secrets of his too great love (Eph. 2. 4). It was by this too great love that God created all things and has plunged us into a mystery of grace that goes beyond all joy, all sorrow and all thanksgiving and can only give rise to complete adoration.

The first to benefit from this fullness of grace was Christ himself, the only one who was predestined and in whom we have all been chosen and are all predestined. The evangelist John spoke of this fullness of grace "that we have all of us received, grace in return for grace" (John 1. 16). Confronted with this mystery, we may ask whether it is possible to discern its point of departure and to follow its route.

We have already mentioned the source of grace. It originates in the mystery of mysteries, the key which opens the door to the supernatural order—the Holy Trinity.

God is. God lives. But he does not live in solitude in his impenetrable and eternal domain. Because he is love and intelligence, he has in himself an irresistible propensity to spread and communicate himself. The Father therefore gives himself totally, keeping nothing back except his privilege as Father, and begets his Son, the Word, his thought, his expression of himself and the perfect image of everything that he is. In turn, the Son receives the entire substance of the Father, having nothing of his own except his sonship. He is a Son who is perfectly open to everything that the Father is. He is completely orientated toward the Father. Father and Son circulate and rest in each other. They embrace each other in a unique way and the end of this embrace is the Holy Spirit.

Everything is a gift and a relationship in God. The Father is light and life: The Son, the Word, is light from light, life from life, and truth from truth: The Holy Spirit, who is the result of the processions of the Trinity and from whom no other person proceeds because he is the ultimate limit of what is without limit the expression of God's life, light, truth and love.

There is, after all, a God without, that exists in addition to a God within a whole created universe, a human race that populates our planet, Earth. Also each individual forms a kind of spiritual universe in himself because of his immortal soul.

The first-fruits of this state of being outside God, that is, of being a member of the human race, was our representative, one who was like us in everything except sin and who was summed up in the person of the Son, the Word, by the eternal wish of the Father and in the great love of the Spirit. There is, therefore, a covenant between God and ourselves that is irrevocable and expresses what the classical theologians of the Church have called the hypostatic union. The mystery of the incarnation is a reality that cannot be measured, a full and unlimited gift made by God to his creature. Thanks to the child who has been born, according to the prophet (Isa. 9. 6), to *us,* a Son who has been given to *us,* there is, in a certain sense, no more outside God and no more beyond. The God who is inaccessible in his transcendence has entered this universe and fills it with his presence and his grace. Even before he appeared in the flesh and after he had gone up to the Father—both before and after—Jesus unites all men and all things in himself, all things in heaven and on earth. When he came down to us he did not leave the Father, and when he went up to his Father he did not leave our earth. Coming down and going up were one single act, a shared immanence by means of which God and man exist forever in each other.

In the incarnation, God experiences our death and we have forever God's glory. "Apart from the person of Christ," a Russian theologian has said, "the divine and the human elements are separated by a total opposition—the opposition that exists between the infinite and the finite, the uncreated and the created elements. It is only if we contemplate Christ that we can ever have the boldness to believe that the divine is not a stranger to everything that is really human. We too, then, are capable of feeling the joy and the strength that spring from the knowledge of this nearness of God, a nearness that no one in the world can ever imagine."[2]

God, then, is present in the God-man Christ and this divine presence constitutes a supreme marriage covenant. All other covenants in the history of man's salvation—the various Old Testament covenants leading up to the covenant between Christ and his Church, the covenant between the Word of God and each individual and all the human and symbolic covenants which extend the body of Christ to the limits of time and space—are summed up and given meaning in this one great covenant. One person, two natures. One union without merging. A distinction without separation, since two are needed to become one and it is necessary to be one so that the two may find, in a unity that is driven to the maximum, joy, rest and infinite fertility.

On the one hand, then, the Word of God has seized hold, totally and definitively, of the humanity and, on the other, the human nature of Jesus is at the same time completely open and receptive in the most perfect freedom. There is, between the two natures which subsist within the person of the Word, a circulation of life, a *perichoresis* in the ontological order. This makes it possible for the two natures to communicate with each other and points to their glorious unity. The divine nature of Christ contains the effusion of what that nature is. The other, human nature assumed by the Word, is enriched by everything that it receives and is, to use a word that the Fathers of the Church loved to employ, "deified." By this, they meant that Christ's human nature was made divine to the limits of his being.

The Church, the bride of Christ and the trustee and hander-on of truth, has attempted to explain what Scripture has said about this mystery. Throughout the first centuries in the history of Christianity, it acted like a lighthouse, sending out successive beams of light from its great councils—Nicaea, Ephesus, Chalcedon and Constantinople. We would undoubtedly accept what Saint Irenaeus said in the second century: "Everything that belongs to the Church should be loved with great love and regarded as the tradition of truth,"[3] but many of us would have to admit that, even though the detailed defi-

nitions made at these early Councils of the Church form the bulwark of our hope, they attract us less than the heat and light that
come to us directly from the fire in the hearth. This is no doubt
because they were formulated at times of danger, to warn us of rocks
in the water through which we were passing. One Church historian
has said in this context:

> These definitions were forged of hard metal in the course of a
> long struggle against subtle errors and are there to protect us
> rather than to nourish us. The Christian who wants to feed his
> spiritual life and warm his heart will inevitably prefer to turn
> to the inspired and inspiring words of Scripture.[4]

The Christian therefore reads Scripture as though he were on
the edge of an abyss of divine love in which everything is one and
is expressed by a single decree that has to be carried out in successive stages. This applies particularly to his reading of the beginning
of the letters to the Ephesians and the Colossians. In these epistles,
the apostle's vision is almost too great and too sublime. He recalls
the mystery of the Father contemplating, with a single and eternal
gaze, his beloved Son. In Paul's vision, the Father is indissolubly
united to the one who is outside him, that is, created man and,
through mankind, the whole universe. He contemplates that reality
in order to fill it with his creative and saving love and to make it
return at last to his own life in the Trinity.

Let us try to express this. The whole of the Trinity is present
in the God-man. The whole of God dwells in him bodily (Col. 2.
9). The Son of God, is the image of the invisible God, born before
any creature and containing within himself all things in heaven and
on earth, all things visible and invisible, everything was created
through him and for him and all things subsist in him who precedes
all things (Col. 1. 15–17).

The origin of grace, then, is, together with the movement from
itself of the essential being of God who is infinite goodness, the eternal decree leading to the incarnation itself. The grace of the Word
becoming man is a blessing and a predestination that embraces the
whole of the human race which is so fallible and disposed to sin. In
the incarnation, grace is subject to the pressure of unbounded love
and operates with the excess that marks Christ's suffering and
death, with the result that it is superabundant. The Father thus sees
the fruit of his eternal begetting at the same time as fruit of the
earth, this insignificant planet lost in the great spaces of the cosmos,

and assuming a human nature among countless others while remaining united with all the others in order to pour out into them the fullness of his gift.

Christ is therefore the only and the complete meeting-place between God and man, the admirable interchange that extends to us of the two natures of which Gregory Nazianzen said: "The one has deified and the other is deified and, I would be bold enough to claim, has become one with God. The one who has anointed became man and the one who is anointed became God."[5]

How did this happen? How did God's begetting of the Word, the Son, extend to the womb of a virgin and how did the eternal man, who existed before the first Adam, appear in the fullness of time? In other words, how did he appear at that moment of time in which all other times, both in the past and in the future, were concentrated, so that he could raise them up together to God in his eternity? What a deep mystery is contained in this double begetting of Christ, both human and divine!

How, then, is God present in the humanity of Jesus in such a way that "the depths of that man are the ultimate depths of God himself and that the inner being of that man in himself is the inner being of God in himself. In other words, how is he a divine person?"[6]

How does the air crossed by the sun become itself sun, while still remaining air? How does coal or iron become incandescent when it enters the fire—how does it become fire itself without losing its substance? How does the "I" of that man, who is so solemn in his majesty and yet so tender and gentle in his humility, call so much for our adoration that it is the same as the "I am" of Yahweh in the burning bush?

How was it that the flame of God did not consume that delicate humanity similar to our own and that it was content to radiate outward by scattering miracles here and there like seed and spreading the power of the word of God from so many treasures of wisdom and knowledge? How did the Son of the living God, who was the "radiant light of God's glory and the perfect copy of his nature" (Heb. 1. 3) succeed in making himself available to us poor mortals, but not in the brilliance, that must have been normal, of his transfiguration? Is this not one of the most striking miracles of his condescendence and *kenosis*?[7]

How was the one who was, according to Pascal, "holy, holy, holy to God, terrible to demons and without sin" and whose slightest gestures, smallest words and most minute drop of blood were perfect and holy able to make himself our brother, our servant and our friend?

Mystery of the incarnation! Sweet and gentle hour of the annunciation! Humble and beautiful appearance at the nativity! We can never celebrate your birth with enough thankfulness, joy and adoration. You are the point at which all God's promises and all our hopes meet. You are the beginning that will never end, the spring-time when all the seeds of the resurrection germinate, the dawn that will initiate the noon of Easter and the glorious sunset of eternal paradise. The Word took flesh in the womb of the immaculate virgin in order to make our poor flesh immaculate. The one who is fullness pours out that fullness so that we may become fullness (Eph. 1. 23). In competition with each other, the Fathers of the Church said again and again, in their different ways, that God became man so that man might become God.

How is it possible for man to become God by participation and by grace and for the end of God's plan to be what Gregory Nazianzen called "God revealed to and united with gods"[8] if there is no communication between God and ourselves, the person of the Word and the humanity that was assumed, the creator and us creatures who are so disposed to sin?

Perhaps we should pause for a while and consider this question of God's coming down to us and entering us in the grace that perfects us and unites us with him.

Are we, then, not predisposed toward this eternal Word who longs to seize hold of us in and through Christ? According to Saint John, who, at the beginning of his gospel, fixed his eagle's eye on him, the creative Logos was the eternal model in accordance with whom we had been made the image of God and the one who had already been named the saviour and redeemer of man and, through man, of the whole of the universe. Is this eternal Word, who is in the very bosom of the three who are consubstantial with each other, not also the expression in God of everything that is God? Is he not, because of this, also the eternal truth that is destined to reveal God to all those who are already open to receive him?

A relationship is therefore set up between God and man by grace as the deep reverberation caused in the soul by the Word. A dialogue between "I" and "thou" is initiated and can continue indefinitely. This dialogue is indispensible to the experience of authentic Christian faith. The Word can only exert his attractive power over us, however, through the humanity that he has assumed and by means of the supreme sacrifice that led him to death on the cross and to resurrection. It is because of this that John the evangelist put into Jesus' mouth, just before his passion, the words: "When I am lifted up from the earth, I shall draw all men to myself" (John 12. 32). Jesus' humanity united with the Word and filled with the Word is therefore the perfect instrument of that Word and is deified by the Word. This deification took place at the moment of the incarnation.

In his great soul and his deeply human consciousness, which was the consciousness of the Word, the Son, Christ was so clearly and profoundly aware of his mission to communicate to men the existence of the light begotten by the eternal Word that his soul was both raised up and at the same time torn apart by it. It was like a great weight crushing him and he could only be borne up by a divine power: "I have come to bring fire to the earth and how I wish it were blazing already!" (Luke 12. 49); "How great is my distress till it is over!" (Luke 12. 50).

This is clearly the echo, in his human nature that was sensitive to God, of the flash of sunlight from the Word that longed to give splendor, life and fruitfulness. It is the cry of the one who is the light of the world. It is the passionate need of a love that is longing to sacrifice itself. To use another image that is as biblical as that of light, it is the irresistible movement of living water flowing from its source, made to run and thirsty to be drunk, as Gregory of Nazianzus said.

If Jesus was, in his humanity, the instrument and the receptacle of the mysterious way in which the Word communicates itself to us, there is also, between that humanity and ourselves, who are destined to be his mystical body, a very deep solidarity that comes from the unlimited perfection which the Word imposes on him.

The person of the Word perfects Jesus' human nature not only at the individual level, but also at the social level. From the individual point of view, Christ is a splendid example of humanity—"Of all men the most handsome," as the psalmist says in his epithalamium of the wedding between Christ and his Church (Ps. 45)—and indeed the crown of God's creation. What interests us here most of all, however, in our consideration of the mystery of grace and the way in which it is communicated to us, is the perfection given by the person of the Word to the social aspect of the human nature assumed by that person. How could it be otherwise? The personal grace of Christ is the same principal grace that he mediates. His human nature contains the fullness of grace and because of this it can only pour it out abundantly, since, in order to possess his supernatural perfection fully, Jesus must, in his humanity, have possessed it with a power to communicate that was a kind of transcendent sociability.[9]

Each one of us is essentially a social being. Every human being is our brother, the object of our concern and one with whom we have spiritual and material dealings. What is more, we are closely connected, beyond our neighbor, to the whole of this universe without a soul which forms the framework of our destiny. Each of us, however, bears the weight of original sin that is expressed as selfishness and division and which has shattered the mirror reflecting the one image of God in the depths of our being. We have through sin become opaque to others and it is only in our heavenly home that we shall be spiritualized and purified and therefore translucent to each other. While we are still on earth, Satan has the opportunity to play us off against each other. Maximus the Confessor wrote about original sin, saying that "it reduced the unity of human nature to a thousand fragments, with the result that we now tear each other to pieces with the ferocity of wild beasts."[10]

The one whom the martyr, Ignatius of Antioch, called "our inseparable life"—Christ—is there and it is in him that we exist and are blessed, chosen and predestined. Influenced by the Word and filled with the grace that flows in him and perfects him, his human nature is full—both in time and in space—of a power of universal expansion. It is above all sociable.

It is because he is also God and rules us from the height at which God dwells that Jesus can penetrate us most profoundly. It is also because he is so open to the fullness of God that he finds us open to receive him and to be filled to overflowing, so long as we give free scope to the action of his grace within us.

It is clear that we are really one with him in a radically interior, physical and ontological unity that binds us most intimately to him. His human nature subsists in the infinite one who is God, but is still individual, although in a manner that is transcendent and without limits. It is because his human nature has been deified and therefore made infinite that it is able to come to us and fill us with God's grace.

When he presented Christ at the moment of his deepest humiliation, Pilate said: *Ecce homo!* These words were misunderstood by those who did not believe. Here is the man—not the man who, like us, has to overcome himself in order to become what he really is, a man. No, here is the man who grew in age and wisdom, but was, even at the moment of his incarnation, the perfect man, the immensely great and deep human reality recapitulating everything in himself by achieving the natural and the supernatural unity of the whole of mankind in his life and by dying for all men and pouring over the whole of mankind the river of his grace.

It is not possible to quote all the texts in which the Fathers of the Church speak of our union with Christ, our Head, the living vine and, through grace, everything that we have.[11] There are so many of these texts that we can do no more here than quote Cyril of Alexandria, who said: "Jesus was anointed and exalted so that grace might be spread by him over all men as a gift made to our nature that will always be preserved by the whole human race. He did not receive holiness for his sake alone. He received it in order to make the whole of nature holy."[12] The same Father also made this remarkably short and striking comment: "In all men, the Word has dwelt by a single man." We are therefore his members, one body with him and our nature has been anointed, assumed and, as it were, made into the Word by him.

Because of the wonder of God's great goodness and his too great love (Eph. 2. 4), we are called to share in this grace of Christ and to share it with our fellow human beings. The Head of our body makes grace flow through his members and it is also his will that we should, in him and through him, give that grace to others and receive it from them. We are in this way united to each other by a great mystery of supernatural solidarity which will not be fully revealed to us until we reach our ultimate home. Then, as Léon Bloy once wrote, it will be the cause of "unimaginable surprises."[13]

While we are still on earth, those who catch a glimpse of this mystery can only respond by adoring this great plan of God's, since it strikes them as a reflection of and a participation in the intimacy of his life in which it is the mutual relationships that result from that plan which make the Father, the Son and the Holy Spirit persons. The family of the three who are consubstantial is both the source of and the model for the great human family, which consists of countless persons created in the image and likeness of the divine persons. The persons in that human family are not really persons if they are not open to give and to receive from each other.

We are in this way confronted by the sublime reality of the communion of saints, which is fundamentally the Church itself.[14] One modern theologian has claimed that it is only possible to understand this doctrine as "an interpenetration between the persons of the Trinity who in turn penetrates them."[15]

Many deeply Christian authors—Léon Bloy, Paul Claudel, Georges Bernanos and Gertrude von LeFort, for example—have considered this doctrine, examined its effects and reflected about its historical development. We may conclude that we did not take our place in this universe for ourselves. We were created by God for another and, in that other person of the Trinity, for the others who are, like ourselves, from him and in him.

Claudel expressed this idea very well when he said:

> Only one thing is necessary—the people to whom we are necessary. Let us go forward! Only one thing is necessary—someone who asks us for everything and to whom we are able to give everything. Let us go forward! The water takes everything. . . . And it is all no longer outside—we are in it. There is something that unites us with everything—a drop of water associated with the sea! The communion of saints![16]

Behind the great number beyond counting and the rich variety of human lives and beyond the successive generations of men in the visible world in which the great river of grace overflows the frontiers dividing Jew from gentile, slave from free man and male from female (Gal. 3. 28; Col. 3. 11), as well as in the invisible world in which our souls move, our slightest action may have unsuspected repercussions. A simple and hardly conscious thought of God, a coin given to the poor or the deepest prayer of the contemplative and the great works of charity performed by a Cottolengo or a John of Kronstadt— all these actions, both small and great, have their repercussions.

We are certainly brought face to face with our responsibilities by this truth, but this should not overwhelm us. On the contrary, it should make us greater and give us a universal soul, without taking away from us any of the simplicity that belongs to a true child of God. All the same, it is impossible not to be struck in all this by the seriousness of the perspective opened up by this question.

We have no destiny in isolation from others. We are interdependent in a way in which only God can understand and that he governs in accordance with his will. We can deliberately overshadow the souls of others by our gloom or fill them with the light with which God enlightens us. We are all present in the only one who is present. Although we misunderstand each other, are divided and cannot see through or into each other, the same under-

Praise (handwritten marginalia)

ground river of grace that springs from God and the fullness of Christ flows in us, through us and among us all. Insofar as we are receptive to God's gift and the terrible, yet sublime gift of freedom does not form an obstacle to God's pouring out of himself, we are able to overflow like the fountain described in the words of the poet C. F. Meyer:

The fountain spreads and falls again,
the basin fills up to the brim.
The water like a slender veil
flows over to a second bowl.
This basin fills another bowl,
a third that is already full.
Each, overflowing, gives and takes.
Each pours away and stays quite full.

Plotinus spoke of the "only one with the only one," God, who, having acquired its real depth in the truth of Christianity, goes back to its source, pours it out and spreads it in its full Catholic splendor. This gives rise to great joy and great hope in the clear light of faith. It also causes a great wish to contribute in all humility to the task of spreading the unfathomable riches of the grace of Christ and to scatter a little of the infinite treasure of silent or visible acts that form part of the fabric of the Church's wedding garment that she will wear, as bride, on the last day. On that day, the song will ring out: "Let us be glad and joyful and give praise to God, because this is the time for the marriage of the Lamb. His bride is ready and she has been able to dress herself in dazzling white linen, because her linen is made of the good deeds of the saints" (Apoc. 19. 7–8).

The dogma of the communion of saints has been greatly neglected, yet it can reveal to us the splendid unity of God's grace and its steady, inexorable aim of making us all one in the one God of the Trinity (John 17. 22–23). There is only one presence in Christ Jesus, our head, and in the Spirit of love who is a gift, communication and union and the knot. This single presence fills all beings and, in the unity of a single body, makes them present to each other. In the mystery of grace, there is only God, carrying out his work of salvation in a series of steps as closely connected as links in a chain. As Paul said: "They are the ones he chose specially long ago and intended to become true images of his Son, so that his Son might be the eldest of many brothers. He called those he intended for this; those he called he justified and with those he justified he shared his glory" (Rom. 8. 30). We are therefore led in this way from the eternity where God keeps us in his mind, his election and his love to the eternity that will consist of being plunged into the perfect expansion of grace, in other words, the eternity of glory.

While we are still on earth looking forward to this ultimate glory, we may already, as a contemporary theologian has pointed out, "share in the nature of God"—this is the effect of grace—and "have access, at least to some extent, to each of the divine persons and above all the relationship between them. We are introduced to love in a way in which separate individuals living a simply natural life could never understand."[17]

NOTES

1. Discourse, 10 July 1963, given to the chaplains of Christian workers.

2. N. Malinovski, *Dogmatic Theology*, II.

3. *Adv. haer.*, *PG* 7. 3. 4. 1.

4. Léonce de Grandmaison, *Jésus-Christ*, II, p. 216. The words quoted are certainly true, but they express a view that has to be given a little more light and shade, since, however dry and uninspiring the dogmas of the Church may appear if examined at a superficial level, the Christian whose faith has been enlightened by the gifts of the Spirit knows that they are full of life. See Emile Mersch, *La Théologie du corps mystique du Christ*, II, pp. 108ff.

5. John Damascene quotes these words in his treatise *De fide orthodoxa*, 3, *PG* 94. 1065.

6. See Emile Mersch, *op. cit.*, II, p. 351.

7. "The Savior came to us not as he was able to do it, but according to our ability to receive him. As far as he himself was concerned, he could certainly have come to us in his eternal splendor. We, however, would not have been able to bear his glory. That is why the perfect bread of the Father was offered like the milk that is given to little children. He wanted us to be fed on his flesh as it were at the breast and, when we had become used to food and drink in this way, by eating and drinking the Word of God, we would then be able to digest the bread of immortality which is the Spirit of the Father." Saint Irenaeus, *op. cit.*, 4. 38. 1.

8. Sermon for Easter, *PG* 36. 627.

9. Thomas Aquinas, *Summa Theologiae*, IIIa, q. 8, a. 5 and *Compendium theolog. ad Reginaldum*, I, 214.

10. *Quaest. ad Thalassium*, *PG* 50. 206.

11. Emile Mersch, *Le Corps mystique du Christ*, I and II, contains many texts on this theme from the Latin and Greek Fathers of the Church. This work, which should not be confused with the same author's *La Théologie du corps mystique du Christ*, is remarkably rich and deep, but the author's untimely death has left it unfinished and still in need of a number of finishing touches.

12. *PG* 75. 355; see also *In Jo.*, 5. 2, *PG* 75. 755–756. Gregory of Nyssa

also commented: "The whole human race forms a united community, with the result that it is assumed as a single whole by the person of the Word yet becomes only one of its elements. The Word is united to this element or part in a very special way in the absolute union of his person. In this way, he becomes the first-fruits or the privileged part of the community and is not separated from the whole of the race. In him and through him, the whole community is attracted by the person of the Word" (*PG* 44. 1317, 1320, 1321).

13. Letter to Elisabeth Joly. In addition to this remarkable document, see also Bloy's *Méditation d'un solitaire* and the second part of his *Le Désespéré.*

14. As Charles Journet, *L'Eglise du Verbe incarné,* II, p. 663, has pointed out, the communion of saints, as distinct from the Church, has figured in the Creed of the Gallican Church since the fifth century. In the ninth century, this practice became common in Italy, Spain and Africa. See p. 662, where the author discusses the text of Nicetas of Remesiana, written around the year 400, on the identification of the doctrine of the communion of saints with the Church.

15. Hans Urs von Balthasar, *Elizabeth of the Trinity and her Spiritual Mission,* p. 148.

16. Paul Claudel, *Le Soulier de satin,* 4th day, X.

17. Hans Urs von Balthasar, *op. cit.,* p. 149.

5

The Presence of Grace

It sometimes happens toward the end of one's life, whether it is long or short, that the soul is bathed in a pure and intense light, a foretaste of the clarity of heaven, and is aware that everything in this world is grace, a gift of God. The whole of one's life becomes bathed in this reality of love. Yes, it is true that everything is grace because everything comes from the goodness of the God who is always present and who always cares and provides for us. Everything is grace because he wants or permits everything and in his mercy lets us be rooted in him, fashions us and goes deeper and deeper into our hearts to discover new spaces in order to fill them. Everything is grace finally because everything points toward an end that is a state of glory.

When this happens, what Jean Guitton has called our intentional will, which has the aim of building us up with a kind of security and exaltation, is replaced by a much deeper and more mysterious form of will—the will to follow a winding way through obstacles, disappointments and difficulties that God has marked out for us, contrary to all our expectations. This second kind of will is something to which we are called to give our consent with the whole of our being. It is also something for which we can be deeply thankful to God.

Alongside the beatific vision of God, this new understanding is certainly grace, but it is grace in the theological sense of the word. It is grace not in the usual sense of a blessing, but in the sense of light and life in us that take us outside and beyond ourselves.

The reader may be surprised by what I have said here. I have spoken about grace without having really defined the term. But how can we confine this immensely rich reality, which has so many different aspects and which is concerned with the most impenetrable essence of God's being and the most purely human part of man, within the framework of a brief, conceptual formula?

But it has, after all, to be defined in some way and we can say that it is a mysterious reality originating in the depths of the life of the Trinity and flowing into us who are members of the human body of Christ, pervading us with his humanity, perfecting our human nature, overcoming all sin in us, recreating us in the image of God in whose likeness we were made, saving us and in the end deifying and glorifying us. Or we can say that it is the reality of which we have the greatest need since, without it, it is not possible for us to fulfill our destiny. And, as immortal creatures of God, we are from eternity predestined to become the sons of God.

This grace is never absent in man. According to Saint Paul, God created man only in order to fill him with his grace and a world without grace is absurd and meaningless. It would, however, not be entirely lacking in beauty and order, since it would be governed by the covenant that God concluded with the just man, Noah (Gen. 11. 19ff). Summer would follow winter, night would follow day and rain would follow sun to make the soil fertile. Because of their rational nature, men would undoubtedly share in the eternal Logos and, benefiting from their experience and gradually becoming more perfect in their actions, they would also succeed more and more as human beings. But what a state of wretchedness their life would be without faith, hope and love and without any glimpse of the eternal reality! Can we have any idea of this state from the teachings of the atheistic existentialists and the despair that they describe so well? Apparently not, since this despair has its origin in the fact that grace, which is life, cannot be reconciled with a doctrine of death.

But grace has always existed in the world. It has been present since God breathed into Adam's breast the breath that gave him natural and supernatural life. The Bible tells us nothing about prehistorical life, but we may assume that since sin, which has never ceased to flourish, first entered the world, grace must have been a weak and colorless element in the lives of cavemen who were totally preoccupied with material existence.

Yet here too, we must be cautious. The cave dweller was undoubtedly aware of good and evil and was, if only obscurely, conscious of God—or gods—who had given him life and continued to keep him alive, supporting him in his hard and unremitting struggle with the hostile elements and in his search for the animals that he needed as food. There was a spark in the depths of his soul below the magic, the idolatry and the human sacrifices which he practiced and which later become what the Bible calls abominations. Although at this stage of his development he hardly knew himself, this spark must have been present in him—the spark of the grace of God who wanted to refashion him gradually in his image. As Tertullian said, "God is patient because he is eternal."

How many centuries it must have taken for God to achieve his aim and to have the first Adam, the living spirit, followed by the second Adam, the life-giving spirit! Waiting patiently, he took this first man in his rudimentary state—man "at the breast" as the Fathers of the Church called him—and led him toward his end. From Adam to Christ, grace was able to unfold its possibilities very slowly and gradually perfect and raise up man. Indeed, grace has unlimited possibilities and its highest points have been recorded in the Bible, from the earliest books onward. It does this by pointing to its effects in a series of Old Testament figures.

After Abel, the first man to die and the cornerstone of the heavenly city in time as well as the figure of Christ in his sacrifice of himself, grace reached its climax in Enoch, the father of Methuselah, who "walked with God." We are told in Genesis 5. 21–25 that Enoch walked with God and that he pleased God, according to Hebrews 11. 5. This clearly points to his piety and his faithfulness and it may even indicate that he was very familiar with God, who took him up from this world in order to keep him more closely in his presence.

Grace reached another high point in Noah, who had great faith, saved renewed humanity and built the ark, which is a figure of the Church borne up on the waters of baptism, the powerful waters of death and life.

Abraham, another Old Testament recipient of God's grace, was called to give up his son in obedience to God. This man of invincible faith was able, through grace, to form the point of departure for a whole history of salvation that began with the law of nature, passed through the Mosaic law and culminated in the pouring out of grace in Christ. Abraham has been called the father of all believers for this reason, although his way of life was primitive and not in accordance with the principles of the gospel. But he was undoubtedly heroic and, from the time that he left Haran until the sacrifice that he was prepared to make on Mount Moriah, his life was passed in an environment of grace that was similar to that in Eden. While revealing himself in mysterious theophanies of a solemn and even terrifying kind, God made covenants with Abraham and was present in his life in a familiar and intimate way.

Abraham was followed in the history of grace by Isaac, the child of the miracle and the promise made by God, and Jacob, the most human of the patriarchs and also the one who, throughout his troubled existence, seems to have been marvelously surrounded by the supernatural. We have only to think of the vision that he had while sleeping at Bethel, when the presence of the most high God on earth, so near and yet so far away, filled his soul with holy fear. "Truly the Lord is in the place and I never knew it!" he cried out, "How awe-inspiring this place is! This is nothing less than the house of God. This is the gate of heaven!" (Gen. 28. 16–17). There is also his struggle with the angel at the ford of Jabbok, his dramatic physical contact with the individual who touched him, during which he learned the most precious of all truths—that we must be conquered by God if we are to conquer him.

Another climax is reached in Joseph, that pure and touching man who prefigured Jesus, innocent, persecuted by his brothers, blessed by God his Father and always forgiving.

God also revealed himself to Moses, the next Old Testament figure in whom grace was abundantly present, in the burning bush, in the desert and on Mount Sinai. He made this strong, solitary man the mediator of a law that reached its fulfillment in Christ. God spoke to Moses so intimately that his love for him could only have been eternal.

Another great man in the history of Israel was David, the prophet king, whose pure, deep and tender religious spirit led to the writing of the psalms, which express the presence of grace so admirably. David, who did not, we know, write all these psalms himself, was magnanimous in success, humble and penitent in sin, fearless in war and always filial in his devotion to his God. He was also and above all in the line that God chose to use for the establishment of the temple of his own body and was also inspired by God to build a temple made by men's hands.

After David—and before him, Samuel—came the prophets of Israel, dominated by the figure of Elijah, who was consumed with zeal for the glory of God. There can be no doubt at all that all these prophets received from God the special charisma that they needed for their mission to accomplish God's eternal plan of salvation. These men, who were destined to lead the people ultimately to the one who is the fullness of grace, Jesus Christ, were also individually recipients of grace—the grace of light and vision and the grace of special power, contained within an unfaltering faith. How great their courage must have been in their mission in an environment of unbelief and wickedness! They succeeded in arousing the Israelites and making them conscious of their destiny so that they eventually turned back to God. Slowly and patiently, using rough but beautiful language and frequently giving way to passionate outbursts, they were able to make the religion of their God, who was both transcendent and personal, penetrate into the stone-like hearts of the people, until they were softened and made open. Yahweh inscribed a law of love in the flesh of the prophets that set them free from the law of slavery.

Their mission preceded that of the glorious Maccabees and the martyrs who died for faith in the true God and whose memory is preserved in Scripture. They were also active long before John the Baptist, the last of their number, at a time of great hardship for the people, tracing the paths of the Lord to the little remnant of Israel that had survived so many disasters. They helped the passage of God's grace into the hearts of Yahweh's poor, the *anawim*, who formed a holy avant-garde for Christ when he came among us, and bore witness to his presence. As for these poor ones of Yahweh, we know that the most shining example was the one who was "full of grace"—the immaculate mother of God, the Church and men, the eternal woman and new Eve, whose name is "Virginity." The spiritual daughter of the prophets, placed at the hinge of the two Testaments, Mary appears, above all in her Magnificat, as the divinely inspired prophetess of the new covenant.

What is the difference between God's grace in the Old Testament and his grace in the New Testament? The author of the fourth gospel provides an answer to this question in his commentary on the words of Jesus: "If any man is thirsty, let him come to me! Let the man come and drink who believes in me! As Scripture says: From his breast shall flow fountains of living water." Saint John has added to this that Jesus was "speaking of the Spirit which those who believed in him were to receive; for there was no Spirit as yet because Jesus had not yet been glorified" (John 7. 38–39).

It should never be forgotten that everything under the old covenant was a movement directed toward the coming of Christ, his redeeming passion, his descent into the underworld, his glorious resurrection, his admirable ascension and finally the pouring out of grace on the world on the day of Pentecost which was to give the Church its ultimate form and its astonishing impetus to overcome the world.

Until this took place, grace had its origin in the chosen people of Israel in what had not been made manifest in history—the infinite merits of the crucified Emmanuel. It directed toward God all those who were waiting for the coming of the Messiah, but it did not lead them to the end of grace. There was certainly a divine splendor that transfigured the souls of those whom God had especially chosen and who, in the words of the psalmist, loved the decrees and the precepts of the Lord more than gold and silver (Ps. 119). But this grace could not be fully effective in them. The full possibilities of man's most intimate relationship with God the Father, Son and Holy Spirit could not begin until the Paraclete sent by the Son had been poured out and the Son's presence among men had been made permanent and the deepest secrets of his heart had been unveiled. As long as the tabernacle of the presence of God remained, the way to the heavenly sanctuary remained closed. In Israel, God continued to be present more in the people as a whole and Moses was their guide and leader. He was present only to a lesser extent in the depths of individual souls. The world had to wait for Jesus' flesh to be torn and mutilated and then glorified before the way to the sanctuary of heaven could be opened wide and the great waters of grace could be poured down on mankind.

This grace was like living water, as the fourth evangelist calls it, but it was enclosed within the narrow walls of a well. How many times wells are mentioned in the Bible! Expressive, symbolic wells! Isaac and Rebecca became betrothed near a well and Jacob first met Rachel beside a well. According to the patristic tradition, these betrothals prefigure the marriage between Christ and his Church. With the coming of Jesus, true God and true man, the depths of the well were plumbed and the walls were broken and the waters were able to spring forth and rise to their heavenly source, spreading everywhere over the earth as they did so. It was no longer a case of God distributing his gifts from the secrecy of his sanctuary, but of God giving himself in and through his Son, in the pouring out of their one Spirit, giving life to everything, making everything fertile and transfiguring and fulfilling everything.

This is why grace, which is as old as the eternal decrees of the most high God and the appearance of man on earth, strikes us, however expected it may be and however well we may prepare ourselves for it, as something intoxicatingly new every time that it appears. As

Christ himself, both announced and prefigured, as king, priest, servant and Messiah or the one who was sent, was a completely new reality, God himself and man, so too was grace, spreading out in the wake of a secular past, a wonderfully new phenomenon. The real meaning of Emmanuel, God-with-us, *Ecce adsum,* "I am there, present," as we celebrate it at Christmas, is precisely this: Christ and his grace. From the time of Christ's coming onward, the waters of grace have risen to heaven and spread everywhere, leading to a flourishing of countless saints, from China and holy Russia to Spain and France, people of every kind of temperament, from the apostles and the martyred bishop of Antioch, Ignatius, to Thérèse of Lisieux and Elizabeth Seton.

Scholars in the East and in the West, with their different attitudes, traditions and propensities, have given their minds to the mystery of God's grace. In the West, the study has been methodical, careful, clear and precise, with the emphasis on sharp distinctions. In the East, it has been more mystical, with great respect for the inexpressible aura with which God has always chosen to surround his being and everything that emanates from him.

It would not be difficult to compare and contrast their writings and to take sides with one or another tradition. But would this perhaps not be the wrong path to follow? Surely it is part of God's providence that the Eastern and the Western traditions exist in order to complement and enrich each other. We have a much better chance of understanding the truth by letting one tradition act as a corrective to the other whenever there seems to be a danger of exaggeration or misunderstanding in the direction followed by Eastern or Western thinking.

It is possible to distinguish two different tendencies underlying the Western doctrine of grace on the one hand and the Eastern doctrine on the other as well as the effects of those doctrines and the kinds of spirituality that they have produced. These two tendencies often counterbalance each other and, what is perhaps more important for us, they can be found in the writings of the great spiritual authors and philosophers whose work has had a lasting influence on later generations.

On the one hand, there is Plato, the idealist whose aim was to set the soul, which had come from the sphere of eternal ideas and was absorbed in eternal and infinite beauty, free from the body in which it was imprisoned and degraded. On the other hand, there is the much more positive and realistic thinker, Aristotle, who was, like Plato, corrected by the biblical and patristic tradition of thought and then baptized by Thomas Aquinas, who was then able to use the scientific structure of his philosophy as a valuable basis for his own theology.

Evagrius Ponticus, a bold thinker and a deeply spiritual writer who was faithful to the Eastern Christian tradition, worked within the framework of neo-Platonistic thought in the fourth century A.D. His counterpart in the West was Augustine, who was despite what has been called his "illuminism"—an aspect of his teaching that was later rectified by Thomas Aquinas—firmly within the Roman tradition.

In contrast to these and many other neo-Platonists were the neo-Aristotelian Christian thinkers. On the one hand, there was Thomas Aquinas, that powerful, serene and wonderfully balanced theologian who in his thought in no sense rejected neo-Platonism, but counterbalanced it. On the other hand, almost a century later, there was the Eastern bishop whom the Byzantine Christians and the Russians call Saint Gregory Palamas, a great thinker and mystic whose work cannot as yet be definitively assessed.

Both Thomas and Gregory were conscious of the deep abyss with which we are confronted in our attempt to reconcile the absolute transcendence of God who is inaccessible over man his physical and spiritual creature with the fact that this same God wants to communicate himself to his creature and even to deify and glorify him. The two theologians, however, differed in their understanding of God's transcendence. Gregory Palamas, in common with most Eastern thinkers, evolved an original synthesis that did not in any way impair the absolute simplicity of God, but which made a distinction between his essence that could not be known, and which should be called his "super-essence," and divine, essential and uncreated actions or energies performed or possessed by God. Whereas God's essence remains inaccessible to all spirits, even if they have been deified by grace, and hidden in the "cloud" or "shadow" that surrounds God's impenetrable light, man is able to share in his actions or energies. These actions or energies are the life of God, the life in which God gives himself and the life that cannot be separated from God's essence and the three persons of the Trinity who form one in this essence. These energies are manifested in the theophanies, the inspiration of the saints and the prophets and the supernatural experiences of the mystics.

This distinction between God's essence and his actions or energies enables us therefore to see that there is only one grace that is uncreated and by means of which God, who is beyond everything and all men, is able to communicate with his creatures. He will always be transcendent and the secret of his divine essence will continue until eternal life when he will take us up, deified, into his glory. The teaching of Gregory Palamas is fully within the tradition that goes back to an authentically biblical Judaism and which has come down to us through the writings of the Cappadocian Fathers and especially those of Gregory Nazianzen, who was acutely aware of the inexpressible nature of God.

Saint Thomas also made a distinction, not in God and not between the essence that preserves the secret of God's being and the energies in which man can share, but between uncreated and created grace, the second being the extension of the first in the soul and a divine quality capable of incorporating the soul into God and enabling it to share in his life.

This is an excellent doctrine, but it can easily be misunderstood. The term "created grace" can give rise, in the minds of those who are too imaginative or too anxious to achieve a mathematical precision, the idea of a second nature, "supernature" superimposed on the original nature. This may result in created grace being seen, as Mersch has said, "as a little being complete in itself, like a spiritual crown which God takes out of his treasure-chest and gives away, takes back again, beautifies or leaves as it is, in accordance with its merits."[1]

We know, however, that grace is not an entity, a thing or a substance that exists in itself and can be isolated. It is above all a unifying factor that cannot be separated from the God who gives it and from whom it emanates and from ourselves whom it beautifies, transforms and deifies. Thomas Aquinas has said that the beauty of grace comes from the splendor of the divine light.[2] It is the pouring out into us of God himself who loves us and who wants to adapt our lives to his. It is our soul itself that has been made sparkling, noble and elevated by this pouring out. As Mersch has said, "It is that through which what God gives to man in a divine manner exists in him [man] in a human manner," adding that "it is more and less than a closed entity, since it is not grace that exists, but man who exists through it." It is therefore an improving, a unifying and a perfecting factor, but because it is transcendent and supernatural, it perfects us by making us true sons of God, similar to God in our being, our lives, our habits and our holiness. Just as, in the mystery of the incarnation, grace made the man-God, so too does it, in a way that is derived from this first grace, make men divine.

Saint Thomas and Gregory Palamas, the Western and the Eastern theologians, used different terms, but complement each other, because both were moved by the same anxiety to safeguard God's inexpressible transcendence and divinity and yet needed to express the irresistible impulse of his love, the love that is his very being, which makes him give himself and raise his creature, man, whom he took from nothingness, up to himself. Both theologians understood that this truth is far removed from all pantheism and from all extrinsicism that might exclude God from his work. The drop of water that I am falls into the divine ocean, but it is not annihilated or absorbed by it. In the immensity of the divine reality, it remains itself a tiny reality that is glad to remain a creature, that is, an empty and open reality, since it can, as such, receive from the one whom it loves and can be plunged deeper and deeper into him.

Both Thomas and Gregory are in agreement about the inaccessibility of the divine essence. Gregory believed that it was impossible to have an adequate knowledge of God and to share in his divinity to the extent that we would ourselves be divine persons. Thomas also believed this and Louis Bouyer has commented that "the participation that he envisaged was no more than an analogous participation and his understanding of the question was not necessarily comprehensive."[3] Even when we see him face to face in the beatific vision, God will preserve his last secret, that of the ground of his being that has no ground because God is God. We shall see him *totus,* but not *totaliter.*

Both Eastern and Western theologians have drawn attention to certain aspects and placed different emphases on the work of God's grace, its effects and the ways in which it fashions and perfects us. It is in their vision of the creation and the incarnation that they seem to have been most influenced by the contrast between Platonic and Aristotelian thought.

Under the inspiration of Plato, Eastern Christians have tended to see in God's creatures a projection into the world of the senses divine ideas that are, like God himself, eternal. For them, the universe is therefore an expression of God and things are shared likenesses of God. In applying this view to the doctrine of grace, they have evolved an understanding of grace that shows it to be a more perfect image of God than the one received by man at his creation. Their view does not fill in the abyss that exists between nature and grace, but it does stress their continuity. And it has to be admitted that many passages in the writings of the Church Fathers—and especially of Saint Irenaeus—support this view.[4]

In the West, on the other hand, care has been taken not to deny the reality of this cause, God himself, and Thomas spoke frequently about it, especially, as we saw in the first chapter of this book, in his commentary on the Letter to the Hebrews (11. 3): "It is by faith that we understand that the world was created by one word from God." All the same, even when his thinking was Platonic, the one whom Chesterton called "Saint Thomas of the Creator" was always under the influence of Aristotle and he was therefore always conscious of the being who exists. He regarded the effective cause, not the formal cause, as of first importance. In his view, the emergence from God's being was at the root of those essences and, before it was a forest of symbols or an epiphany of the invisible world beyond this world, the world was a world of natures and causes that was autonomous, had its own value and enveloped thanks to the germs that God placed in it when he created it.

According to this view, grace is a power, helping and making up the deficiencies of nature and reaching what nature cannot in itself achieve—union with God, the creator. The dividing line is quite clear, since nature is unable to achieve this end by following its own course. The power from above is necessary if it is to be perfected and to reach the end that it is destined to reach. Grace can therefore be defined as a new power added to nature.

Even though this clear distinction between the natural and the supernatural orders was not made at the very beginning of the Christian era, it is still an important reality that must be carefully preserved and regarded as very precious. It serves in the first place to protect Christian teaching against a number of dangerous errors and it is secondly a light that throws the infinite wisdom of God and the harmony of his plans into sharp relief.

God has only one intention, one idea and one single will—to lead his creation forward, by gradually perfecting and deifying it, to glory. To achieve this end, his love and faithfulness are always at work and he gives gratuitously and generously without ceasing. For us, however, it is quite different to be taken out of the hands of our creator with all that is needed for our natural being to develop and to be given back, through the mediation and recapitulation of Christ, to the same creator and allowed to enter the secret of his life and enjoy the most delicate and intimate of relationships with the three persons of the blessed Trinity.

What we have to do, then, is to retain what is true and good in both these traditions. We have to be mindful with Saint Thomas and those who have followed him of the distinction between nature and grace. At the same time, we should also bear in mind, with Saint Irenaeus, the Cappadocian Fathers and the Eastern mystics, the sense of continuity between the work of God who loves us and wants to save us, that work which never ceases and is never interrupted so long as we do not prevent God, who has created this nature to support and contain his grace, from carrying it out, and the grace that he so abundantly gives in order to complete and crown nature.

We may say with conviction that these two different ways of interpreting grace reinforce each other. The Eastern tradition places the emphasis on the formal cause of beings in accordance with the Platonic way of thinking, and the Western teaching stresses the effective cause of creatures in the tradition of Aristotelian realism. This has resulted in the being of things being regarded in the Christian East as likenesses of God and the West attaching great importance to their activity as coming from what God has placed in them in the twofold gift of nature and grace. The two traditional teachings, which have led to two different forms of spirituality that are not so much contradictory as mutually complementary by virtue of their special emphases, can therefore be summarized as the order of being and the order of operation.

There is clear evidence of a great longing, even an obsession, in Hellenic Christian literature, present in man, who has been created in the image of God, to rediscover in a brilliant and pure form the likeness that he lost in original sin. He is concious of the fact that he belongs to God's "race," that he is "consubstantial" with God and that he will be deified by the Spirit seizing hold of his own spirit. This deification of man goes as far as the transfiguration of his body, thanks to a light which, arising from within, is a sharing in the light revealed on Mount Tabor.

Man's nature was originally "theophorous"—bearing God—and it should become this once again, rediscovering, in the clarity of a reborn innocence, perfect harmony with the creator, with itself, with other men and with the whole of the cosmos. It should once more become the faithful reflection of the Trinity. It should also complete God's great plan that was disrupted by original sin and, in the process of deification, take with it the whole world with which it is united. The ultimate end of this process is, after all, a glorification that extends to even the most humble aspects of God's creation.

The word "deification" is not regarded by the Eastern Christians as too strong a term for the progressive illumination of man's nature under the action of the Holy Spirit and the grace of Christ. It expresses the spiritual message of Easter and the resurrection. Seraphim of Sarov, the Russian mystic, repeated incessantly: "Christ, my joy, has risen!" and appeared to his disciple Motovilov in a radiance of light. This story is a good illustration of the Eastern Christian search for God.[5]

In the West too, we are also constantly looking for a paschal form of spirituality, and perhaps the highest expression of this is to be found in the liturgy of the resurrection, with its vigil and the *Exultet*. Gregory Nazianzen called the Easter liturgy the "solemnity of solemnities."

This spirituality is, however, different in quality from that of the East in that the concepts of deification and likeness are replaced in the West by the corresponding ideas of beatitude and operation or activity. Western Christians have always seen grace as an activity of God's being or a principle of supernatural operations. For them, glory, the perfect opening out of grace, is also the "effective principle of a beatifying act by means of which we shall see God as he sees himself."[6] According to Western thinkers, then, when we are in the heavenly paradise, all that we shall do is to share in this divine operation in which God contemplates himself and takes himself as the object of his own vision. We shall both operate like God and see God.

These two ways of considering God's grace, then, are derived from two different views of man that are not in opposition to each other, even though they differ remarkably from one another. Above all, they complement each other. The Western view of man, which is based largely on his activity, is primarily a moral one. The blessed vision of God is achieved, according to this Western anthropology, through divine and human holy actions. An important part is played by merit. The Eastern anthropological teaching, on the other hand, emphasizes the essentially religious and mystical aspect of man who is "theophorous" and created in the image of God. The psychological and ascetic aspects are much more strongly stressed in the West, but the mystical element is present and, in the depths of his being, the Western saint is very similar indeed to his counterpart in the

East. His mysticism, however, is always closely linked to morality and it is always directed toward the end, which is blessedness in the vision of God. The term that is used in the West is "divinization," rather than "deification."[7]

These are subtle differences and they should not be exaggerated. It would, however, be difficult to imagine that certain methodical treatises, dealing more fully with morality than with faith, writings that have been so common in the Western tradition of Christianity, could ever have come from the same environment as the work of Sergei of Radoniezh or even that of Vladimir Soloviev, who is undoubtedly the Russian theologian and mystic who is closest to us in the West.

It must be an act of providence on God's part that we have these differences and shades of interpretation, however, and it would be valuable if the two different traditions could be reconciled with each other. They would be mutually enriched. The Eastern teaching, based as it is on man's natural nobility and inspired by a fervent longing to go back to the original source and a powerful desire for the transfiguration of all being even before the resurrection at the end of time, brought about by the life-giving action of the Spirit of the risen Christ, would have much to give to and receive from the Western tradition with its moral preoccupations and its stress on the need to imitate the virtues of Jesus and to perform actions that are increasingly worthy and meritorious and therefore capable of bringing man further on the way toward the blessed life that is waiting for him beyond death.

All this constitutes grace and forms part of the essential mystery of the incarnation by which man is redeemed. But this very mystery has also been considered by the East and the West in the light of their different traditions and attitudes. It is true to say that, for both Eastern and Western Christians, Christ is the Word made flesh, the man-God, the mediator and the savior of mankind. But, for Western Christians, he is also the one who came to redeem us by his suffering and death, to annihilate sin, obtain forgiveness for us and reestablish between us and our Father in heaven a relationship of friendship that would take us into the kingdom of God.

For Eastern Christians, however, it is less important to find in Jesus a way of making good an offense against God and more urgent to see Jesus as the source of the grace that will enable man's nature to be restored to its original state, to become again capable of bearing God and to be consubstantial with the divine nature. Eastern Christianity teaches above all the need to be recreated and respiritualized.

It emphasizes that man must rediscover his true nature by means of a germ of incorruptibility that will make him immortal and, thanks to the leaven of the Eucharist, will ensure the resurrection of his body.

All this is true and all this is grace. We are saved by Jesus and taken back, repentant, to the house of our Father like the prodigal son. We are also recreated, as the apostle Paul said, by our whole being being taken up into the one who has recapitulated all things, the living vine and our Head. We are really deified in this way and made children of the light. Because we have access to the writings of John and Paul, we are able to know more than Nicodemus, for example, about this taking up into Jesus and this rebirth which is the fruit of God's grace. We should also remember that what is derived from this is a morality that aims to make us, who are grafted onto Christ himself, perform actions that are divinely human. These actions are also the principle of our transformation—as John the Evangelist said, "The man who lives by the truth comes out into the light" (John 3. 21)—and at the same time the sign and the promise of our blessedness that is to come.

We may also say that these two ideas—the Eastern concept of deification and likeness and the Western one of beatitude and operation or activity—have given rise to two different ways of regarding, within the framework of grace given to man, the cosmos which, in unity with man's destiny, is "groaning" while it is "eagerly awaiting" to be set free (Rom. 8. 19–22).

Far too often the Western Christian regards the cosmos and man's religion as quite separate entities. According to Barsotti, he seems to have overlooked the divinization of the world and the flesh in his preoccupation with the salvation of the soul. He tries to use and control the cosmos for the good of his fellow-men and in the service of God, whose word of truth he wants to take to the ends of the earth. A change seems, however, to be taking place in his attitude to the world and man is clearly becoming aware of a wider and greater reality.

The East can also teach him here to consider the salvation of the world. The soul is seen in the Eastern tradition as progressively illuminated by grace and, because of a mysterious solidarity with the universe, the latter is also transformed into a new heaven and a new earth, the new universe transfigured by God and his saints, as proclaimed by John in his Apocalypse (Rev. 21. 1). Man, then, is seen in the East as in communion with this world of animate and inanimate beings that God created for him and which is the con-

stant accompaniment of his highest plans. Soloviev, whose writings
on this subject are impressive and even apocalyptic, has said that
"God does not exist without the world and the world does not exist
without God. God and the world form a single whole."

All the mystics of the West are conscious of this and we can
share the immensity of their vision. We can name here only two examples—Francis of Assisi and John of the Cross—of men who were
led by divine grace to break every carnal link with the world and
other men and seek an extreme form of solitude. Following in the
wake of this grace, the gift of wisdom, these saints found that this
carnal link was replaced by a sacred one of great strength and beauty
between themselves and the universe, forged by the all-powerful
love of their creator.

How could this universe not be worthy to receive man, its king,
even before he appeared on earth? It consisted, after all, of those minute particles that were transfigured by grace and glory, the fragments that were to form the flesh of Christ and his immaculate
mother and to produce the bread and wine that were destined to be
transubstantiated into the body and blood of Christ. The earth was
saturated with that blood, making it the first-fruits of the blood of
so many martyrs. The water and oil of the cosmos, nourished by the
Word, were channels of grace. The same cosmos also fed the flesh
of God's elect, who were destined to rise again. The mystical vine
that was made for eternity and which came from the great living and
life-giving stock was also the produce of the cosmos. This cosmos,
with all its great and familiar changes, its heaven studded with
countless planets and stars, its alternating seasons and its dawns and
sunsets—surely this world radiates God's splendor and reveals his
very being.

Grace, then, reveals the immensities of God and his infinite
mystery to us by making us aware of his universe and his countless
creatures and invites us to ascend to God himself. It also tends to
expand our souls to embrace the dimension of the reality of which
it is the image and to unite us with the whole of creation. It is therefore important for us to go back to that place close to our souls
where grace is born if we are to try to define as precisely as possible
the part that it plays and the relationship that exists between the
presence of immensity and the presence of grace. Both these kinds
of presence exist together in us and neither can exist independently
of the other. We know too that the presence of immensity is the pri-
or condition for the presence of grace, but it does not necessarily

presuppose Augustine's "with God." Grace, then, is based on nature, but it transcends it infinitely.

Both kinds of presence come from the goodness of God and both are there in the soul of the just man. God is there as he is in a stone, a bird that chirps or a rose-tree in flower. He gives existence and movement. Like living water, a light or energy, his grace penetrates me. He is much more for me than the effective cause who created me and who continues to keep me in existence. He is a reality that is always new and admirable. He reveals and offers himself to me and lets himself be grasped by me. He wants to be the object of my love, known intimately to me. He seeks me out, tries to gain my freedom and to arouse desire in me. He has known me and loved me from eternity and calls on my spirit, my heart and my strength to cling to him in that small part of time and space where I exist by virtue of his eternal will.

Through his grace, then, God is substantially present in my soul as he is in all things and my soul in turn goes out to meet him. Grace therefore makes me look for, join and seize hold of God and there is no need to make him come down from heaven or come up from the depths of the earth in order to find him. He is already there, more intimate to myself than I am, in the depths of my own being. If I want him and if I answer his call, he is there and I am with him as he is already with me. Our glances and our wills are united through the density of creation and despite the reticence of a nature that prefers to be anonymous. Instead of being a stranger to me, he is able to be everything—my Father, brother, friend, host and spouse. As the object of my love and knowledge, he imposes no limits on that love and that knowledge. He is also able to reveal himself to me in the intimacy of his own life, in the depths where such intercourse takes place and at the point where the three persons of the Trinity cross each other and rest in each other. In this way, he can involve me in his trinitarian relationships. These three persons do not act independently of each other with me. The nature of God is revealed in three faces—those of the Father, the Son and the Spirit—and this is the principle of all divine activity. It is in their essential unity that these three persons created me and redeemed me when I became a sinner, and all three have poured into me that grace which enables me to regard them as my royal family with an infinite respect mixed with a sense of privacy and to share in their relationship.

I do not intend to discuss any controversial issues regarding grace and its prerogatives here, as I am not competent to do so. But

I think that it is certainly possible to accept the teaching that I have tried to outline here in this chapter, a doctrine based on the work of one of Thomas Aquinas's best commentators, John of Saint Thomas, and Father Gardeil's elaboration of this in his book, *La Structure de l'âme.* The relationship between the presence of immensity and the presence of grace does not necessarily have to be distorted by making grace replace the presence of immensity and claiming that, if the latter did not, by some remote possibility, exist, grace would still be present to make up for the deficiency. This assumption—"if by some remote possibility"—is in itself not possible. We have no need of such statements in order to give a high status to grace, when the prerogatives of grace are in themselves unlimited and immense.

So, we may conclude, God is in the creature that he has made in his own image through his presence, his power and his essence. As Saint Paul told the Athenians: "It is in him that we live and move and exist" (Acts 17. 28). This pronouncement can be transferred to the purely supernatural realm and we can say with William of Saint-Thierry that we are not in the Lord our God as we are in the air that surrounds us, but that we live in him through faith, move in him through hope and exist in him through love. Or we may say that we live in him thanks to the Spirit, the soul of our soul, who, in incorporating us into Jesus Christ, moves us toward the Father in whose bosom we, having become true sons of God and having found our true self, the self that God intended for us, exist.

NOTES

1. E. Mersch, *La Théologie du corps mystique,* II, pp. 252ff.
2. *Summa Theologiae,* IIa, IIae, q. 109, a. 7.
3. *Introduction à la vie spirituelle,* p. 157.
4. Especially in *Adv. haer.,* 4.38, 1–4.
5. See *La Vie spirituelle,* August-September 1952, Motovilov, "Comment l'Esprit de Dieu se manifeste en saint Séraphin de Sarov" and Divo Barsotti, *Le Christianisme russe,* p. 77.
6. For this difference in view between the East and the West, see Yves Congar, "La déification dans la tradition spirituelle de l'Orient," *La Vie spirituelle,* May 1935, pp. 91ff.
7. The two words "deification" and "divinization" are not completely synonymous. The first, which is derived from the noun *Deus,* is stronger than the second, which is derived from the adjective *divinus.* It implies that God seizes hold of us and makes gods of us (clearly by participation). The second implies a divine action that raises our human nature gradually up to God and has us taken up into a divine way of life by transforming us into his image.

6

God's Presence in Us Through Our Supernatural Organism

We have, by God's grace, been torn away from the power of darkness, raised above our nature and taken into a kingdom of light and life, a mystery which is God himself, God revealed and given in his beloved Son. It is, however, clear that, if we are to live in this kingdom, we must have a way of life that is the way of life of our Father. We must once again have the image of God which cannot be lost, that of Christ Jesus, and become new men. We must allow ourselves consciously to be seized by God, who is always ready to communicate with us and be "everything to everyone" (1 Cor. 15. 28), and let him be present in us. If, however, we are to respond fully to this appeal and know the vision of this presence and if we are to obey the demands made by God docilely and in the full freedom of our souls, we must have a supernatural organism that is as perfectly sufficient and harmonious as our natural organism is in its own sphere. Let us look a little more closely at this organism that has been introduced into our being by the grace of baptism.

The word "organism" is used here, but regretfully, since it inevitably calls to mind a material or physical reality. What we are considering here, however, is purely spiritual. We must therefore banish from our minds all the limited and spatial associations of the word and any relationship that it has with the senses. At the same time, we should retain its expressiveness and the rich complexity of meaning that it has in its application to our natural organism.

What, then, is an organism? It is, surely, a whole formed of various parts, each differently structured, hierarchically ordered and capable of carrying out special functions, but despite their differences, all tending toward the same end—the good of the living being.

If God has achieved this in such a splendid way both in plants and animals and in the moral dispensation, then surely he can do the same in the supernatural order. Let us consider for a moment the organism of the plant—to achieve its aim, which is to produce fruit, it has been made by God the creator a whole consisting of roots, stem, branches and leaves. In the same way, the human body is formed of limbs and organs all adapted to carry out certain physiological functions in unity with each other and all contributing to the upkeep and development of human life. All this has the aim of fulfilling healthy life.

By analogy with the natural and moral order, the soul also, we may say, has an organism, since it is a substance of spiritual nature that tends toward an end, which is, in its case, the good that it has to accomplish in its acts. In order that it should reach this end, God has provided it with various faculties, each with the function of carrying out different actions. These faculties include, for example, intelligence, which is capable of grasping truth, the will, which is directed toward good, and the senses, which if they are guided by reason and the will, are intended to enable us to perceive those realities that address themselves to our sensual being and to which our senses, which Chesterton, following Saint Thomas, called the windows of the soul, lead us.

God, who in his infinite wisdom, acts gently but with strength, with the aim of ordering all means to their end, wanted this inner organization of the soul that he created in his image to be found in a mysterious way at a higher level, that is, in the pure supernatural sphere. It was his plan from the beginning that the soul should share in his eternal happiness through the glorious vision of his essence. For this reason, he wanted the soul, which he created capable of carrying out actions that would prepare for this contemplation of God, to be at the same time able to know and love God even in this world as he knows and loves himself. If, however, the soul is to have this supernatural knowledge and love of God and share, through its actions, in God's life, it must have a complex of faculties, powers and mystical organs. These have, in fact, been given to the soul by God in a supreme act of love.

What comes from this great resource of grace and this participation in God's nature, in accordance with the essence that is infused at the most intimate level of being into what Saint Thomas, following Saint Augustine, called the *mens,* are the infused virtues and the gifts of the Holy Spirit. These amount to a participation in God's nature in accordance with the powers introduced into the faculties. When this happens, we witness the splendid harmony between grace and the natural order, in which grace blends in with the outline of nature to such an extent that, when the soul has been fully deified, nature seems to be present only as a framework supporting grace. God himself hands over his divinity, the intimacy of his life in the Trinity, both through and with us—since, as Scripture tells us, he treats us with great respect—to the soul that tends toward him, whose beauty draws to itself everything that goes from it. This beauty, which is nothing more or less than the whole complex of God's perfections closely interwoven into each other and the unique splendor from the unique agglomerate of God's attributes, is the center from which all movement, all order and all desire flow to him.

Let us now turn our attention to this supernatural organism. We will consider it first as a whole and then we will look at the different mechanisms, if I may be allowed to use this word, that contribute to its activity.

At the summit of this organism is the transcendent principle that moves, directs, regulates and watches over everything—the third person of the Trinity, the Spirit of love. Saint Irenaeus tells us that, whereas the Spirit is the third person with regard to God coming to us, he is certainly the first with regard to our ascension and our return to God.[1] He makes us holy by uniting us with and incorporating us into Christ Jesus, who breathes the Spirit into us with his Father. Christ Jesus also takes us, as sons in the one Son, to his Father. This divine person, the Holy Spirit, who forms the end of the cycle of activities of the Trinity, has received from God the mission to be fertile here on earth by acquiring an unlimited number of adopted sons for the Father. Although we shall consider this question more closely later, it is important to note here and now that the Spirit of truth and love, thanks to his ability to persuade us to be led by him, plays the important part in our supernatural organism that reason plays in our natural organism.

Charity is at the heart of this supernatural organism, in which it is spread by the Holy Spirit, from whom it comes as the effect comes from its cause. As Saint Paul has said, "the love of God has been poured into our hearts by the Holy Spirit which has been given to us" (Rom. 5. 5). This charity is the center from which two sets of seven virtues or gifts come—the three theological and the four cardinal virtues which are made supernatural by charity on the one hand and the seven gifts of the Spirit on the other. Charity is the dynamic unity at the center of this double septenarium, linking together the different operations. Everything radiates charity, which in turn moves and harmonizes everything. It is also the spiritual mortar which makes the building solid and a single, beautiful whole.

The other two theological virtues are also central to this supernatural organism and they are certainly of greater importance in the structure as a whole than the other virtues. Their function is above all to unite the soul directly with God. Faith has, as its formal objective, God himself, and by faith we are able to know God as he knows himself in his eternal Word who became man for us and thus initiated our faith. As the author of the epistle to the Hebrews says, he "leads us in our faith and brings it to perfection" (Heb. 12. 2). Hope, the formal object of which is also God, is the third central theological virtue. God will never disappoint our hope, as his faithfulness and goodness are as unfailing as his omnipotence.

These three theological virtues are joined together in unbreakable unity. Charity receives from faith light that it transforms into warmth. In return, it gives life to faith and leads it to its final completion. Hope fulfills charity by expanding the beatifying aspect of its object that love, which is entirely disinterested with regard to the infinitely lovable character of its object, cannot make explicit.

Charity also deeply influences the moral virtues that come from it. The aim of these virtues, which are inferior to the three theological virtues that enable us to cling directly to God, is to regulate our relationships with our fellow-men and the outside world, but this aim is contained within the other, superior aim of our supernatural destiny. It would be true to say that, in this sphere too, everything has love as its point of departure and as its end-point.

What, then, is temperance? It is, surely, love that preserves itself integrally for the loved one. What is fortitude? It is love that easily undergoes all tests for the sake of the loved one. Justice is also love of the kind that rules over all creatures in the service of its unique object and in order to make sure of this service. Finally, the fourth of these virtues, prudence, is a love that is clearly aware of everything that will allow it to flourish and which will remove all obstacles to that flourishing. Prudence is undoubtedly the leading cardinal virtue, because, in the light of faith and the ardor of charity, it decides what the other three virtues of justice, fortitude and temperance have to achieve.

In this way, because of the inflowing of charity coming from the Holy Spirit, there is a wonderful intermingling of the theological with the moral virtues. The theological virtues are like three heavenly bodies situated at the summit of our inner life or the peak of our faculties. They pour their light and warmth on the cardinal virtues, which in turn make God's grace penetrate into our way of life and habits and even into the complexity of our social life.

The seven virtues, then, are like channels through which the Holy Spirit is able to spread throughout the whole of man both intelligence and will and a great love in such a way, moreover, that the person who experiences this can say in all truth with the psalmist: "Bless the Lord, my soul, all that is in me, bless his holy name!" (Ps. 103).

This indirect action of the Holy Spirit in us through the charity that he pours into us is, of course, excellent, but the total reality of our supernatural organism is even more excellent, since that reality is able to respond to the wisdom of God, who surely cannot want our supernatural organism to be less perfect than our natural organism.

If the Holy Spirit is at the root of our being and present in us as the heart of our heart, our cool reason will still remain in control of our moral life, even though this has already been raised to the supernatural level of existence by charity. The Spirit is still free to act in us by means of the virtues, while at the same time being, as it were, the prisoner of that created love which inevitably feels the effects of the obscurity of our faith. In its attempts to expand beyond itself, its movement is blocked by the necessary, but fatal indwelling of the three theological virtues in our human faculties, even though those virtues are really the ultimate fulfillment of our own faculties.

If we are to understand what our supernatural organism must inevitably have in order to achieve its aim, we should consider our human organism. We have, in the first place, full possession of our reason, which is the principle of our human organism, and of the virtues, which permanently help our reason to shed its light on our moral life. Our human constitution in itself requires this. The Holy Spirit, however, is at the summit of our supernatural organism and is therefore far above us, living in sovereign transcendence. The theological virtues too are far above the natural moral virtues in the dignity of their being and the nobility of their aim, which is the immediate knowledge of God. Our possession of these three virtues is, however, very imperfect, if only because they are present in us as the gift of another. Although our supernatural perfection is infinitely superior to our natural perfection, because it is a divine reality, it is therefore less fully interiorized, in that it is less perfect "in us."

It is precisely because they are interior and con-natural that the natural virtues are able to act dynamically. This is why Father Lajeunie said that

> Our reason has a deep and natural effect, at least when it begins to function. It easily becomes dominant and powerful, especially in the case of the virtuous person. This interiority is not, however, perfect in us in the case of the supernatural virtues. The light shed in us by these virtues has to become, as it were, acclimatized in the soul. It is too sublime and immeasurable. Although it is con-natural with our first knowledge of it, it can never in itself be con-natural with our human understanding. It will never spring up inside us in a perfectly instinctive way. These supernatural habits will consequently never be perfect skills or complete powers.[2]

Because of their sublimity, then, the three theological virtues, which are fully acclimatized to the eternal, but not to the human mode of being, are not at ease in us and consequently not capable of producing a perfectly harmonious relationship between us and God. They are present at the summit of our faculties like three splendid planets, but they are austere and too high for our poor faculties, with the result that they are constrained to act at the level of our human mode of being. They are certainly present in our most intimate depths, working almost exclusively for our union with God, but they always remain isolated in us. Faith is a light in us, but left in its pure state, it is like a lamp shining in a dark place. What a great gap there is between the truths of faith expressed in the human formulas of our creeds and the truth itself in its glowing reality! However carefully I might observe everything to do with my faith, the mystery remains impenetrable and the God in whom I believe continues to be the hidden God. Faith, then, is in this sense imperfect, as are hope and charity. Deprived of help, these two theological virtues inevitably tend to let the soul sink into a permanent state of relaxation and give way to natural activities of a lower and easier kind.

The same defect can also be perceived in the operation of the infused moral virtues. Even though they are filled with charity and raised up because of their supernatural end, they still continue to be dependent on our reason, which watches over them and guides them. We know too that man's natural reason tends to see the perfect way of life as a golden mean placed equally between the two extremes. This has been described as the *mediocritas aurea* of the pagan world. This mean can, however, be raised to the height of our divine end, when it consists of an ordering of our passions and our activities so that they are directed toward that end and a reduction of all excesses and a giving of correct dimensions so that they are able to achieve their proper aim. The Holy Spirit can therefore be said to act hidden in this obscurity and within the golden mean. This activity is gentle and at the same time energetic. It wants, as the source of grace in our being, to take everything along with it and to submerge everything.

God has provided for everything. He did not want the thrust of the Spirit in us to be in any way impeded or even reduced. Nor did he want this great desire to embrace him to remain unawakened in us. It was his will that we should not only see him face to face in the eternal vision, but also that we should possess him even now, in this life, in an immediate way. The children of light after all should be able to contemplate their Father with their eyes enlightened by their hearts and believe in love, if they have already experienced, intimately and personally, that God is love. God did not, moreover, want us, as poor fallen beings, to remain at a far lower level than the end to which we are moving. Finally, he was anxious that we should not be incapable of fulfilling the requirements of our duties, which call for heroic virtue at times and plain faithfulness always. Yet we are so vulnerable in the presence of temptations, which are frequently quite violent because our human nature is always inclined to satisfy our senses and to seek carnal pleasure that even simple faithfulness is made very difficult by what Pope Pius XI once called the suffocating fumes of everyday life. We have been given the gifts of God's Holy Spirit in order that we should be strengthened and at the same time raised up to him, in spite of all the obstacles both inside us and in the world outside.

These gifts are not sources of activity like the virtues that we have been discussing, but wonderfully receptive factors that place us under the domination of our reason, thus subjecting us to the direct influence of the Spirit of truth and love. Just as there are seven infused virtues, so too are there seven of these gifts of the Holy Spirit and they point, not to a limitation, but to a fullness and a great diversity. They should not be confused with the activity of the Holy Spirit himself, although these gifts set this activity in motion, by their supple, prompt, docile and available character making us passive under the action of the Holy Spirit and handing us over to him like a great field of action unfolding itself, or a sensitive instrument ready to be used by the inspired artist. With respect to the activity of the Holy Spirit, these gifts occupy a similar place to that occupied by man's moral virtues with respect to his reason. This means, in other words, that they permanently help the Spirit of God, who can, from his place at the root of our love, freely pour out his being into our being and make us true sons of God in the one Son.

Through the virtues, the Spirit is able to spread out in us like a fire warming the heart, a gentle light illuminating our being without revealing the source from which it comes or oil flowing over the limbs strengthening and softening the joints. In this, the Spirit takes on the shape of our reason and our human love.

When the seven gifts are bestowed on us, however, everything is brought to life, opened out and transfigured. They function as a glowing hearth, whose flames heat everything in us or as a strong light from the face of God shining on our own, penetrating to the depths of our being, transforming us and communicating to us God's own joy. When this happens, our heart becomes a sun, spreading its rays around us. The whole of our inner world—not only the depths, but also the approaches—is activated by the Spirit of God with the reception of the seven gifts and it may even happen that what the psalmist described takes place in us: "My heart and my flesh sing for joy to the living God!" (Ps. 84. 2).

We should not think, however, that the Spirit always acts in a brilliant and striking way. He makes himself felt above all in ordinary, everyday life with a discretion that is worthy of God, and his action is therefore as often silent as it is obvious. The soul has to be very attentive to catch the murmur of this living water flowing quietly from the depths of the Trinity. At the same time, it is true to say that we are constantly subject to the action of these gifts, which have an effect similar to that of direct heat from the fire of the Spirit, although that heat is to some extent made bearable by being tempered by the virtues that are perfected in this process.

We have already seen how imperfectly the theological virtues function in us because of their sublimity and their need to conform to the way that our own human faculties act. The gifts of the Spirit have the effect, however, of making the virtues interior within us and of enabling us to feel the presence of the eternal God immanently. Their function, in a word, is to make God's life in us as easy, as con-natural and as perfectly our own as our rational life is in our natural being. In this way, the seven gifts raise the seven virtues above the human mode of being and, by filling them with their fire and their gentle unction, make them flourish with a vitality that they could never otherwise have: "Awake, north wind! Come, wind of the south! Breathe over my garden to spread its sweet smell around" (Song of Songs 4. 16). It is because of the breath of the Spirit that the three heavenly bodies, faith, hope and charity, which would otherwise be rough and severe, are covered with sweetly smelling flowers, succulent fruit and tender vegetables. Thanks to the gifts of understanding, knowledge and wisdom, they are freed from all human impurity and able to impress on the soul the virginity of the spirit that Saint Augustine discussed in his commentary on the gospel of Saint John: "What is this virginity of the spirit? It is entire faith, firm hope and sincere charity" (*In Ev. Joh., Tract.* 13).

The gift of understanding, unlike reason, is essentially a simple insight or intuition. Through it, the darkness of faith is illuminated by a light that is a source of great delight. As the psalmist says: "To you night would be as light as day" (Ps. 139. 12).

The gift of knowledge reveals God to us through and beyond his creation and enables us to be detached from creatures and rest in God. Our hope is not directed toward an inaccessible and remote object, but becomes confident and secure, wrapping us in warmth and tenderness of a kind that clearly come from God. Here too the psalmist has said: "You find shelter beneath his wings. . . . His faithfulness is a shield and buckler" (Ps. 91. 4).

Through the gift of wisdom we can taste and experience God and see all creatures and, at their source, God as their first and most eminent cause. Wisdom is transfigured in the love of God which is stronger than death and whose flame cannot be extinguished by the waters of suffering. The author of the Song of Songs has said: "For love is as strong as death . . . love no flood can quench, no torrents drown" (Song of Songs 8. 6–7).

The virtues of prudence and fortitude are perfected by the gifts of counsel and fortitude. The gift of piety makes the virtue of justice lovingly submissive, respectful and grateful and we are in turn made even more than servants of God—we become true children of God.

Finally, the gift of fear helps the virtue of temperance by putting us on our guard against the emotions aroused by the boldest attacks of sinfulness. In this way, then, thanks to the gifts of the Holy Spirit and the effects of the three theological virtues, the infused moral virtues give the Christian an ease and a heroism that enable him to be a divine man.

The activity of these gifts remains hidden and secret, like sap working inside the growing trunk of the tree of life, forcing its bark open as new branches grow out—new life bearing leaves, flowers and fruit. This sap is essential to what Bossuet called the "incomprehensibly serious aspect of Christian life," that note of spontaneity, freshness and youth which characterizes those who, following Christ and his grace, are born again and again in the Spirit by drawing incessantly on the treasure of baptism. This permanently new aspect of Christian life enables us to perform the simplest tasks with greatness because of the majesty of God dwelling in us and to accomplish the most difficult and strenuous work easily because of God's omnipotence operating in us.

The gifts of the Spirit do not, however, have the same effect on the theological virtues as they have on the moral virtues. In the case of the first, they constitute not a sovereignty, but a service because of the dignity of the three theological virtues which bind us directly to God. In the case of the second, they have a guiding and even a dominating influence.

In this context, it is worth noting how freely and in what an infinite variety of ways the Spirit comes to us. He measures out the strength of his breath as he will. Sometimes it comes as a great wind, sweeping, as it were from the high seas, and carrying everything with it. At others, it is no more than a gentle breeze that can only be heard by the ear of the heart. The storm and the whisper—Moses on Mount Sinai and Elijah on Horeb—both make the strings of the musical instrument of our virtues and gifts vibrate in different ways and with a different volume of sound.

As Father Gardeil has said,

Sometimes the Spirit lets charity and the moral virtues continue on their course and does no more than simply watch over them. Sometimes he intervenes in their progress with his gifts and strengthens or corrects them. Sometimes he makes the gift act without the virtue by means of an inspiration. Sometimes he directs a virtue by means of a gift or directs that gift by means of a superior gift. In this way the Holy Spirit uses a great variety of means and his benefits are infintely rich.

The activity of the Holy Spirit which is, as we have seen, so infinitely varied, is expressed in all these holy realities that together form the network of the life of the real Christian. What, then, are the fruits of the Spirit, the ways in which he makes his being powerfully present? These fruits are manifested in many different ways. We can mention here, for example, the sacrifices accomplished with love that mark the steps in which the soul is purified and makes its gradual ascent to God. We can also include the resolutions, correct actions, wise counsels, delicate acts of piety, penetrating insights and good decisions made by the serious Christian and his patience, sense of God's presence and calm, wise enthusiasm. Saint Paul enumerates several such "fruits" in which the just man experiences deep spiritual pleasure in his letter to the Galatians (5. 22). Among these are peace, joy and chastity. The beatitudes of the Sermon on the Mount (Matt. 5. 3–11) are also fruits of the Holy Spirit. These works perfect the Christian in holiness and transport him to a world that is entirely new, the world which we call the kingdom of God and which is to be found in the depths of his being, where the values of this present world are reversed: "Happy are the poor . . . Happy are those who mourn . . . Happy are those who are persecuted. . . ."

Finally, the obscurity and the golden mean favored by pagan thinkers in the context of the virtues seem to disappear under the influence of the gifts of the Spirit. God, who is mystery itself, will, however, always remain the God who is seen in this life only as an enigma in a mirror, and we know how he has made even those who are powerfully moved by the Spirit of his love pass through the experience of night. Nonetheless, when he is pleased to do so and even when we are in the deepest darkness of the soul, we are sometimes allowed to experience him. In spite of his transcendence, he wants to be tasted and touched and the veil that conceals him from our gaze is so thin and transparent that the just man, following Moses, is able to stand in front of him who is invisible as though he can see him (see Heb. 11. 27).

The golden mean of pagan thinkers also to some extent disappears, or at least it disappears in the form in which we spoke of it above, as a middle course placed equidistantly between two extremes, those of excess on the one hand and total absence on the other. It has been correctly pointed out that Christian truth differs from all other teachings in that it does not accord a mediocre neutrality to wisdom, but endows it with attributes that are apparently contradictory and filled with an extreme intensity of meaning. In Christian teaching, wisdom is magnanimous and humble at the same time, strong and yet gentle, austere and tender, joyful and penitent, able to love and to renounce. . . . These extremes appear to contradict each other, but there is no real contradiction. They act as counterbalances to each other and give an inner equilibrium to man that enables him to live fully in accordance with both nature and grace. Stretched out, as it were, on a cross, man lives in a state of tension. All that he has to do is to extend his arms and he can become one with this cross and in this way adapt himself inwardly to the mystery.

It is especially in the beatitudes, which anticipate the happiness of eternity, that the opposite poles are united. Mercy, a quality that is without limits, is united to our hunger and thirst for justice. Poverty, which penetrates to the deepest recesses of our soul, is made one with the possession of the wealth of the kingdom of God. Mourning, caused both by need and by vanity, is closely associated with the perfect joy of God's consolation.

"You must be perfect just as your heavenly Father is perfect" (Matt. 5. 48). In fulfilling this commandment, man shares in the mystery of these apparent contradictions in which we see in God an identification of attributes that would seem to be quite irreconcilable—God is apparently both unchangeably absolute and perfectly free, the source of enjoyment and yet supremely wise and finally unfailingly just and yet infinitely merciful. The Christian who has been recreated in the image of the Son by the Spirit is able, in all that he experiences and does that is similar to his model in the heavenly Father, to conform to this calling to be a son of God. Who are the peacemakers who are called sons of God? They are those who radiate the tranquillity of inner order, the fruit of the normal, free and happy expansion of all the splendor of new life received in baptism. This inner order consists of a calm power found in the superabundance of wealth already possessed: "Peace inside your city walls! Prosperity to your palaces!" (Ps. 122. 7).

This wish expressed by the psalmist that Jerusalem here on earth, which is, of course, the type of heavenly Jerusalem, should be prosperous and peaceful can clearly be applied to the peacemakers mentioned in the Sermon on the Mount. Because of its purity, beauty, clarity, unity and energy, the soul, in a state of grace and fortified by the virtues and the gifts of the Spirit, is an image of the city and the bride that appeared to the prophet of Patmos. Saint Bonaventure said that we have ourselves to be a heavenly Jerusalem if we are to be allowed to enter the eternal Zion. The treasures described in the vision of the Apocalypse (chapter 21) can therefore with justice be applied to the soul that has been baptized.

Saint John speaks of the holy city coming down from heaven and appearing on the top of a mountain as a single, brilliant whole. In the same way, grace comes down on us from the sanctuary of the Trinity in heaven and rests on the summit of our soul with all its riches, setting up its abode with us as a single whole with its virtues and gifts. Unlike the natural virtues, which we make our own by practicing them, the supernatural energies become established in us at once, as if they had been grafted by God as a whole and with all their natural dynamism onto the active stock of our own nature. Our supernatural organism rules over both our natural being and the created world from this summit.

But what is the river of living water, clear as crystal, which Saint John describes as flowing from the throne of the Lamb down through the whole city? It is the Holy Spirit, the source and the fertile motivating force of our supernatural organism, the Spirit compared by Jesus Christ himself, following the prophets, compared with living water flowing from the depths of God's being (John 7. 38) and welling up to eternal life (John 4. 14).

What is the tree of life placed in the center of the city and watered by the river beside which it is growing, the tree that bears fruit continuously throughout the year? It is charity at the heart of our supernatural dynamism, its effects being felt without ceasing.

What is the gold of which the city is built? It too is charity, seen in its unifying character and as a universal spiritual power. It is not, after all, seen as opaque, but as transparent gold that lets the eternal and unfailing light of God and the Lamb shine through without in any way dimming its brilliance.

Finally, what are the gates at each of the four points of the compass, connecting the city with the outside world? They are the four moral virtues that form the link between us and the world.

The vision of Saint John provides us above all with an impression of balance and at the same time of brilliance. The city that comes down as a bride is perfectly square and this is reflected in ourselves—there are seven gifts and seven virtues. All the stones used in its construction gleam and sparkle in their different colors, but the dominant color is green. Green is the symbol of eternal youth, which is here applied to the Church and the redeemed soul of the Christian which is constantly bathed in hope, living in the freshness

of repeated regeneration, watered by the Spirit, made fruitful by the
tree of life and enlightened by the clear light of the eternal present.

In contemplating the unbelievable greatness and beauty of the
eternal city, we should not, however, overlook its intimate aspect.
This city is emphatically described as the bride dressed for her husband. Saint John also says: "Here God lives among men." We are his
and he is ours. In the city there is nothing but joy and tenderness
and God himself wipes away all the tears from the eyes of those who
are intimately united with him. There is no more death and no more
sadness in this tabernacle. Only love has a place here.

In this world, on the other hand, we are born poor and naked,
even though we are created in the image of God. God did not spare
his own Son, but gave him up to benefit us all, Saint Paul said and
added, in view of this, we may be sure that he will also give us all
things with Christ (Rom. 8. 32). Unfortunately, however, Bossuet's
melancholy observation is all too true: "There are so many things
in us that we do not possess!" But we may be more positive and
thank God for the treasures of grace in our being that we have received from the deep silence of the Father, the full divinity and humanity of the Son and the abundant pouring out of their one Spirit.
Despite the many tests that we have to undergo, each of us is, however commonplace our life may seem to be, a heaven filled to overflowing with the presence of God and his gifts, a heaven in which
there is no place for fear. Each of us can say confidently with Saint
Paul: "There is nothing I cannot master with the help of the one
who gives me strength" (Phil. 4. 13).

Possessed by the Spirit, the city and bride of our soul looks forward to the victorious parousia of the one whose face we are constantly seeking. In the words of the author of the book of Revelation, we too can say: "Come, Lord Jesus!" (Rev. 22. 20). One day
we shall grasp him as he has already grasped us here on earth. The
countless supernatural organisms that are no more or less than universes will become one single organism without losing anything of
their individual originality. They will become the body of Jesus
Christ in its final perfection, an immense body of which he is the
head and the Holy Spirit is the soul.

"Know your dignity, Christian," Saint Leo said. "You share in
God's nature and you should not return to the lower state that you
had before by a life that is unworthy of your real condition. Always
remember the head to whom you belong and the body of which you
are a member. Do not forget that you were taken from the power

of darkness and transported into the light and the kingdom of God."[3]

NOTES

1. *Demonstration*, 7; *Adv. haer.*, 4. 20, 5; 36, 2.
2. *La Vie spirituelle*, June 1937.
3. *Sermon*, 21, 3.

7

Christian Life in the Presence of God

According to Saint Bonaventure, we ourselves have to be a heavenly Jerusalem if we are to enter the city and bride of which the visionary on the island of Patmos caught a glimpse. In this, we are not thiking exclusively of the soul in all the splendor and holiness given to it by the grace of baptism. We are reminded rather of the soul united in marriage to God by the full expansion of all the wealth that God has given it in sanctifying grace. Our supernatural organism is perfect in itself, since it contains all that it needs to achieve the fullness of divine life that constitutes holiness. The perfection of the Christian who is still on the way as a traveler (*viator*) on earth is not normally the same as the definitive and full perfection of the creature who has been restored to original innocence and is in possession of the end toward which it has been tending for so long. Holiness is the fruit of a slow, progressive conquest that includes a great number of actions, each one going further than the last and making up for the defects of the last. Life in the presence of God is therefore very far from being a static reality. It is essentially dynamic. It is movement, becoming, progress and ultimately consummation.

It is important for us to make full use of this wealth that is grafted onto our most intimate being, to give it full scope and allow it to expand and increase without limitation. The vigor and intensity of life that this wealth of grace gives us should be encouraged to spread. It is a fire that Jesus came to light on earth and it must burn in our hearts. It is a stream of living water flowing in him, in his Church and in each one of us, in whom it must become a spring of eternal life (Luke 12. 49; John 4. 14).

Living is becoming conscious of everything that God has done through love, and through his Christ, outside us and without us, once and for all time—the incarnation, the passion and the resurrection above all. The mystery of Christ will be realized in and for us only by means of the daily faithfulness and love of an existence that is given to us ultimately only for this purpose. As Augustine said, "God who created us without us will not save us without us."

If the fire that Jesus came to spread is to burn and if the living water is to return to the spring from which it flows, we must want this to happen. It is at this point that we encounter the important question of our freedom. It is a terrible but wonderful thing that, if it is really true that God is all-powerful, then it must also be true that he can do nothing without us. As Paul Claudel says in *The Hostage:* "Oh my child, what is weaker and more defenseless than God, when he cannot do anything without us?" Our freedom, which is the seal of our human dignity as creatures made in God's image, is the indispensable condition of our acceptance of God's grace. That is why, in every man's life, there is one moment, perhaps the most serious of all, when we are able to decide between the two ways, the good way and the way of evil.

We are extremely simple at the source of our being, where there is a plain "yes" and a "no" which can only be intermingled or confused if we make concessions to a sinful world that is composed of vanity and lies. As soon as we reach what Thomas Aquinas called the age of reason—and that may be as children, before we are mature—we have to choose between the way of duty that leads to God, our sovereign good, and the way of desire that will lead us away from God and make us love ourselves above everything else. At that moment of choice, the child's soul is helped by prevenient grace and so long as he does not resist that grace, he is bound to take the right path which, Saint Thomas assures us, leads from grace to grace until the final grace of a good death and salvation is achieved.

God never ceases to follow us on the winding path of our life, as we fall and again and again get up, with his grace. He acts in the first place in order to orientate us toward our final end and after that he allows us to move freely toward him.

Really great decisions that set us on the path of heroic sacrifice are, of course, rare and when they have to be made the soul enters into combat with God. It is then as if two swords flash and strike each other until man eventually gives up, conquered and conquering, like the patriarch Jacob with the angel at the ford of the Jabbok.

More often, however, it is in the course of apparently dull, everyday life that the soul is wooed by grace, which calls to us in the depths of our being as it called to the Maid of Orléans: "Daughter of God, come! I am with you!" But, however compelling the voice of grace may be, it never ceases to say: "You are free; but if you want to be perfect as your heavenly Father is perfect, if you want to be my disciple, my friend, my sister, my bride, come—follow me!"

Everything in our supernatural organism is formed with admirable skill to ensure that we retain our full freedom in all that we do when we are confronted with God's initial act. Supernatural charity and the Holy Spirit, who acts as the soul of our own soul, spreading this charity in our hearts, are inseparably tied to each other, although they remain different. The just man performs good actions with an ease, a spontaneity and a joy that prove that everything flows from its source because it is impelled by God who is more ourselves than we are and who inspires and impels us forward.

God and man—grace and freedom—are made to work together. We should not oppose this collaboration, but make sure that it functions with admirable harmony at two different levels, the uncreated and the created levels. Who makes the rose open and flower? Obviously it is God the creator, but it is also the rose-tree. "Without me you can do nothing," Jesus said, but the apostle Paul adds something to this which illuminates it powerfully: "Work for your salvation in fear and trembling, for it is God, for his own loving purpose, who puts both the will and the action into you" (Phil. 2. 13).

As Matthias Joseph Scheeben pointed out, a great mystery is contained within this text. Does it not show us clearly that the reason that the apostle gives for our fear is at the same time the reason for our hope and our trust? It is because the will and the action both depend on God's grace that we have to work out our salvation in fear and trembling, in other words, in a kind of holy terror. The soul is in the presence of God who never ceases to work with it, help it and remain with it. It knows that God will, as Paul also said, one day finish the good work that he has begun in us, namely on "the day of Christ Jesus" (Phil. 1. 6). So what does our own weakness matter? We know that, if we respond faithfully to the help that God always gives us, we shall preserve within us the grace that will lead us to our end.

It is therefore true that our human freedom is subject to God's action and that our will is dependent on grace and its free will and the persistent, efficacious and con-natural exercise of God's will. Our good works are certainly our own, but it is God who performs them in us in order to accomplish his eternal plans through us. The way in which our meritorious acts are harmonized with God's eternal and unfailing decrees is a great mystery, but how is it possible for the Christian who considers this mystery in the clear light of a living faith to be troubled by it? Surely this subjection of our free will to God's will and to the movement of his grace should be an unending source of security, peace and happiness. This divine inflowing of grace, which embraces and penetrates our freedom and which orientates us toward good by investing that good with a great power to attract or, if that attraction is not there, by giving us the strength to break through our reluctance, is quite different from any fatal feeling weighing down on us. We cannot escape God! The very idea is capable of impelling us forward! We have, after all, the certainty that God is love, that all his ways are, as the psalmist said, mercy and truth, that his pleasure, far from being arbitrary, is tender and wise and that this infinite tenderness and wisdom of God are also infinitely powerful.

It is possible for us to be raised up by this combination of love, wisdom and infinite power that enclose our poverty and weakness as creatures on all sides and increase in us the virtue of humility. God treats us always with great respect and tenderness. He who is not in the mighty wind, the earthquake and the fire is to be found in gentleness and it is with gentleness that he, who has recreated us in the blood of the one who is meek and humble of heart, treats us. We are led both gently and powerfully—*suaviter fortiterque.* Grace grants us all that we need so that we may reach the haven of blessedness. At the same time, it also gives us the joy of conquest, even though it is the first cause of that conquest and the only reward that God gives us for the victory is the recognition of his own gifts.

God acts in us, then, like a magnanimous father and this can surely only fill us with gratitude. It seems to me that, beyond the gift of being and life, a debt hangs over us that can never be paid. It may be one of the greatest forms of glory that we can give to God simply to acknowledge that debt and to tell him that we recognize it.

In addition to this humility and gratitude, there is another attitude that is developed as a result of our absolute dependence on God's grace. This is the attitude of total self-abandonment. It is difficult for us to place our heart and will fully in God's hands in the knowledge that he orders all things for our good (Rom. 8. 28), without at the same time wanting to hand over to him, in a great act of freedom, that mark of our human dignity, our will.

What is this total self-abandonment? It is being quite supple in God's arms, consenting with the whole of one's life, clinging to his will, never disappointing the Spirit that moves us and accepting completely that we cannot return to ourselves and at the same time become "as little children." What is the end of this self-abandonment? It is a being plunged into the mystery of God's love and fatherhood.

A little child freely puts his hand into the firm, gentle hand of his father in order to find support for his weakness in his father's strength. In the same way, we place our soul in God's hands freely and trustingly in the midst of the vicissitudes that we experience on earth, knowing that he will lead us to eternal splendor. If there are obstacles on the path or if the climb is steep and rocky to the top of the mountain, the child does not simply walk with his hand in his father's. He is happy to let himself be carried in his father's arms. In this way, he can be sure of arriving safely at the summit, which is the home of the three consubstantial persons of the Trinity. The gift of his natural being has, as it were, put him out of this home, but the gift of supernatural grace has also gradually led him back to it. This takes place after many ascents in his heart, the last of which ends in his entering paradise.

If we are borne up by God, we can always set out on the divine adventure of life and plunge into the unknown. We do not, of course, like the unknown because we are not really aware of the risk involved in faith and the great inner wealth that comes from an absence of all security in the human sense. When we abandon ourselves completely, we are really children of the one Father and brothers and disciples of Jesus, who receives everything from the Father and is related to him in every way. We are also possessed by the Holy Spirit, who breathes in our soul and guides it. If, then, we abandon our free will to the great will of the Father who, with his Son and Holy Spirit, is seeking, desiring and loving himself through us, we shall find a much more radical and fundamental freedom than the freedom that consists in choosing between good and evil—the pure freedom of love. "Where the Spirit of the Lord is, there is freedom," Saint Paul tells us (2 Cor. 3. 17) and for him going toward evil was slavery.

What we have therefore to do is to rediscover, in openness to

the Spirit, that original freedom which, for Adam in a state of innocence, merged into instinct that drew him irresistibly toward his
end in blessedness. We, in a state of sin, can also be aware of this
free activity of love that enables our soul to be drawn down into the
depths of God, like a stone rolling down a slope. To make it our
own, however, we must first achieve freedom from the flesh and its
activity which is hostile to God and leads to death. At the same
time, we must also escape from the stifling pressure that drives us
to do the evil that we do not want and prevents us from doing the
good that we do want (see Rom. 7. 19ff). Living in this freedom of
love is also, of course, living in a way that cannot be reconciled with
the life of the world, that is, a life of worldly desires and a life given
over to the weaknesses and disorders of a nature in which the senses
have not been subjected to reason and reason has not been subjected
to God. It is also being made able to share in God's nature and to
be indifferent to lower things. The whole drama of man's life on
earth is to be found in this life of freedom—our gradual liberation
from the dualism of flesh and spirit which tears us apart and our
eventual achievement of that liberation and the simplicity of our first
vocation as children of God whom the grace of Jesus Christ, even
if it radiates through him, has separated from this body given over
to death: "Who will rescue me from this body doomed to death?
Thanks be to God through Jesus Christ our Lord!" (Rom. 7. 24–25).

This liberation is life that really allows man to glorify God,
since God has become in the soul and for the soul what only God
can and wants to become in us—a sovereign and absolute freedom
that has given itself over completely to him, since, as Jacques Maritain pointed out, man in fact only wants what is good, God therefore makes man want everything that he wants and indeed everything that they both want, since the two wills are no longer distin-
guishable in practice.

The whole soul thus becomes similar to God whose image it is.
"God is love" (1 John 4. 8) and the soul is also love and nothing
but love. Its weak, creature's life, which is consumed in the life of
God who enters it in order to draw it into his infinity, expands,
finds itself and is lost. "Life is no more than a little stream," Saint
Ephraem said and suggested that we should "try to direct its flow
toward God, so that, when it flows into him, it will become an
ocean for us." These words are similar to those of Thomas Aquinas,
who insisted that, just as the whole of the universe could be contained within the smallest of its parts, if that part was knowing, so
too could God's eternal and infinite life fill the least of his creatures,

if that creature was loving and let love act freely in it, since love passed through the creature in order that God should be able to love himself in the creature. "O God," William of Saint-Thierry declared, "you love yourself in us when we love you through you."

"No longer are you to be named 'Forsaken' . . . but you shall be called 'My delight'. . . . Just as the bridegroom rejoices in his bride, so will your God rejoice in you" (Isa. 62. 4–5). These words that the prophet Isaiah, in a vision, the horizons of which were lost in the splendors of eternity, addressed to Jerusalem in its captivity describe very well what takes place in the soul. The soul is, of course, also a type of the heavenly city and bride that has finally been set free by the opening out of all the energies of grace and which is the place of delight and happiness for God.

This end is not usually reached, however, until one has passed through many stages on a long journey, since as long as we are here on earth we are still far from the Lord (see 2 Cor. 5. 6). If, by grace, we have the possibility of seizing hold of God and clinging to him in the unity of the Spirit, we must recognize that this union will not be perfect until we reach our final home and God, who during this life always comes toward us, runs to meet us. It is possible to say that he wants to tie us down to an endless pursuit in order to draw us into his infinity.

It would seem, then, that God draws the soul to himself by means of the activity of the virtues and the gifts described in the previous chapter in two principal and closely related ways—the way of "going out" and the way of "walking." These are certainly the ways revealed to us in the Old and New Testaments. Let us consider for a moment the call of our father in faith, Abraham. This can easily be summarized under the two commandments given to him by Yahweh: "go out" and "walk": "Leave your country, your family and your father's house, and go to the land I will show you" (Gen. 12. 1). In other words, Abraham has to flee and forget—he has to flee from idols and sin and forget the attractions of his human life that enslave his heart of flesh. "Walk in my presence and be blameless" (Gen. 17. 1). When Yahweh said this to Abraham, he meant that he was to walk in a faith and a hope that would overcome all obstacles. He hoped and believed against hope (Rom. 4. 18), with a charity that was to prove, through heroic and boundless obedience, that it was also boundless (see Gen. 22. 1–18).

"Walk in my presence"—this meant having as his objective and his ideal not a system or a law, but a personal being, an eye that sees as he saw Hagar in the desert (Gen. 16. 14), an arm that supports, a heart that loves, an intelligence that decides and a being who knows and understands. In this context, an "understanding" being means one who penetrates, envelops and possesses.

Although the psalms are so representative of Israel's attitude, it would take too long to examine them for evidence of going out and walking in God's way. We can, however, give one or two examples out of many. According to Psalm 25, Yahweh himself teaches his way to the poor and humble, in other words, to those who have let themselves be pacified and overcome by the truth and tenderness of their God. The long psalm (119) is fundamentally a prayer for understanding and knowledge of God's way in which eternity is expressed. The psalmist stresses how good it is to walk in God's presence and how walking becomes running when the soul is filled with love. The worst situation in which the soul can find itself is when it is unable to move forward, fixed in an attitude of death.

Jesus Christ did not speak to men in a way that was radically different from the way in which Yahweh spoke to the father of faith and the prophets. In the parable of the bridesmaids, in which the conditions of our entering the kingdom of God are outlined, Jesus, the bridegroom is announced: "The bridegroom is here! Go out and meet him!" (Matt. 25. 7). The one who is eternally present comes, then, to invite us to the eternal wedding feast. He comes ahead of us by his incarnation and we go out to meet him by grace. Human life is this going out and walking a long or a short way from our home to that of the royal Son of God and his trinitarian glory. The duet begins here on earth. It will end in the home of the bridegroom, in the huge choir of the bridegroom's friends—a scene that is evoked in Bach's great cantata on this parable.

This wedding scene, which is described so vividly in the gospel and which gives us a remarkable glimpse into the practices of the period, is followed closely by the story of Jesus' suffering and death. On the eve of his self-sacrifice, Jesus tells us that we should "walk while we have the light," in case we are overtaken by the dark, in which it is impossible for us to find our way (John 12. 35). We know, of course, that this light that directs our steps as we walk is the eternal Word himself.

Jesus is always present and wants to be not only the principle and the end of our way, but also its model and plan and indeed the way itself along which we walk. We may go further and say that, in order to achieve this aim, he himself, while remaining in a state of rest that is perfectly unchanging, also wanted to go out and walk.

If he is the way, it is because he went out from the Father to come into the world and because, at the end of his life on earth, he went out of the tomb in victory and went up to his Father (John 16. 28), so that we might go out of sin and death and enter a life of holiness and resurrection.

Between these two "goings out," he leaped like a giant who had completed his race (Ps. 19) so that we might also be able to walk as he had walked, while still remaining in him and, like him, never ceasing to remain in the Father.

Saint Paul spoke a great deal about this walk in Christ, filled with the Holy Spirit, but the most personal and most characteristic account is to be found in the epistle to the Philippians. Although the apostle speaks of running rather than walking, the idea is the same: "I have not become perfect yet, nor have I yet won, but I am still running, trying to capture the prize for which Christ Jesus captured me . . . All that I can say is that I forget the past and I strain ahead for what is still to come; I am racing for the finish, for the prize to which God calls us upwards to receive in Christ Jesus" (Phi. 3. 12ff).

In this text, Saint Paul calls vividly to mind the image of a competitor in the ancient games, stripped of everything that might slow him down and following his course in the stadium. It expresses in a wonderful way the rapid and unbroken movement forward to the goal that ought to characterize the inner life of every Christian. But we are bound to say at once that the going out and the walking— or running—are not two different realities here, taking place one after the other, as usually happens in ordinary life. No, what we have here—not only in Saint Paul's account, but in the life of the Spirit generally—is only one movement. Every going out coincides with a walk and every walk involves a new going out.

These two terms, however,—"going out" and "walking"—have the advantage of stressing two different aspects of the same life. Our going out is a movement out of the world and the superficial realities of ourselves into a the diaphanous region of God's life. Our walking is an undefined progress toward God which is both accomplished and fleeting. These two movements coincide in the one reality of a continuous transcendence of ourselves in, for and toward God. This is the life of the Christian.

If the going out and the walking on the way coincide, so too do their aims. The end of both is God and the depths of our being— the ascent and the descent coincide. We descend, impelled by the Spirit, to conquer our inner man who, at the expense of the outer man, opens out and grows strong. In the words of the apostle Paul, "Out of his infinite glory, may the Father give you the power through his Spirit for your hidden self to grow strong." We ascend at the same time to God who is both in heaven and in our innermost self.

But what is this inner man of whom only God has the secret and who is the most precious and authentic part of ourselves? According to Father Allo, who has commented on this text of Saint Paul, the apostle was making a contrast between the outer man who can be seen by everyone and who gradually deteriorates and the inner man who is renewed from day to day (2 Cor. 4. 16). The inner man functions through his pneuma, that is, in accordance with a spiritual reality which is always present, even in the sinner. This man is visible only to God and is able to see himself only confusedly.

If we combine this general idea of the inner man with the more particular notion of the "new man" that is also found in Saint Paul's teaching, we see that the apostle is concerned with the human personality, not as it is exposed to the contingencies of life and death, but as regenerated and transformed by supernatural contact with God. This is something that is not, of course, visible externally. It is man at the deepest level of his reality, on the way to perfection. This perfection is a process that takes place through the grace of Christ who lives in man by faith and through whom man is rooted and founded in a boundless charity which goes beyond all knowledge until man is filled with the fullness of God (Eph. 3. 16).

When we descend, then, into our deepest and innermost self, we reach a point where we are far from all visible things and from our superficial personality. In this deep center of our being, we are the pure mirror of the God who created us in his own image and re-created us in the eternal image of himself, that of the Word, the Son. In this situation, the "image is given back to the Image," as Gregory Nazianzen said. This conquest of our deepest and most fundamental self, in a process by means of which we are united to God, who is more intimate to ourselves that we are, and are able to rest in him, is surely the true life.

Should not all Christian asceticism end here? After all, asceticism is no more than the means through which our fallen nature can achieve holiness in unity with the only holy one, God himself. This is what makes asceticism a work of restoration rather than a work of destruction.[1] If we consent to lose our soul, it is in order to gain it. If we die every day, it is in order to live forever. If we let ourselves be torn from ourselves, it is in order to find our authentic personality in eternity and, with it, that paradise of innocence and happiness where we shall rediscover in God all his creatures transfigured and made our own: "The world, life and death, the present and the future, are all your servants, but you belong to Christ and Christ belongs to God" (1 Cor. 3. 23). If we consent to all these obscurities, it is in order to be transformed by brightness into brightness by the Spirit, our hearts illuminated by the light that shines on the face of Christ (2 Cor. 3. 18; 4. 6). Jesus is the author of our faith and it is he who perfects it (Heb. 12. 2). He is the splendor and the glory of the Father (Heb. 1. 3). This is surely life itself.

A number of stages can be distinguished in this living way that leads to life. Without weakening the value of the classical distinction between the three ways of purgation, illumination and unity, it is also possible, however, to make an initial distinction here. Is our going along this way not directly linked with our supernatural organism and the activity of the virtues and the gifts of the Spirit? Is it not in accordance with an experience that is indispensable to us at the end of our human life?

In the first place, our soul moves toward God by following the call of the infused virtues. The gifts of the Holy Spirit are certainly present, but they operate discreetly, so that the soul always acts in accordance with reason in a zone of brightness that enables it to follow itself in its course. It knows where it is going. It is in control of itself. God helps it visibly, both directly and by means of human intermediaries whom he uses as his instruments. It cannot, moreover, be denied that man can be raised up by the experience of following his own progress on the way of good and by building himself up and seeing himself, in this collaboration with God's grace, as the master of his own destiny. What better activity can there be, then, to encourage him to continue?

The soul lives in God more than God lives in it, since, if it is true that it is really orientated toward God, it is also true that it takes an initiative in trying to understand what it must do in order to please God and in what direction it must go in order to reach its goal. God is always present, helping and encouraging and, in his mysterious and merciful condescension, he also adapts himself to the soul and reveals himself to its understanding according to the concepts available to the soul, to its heart according to its aspirations and to its will, taking into account its weaknesses. In this, he acts like a mother guiding her child's steps and bending down to her child's level to walk gently and slowly at the child's own pace.

This situation is not, however, necessarily definitive. If it is God's will, the soul will be handed over to the Spirit, who will guide it with his breath powerfully and mysteriously along unknown ways and only wait for the soul's consent to invade it. How could the Spirit not invade the heart of man when it is ready to receive him? The psalmist cried out: "My heart is ready, God, my heart is ready; I mean to sing and play for you; awake, my muse, awake, lyre and harp, I mean to wake the dawn!" (Ps. 57. 7–8; 108. 1–2).

As the great theologian and mystic John of Saint Thomas said, we cannot arouse our soul at will, although it can and should always be ready to obey and to be in harmony with God's will. There is also no more excellent harmony than that of the soul moved by the Spirit when the latter uses it as an instrument and causes it to cry out, with the psalmist: "My mouth is full of your praises!" (Ps. 71. 8).

God therefore takes the soul away from a path that has been active and transfers it to a way that is passive but at the same time supremely active because of the guidance and movement of the Spirit. On this way, God does not adapt himself to the soul—it is the soul that adapts itself to God. It no longer lives in God—God rather lives in it and founds it more and more deeply in truth, the truth that is one with love. The Spirit always acts like a mother, but not as a mother who bends down to the level of her child to guide his first steps. Now the Spirit is like a mother who takes the child firmly in her arms and lifts him up to her face and, when walking, makes his steps fit in with hers.

We too have to abandon all certainty and all security in this climate of heroic faith. The Spirit, whose origin, movement and destiny we do not know, is the only one capable of fathoming the secret depths of God and the soul: "The Spirit reaches the depths of everything, even the depths of God" (1 Cor. 2.10).

The soul that does not lean directly on God will question itself and be anxious. It is, John of Saint Thomas said, like the ancient Israelites who were restless and lacking in trust and therefore paralyzed with fear. They were told by the prophet Isaiah: "How can you say, Israel, 'My destiny is hidden from Yahweh, my rights are ignored by my God'? Did you not know? Had you not heard? Yahweh is an everlasting God, he created the boundaries of the earth. He does not grow tired or weary, his understanding is beyond fathoming. He gives strength to the wearied, he strengthens the powerless. Young men may grow tired and weary, youths may stumble, but those who hope in Yahweh renew their strength, they put out wings like eagles. They run and do not grow weary, walk and never tire!'' (40. 28–31). John of Saint Thomas concluded from this that ''It is not without good reason that those who hope in God are promised eagles' wings and that it is not said that they fly. They are, on the contrary, said to run and walk, as men still living on earth. But they are moved by the wings of the Eagle who descends from on high'' (*The Gifts of the Holy Spirit*).

The words of Jesus to Peter echo the prophetic words of Isaiah: ''When you were young, you put on your own belt and walked where you liked; but when you grow old, you will stretch out your hands and somebody else will put a belt around you and take you where you would rather not go'' (John 21. 18). When the soul is handed over to itself and tries to follow the path of virtue, it chooses the means to reach the end of the road. When it is really mature, however, and has really become a child of God, it allows itself to be guided exclusively by him. God puts a belt around the soul, penetrates it, surrounds it mysteriously with his grace and providential care, supports it from below without letting it see his arm and holds it prisoner with his strong right arm as a captive of his love and good pleasure. The soul could say, in this situation, with the bride of the Song of Songs: ''His left arm is under my head; his right embraces me'' (2. 6). In this way, the soul goes where it does not want to go— in a direction that is not marked by any path.

Going in this direction, it enters the ''blessed jungle of love''[2] where there are no maps, no routes, no compass and no landmarks and where it is only possible to live from day to day in the bosom of the one who is unforeseeable and unknown. In the words of Saint John of the Cross: ''To go toward what you do not know, you must pass through what you do not know; to go toward what you do not possess, you must pass through what you do not possess.''[3]

The soul is therefore a true virgin and a true bride. It is all suppleness and submission. It allows itself to be gradually fashioned by its beloved. God knows that he can ask and expect everything from it. Sometimes his grace comes as a flash and when it disappears the soul is quite changed. The soul should not attempt to cling to grace of this kind, because its fruit is given in due season and should not leave any trace other than deep gratitude. Sometimes, however, the soul is tested by a painful absence, the purpose of which is to purify it from too great an attachment to human ideas and comforts and to prepare it for a deeper and more authentic presence. We have, after all, to approach more and more closely the one who is both beyond and above everything and everyone in the transcendent fullness that takes him away from us into the cloud and at the same time most completely close to us in his mysterious immanence. When we approach God in this way, we are like Moses on Mount Sinai.

Immanence and transcendence—it is in the inseparable union of this double mystery that the secret of God's presence is to be found. It is precisely because he is both infinitely distant and infinitely near—so near to us that, if we were fully conscious of his proximity, our hearts would burst with fear and joy—that God invites us to go toward him with our eyes closed, under his gaze that passes through us and with a self-abandonment which is boundless, which has no plans or projects and which wants only to fulfill perfectly God's eternal plan for us in the way that will please him most and at the time that will please him.

Father de Caussade said that we should

act when it is the right moment to act, stop when it is the right moment to stop and lose when it is the right moment to lose. In this way, imperceptibly, acting and ceasing to act by attraction and by abandonment, we may read, put our book aside, be quiet; or we may write, stop writing and not know what may follow. After several transformations, the soul will be fulfilled and be given wings to fly up into heaven, leaving on earth a fertile seed which will continue its fulfilled state in other souls.[4]

It is, then, in a zone of complete simplicity, recollection and silence, in which all our powers are concentrated in the most intimate depths of our being, that we find the perfect image of our creator deep within us. How does this happen? It comes about through love and the practice of the virtues, especially the specifically Christian virtue of patience, and the fulfillment of the commandment to be perfect as the heavenly Father is perfect. It comes about too through our incorporation into Christ Jesus under the activity of the Spirit of Christ, in the depths of whose heart are all the virtues. It also happens, perhaps most of all, because we are situated at the opposite pole from God and are emptiness waiting to be filled by him.

That is the wonder—we become like God by being quite passive in love and freedom in the presence of his pure activity, since there is, between God and us, a wonderful similarity which God gives boundlessly, as much as we can receive and more, and which we are able to receive, because, as Tauler said, "we are able to suffer unlimitedly as he is able to act omnipotently." God can pour himself out endlessly into our soul and we can become deeper and deeper to receive him. One abyss calls, as it were, to another abyss and this makes the encounter between the two extremes that are made for each other possible. These two are, of course, the soul and God. God makes it possible for the soul to walk more quickly toward him and to be more and more mysteriously attracted to him the closer it comes. The soul and God are two infinities interpenetrating each other and constantly moving toward each other. Resting in God, the soul derives new power from this rest, allowing it to continue on its course with a spiritual energy that increases the more active it is and has the ability to replenish itself as it expends itself and to add to its strength as it uses itself up.

Thus, the more firmly the soul is established in God, the more rapidly it will advance along the way of virtue. As Gregory of Nyssa said, "the soul's stability is like an eagle flying into the mountains. It takes flight because it is so firmly established in good. When he showed Moses the extent of space, God encouraged him to run. Thus, by promising to establish him on the rock—which is Christ—he showed him how to run" (*The Life of Moses*).

Christian perfection is therefore the movement that takes us to God and within which we continue to be transformed by sharing increasingly in God's life. If we are to find God and become "gods" by becoming children of God and being united with him, we must look unceasingly and insatiably and we must be filled to overflowing with him. The more he reveals himself and gives himself to us, the more deeply and intimately we shall be united with him.

Will this be the same when we have died and God has introduced us to the beatific vision of his essential being? It would seem that this will be the case, at least according to certain Church Fathers and those spiritual writers and theologians who have accepted their teaching. It is not difficult to understand this.

In the infinity of his being and his perfections, God is inexhaustible. He can only be exhausted, in other words, complete, when he contemplates his Word, who breathes with him their one Spirit of love. For us—and not only for us pilgrims here on earth, but also for his chosen ones and his angels in heaven—he the inexhaustible, inexpressible mystery that transcends all reality.

The author of *The Divine Comedy* wrote: "O eternal light, dwelling only in you, hearing only you, understood by you and understanding you, loving you and smiling at you" (*Paradise*, 33). Saint John of the Cross, commenting on these words of his *Spiritual Canticle*, wrote:

> It should not surprise us if God seems extraordinary to men who have not seen him. He is the same for the angels and the souls who contemplate him. These blessed ones will never succeed in seeing him completely. Until the last day of judgment they will continue to see in him such great and new aspects concerning the unfathomable secrets that govern his works of goodness and justice that they will always be surprised and made to wonder more and more. Not only men, but also the angels may well call him the "extraordinary islands." God is the only one who is not astonished by this. He is the only one who sees nothing new in himself.

Will it be different after the last judgment when, in full possession of our risen body, we shall contemplate God as "everything to everyone" (1 Cor. 15. 28)? Then we shall see God in himself and his presence will fill not only his own, but also the new heaven and the new earth. The whole universe will be transfigured in his glory.

There is no reason to think that it will be different. The universe, with its countless planets and stars moving in space, that has no limits and with a speed that defies imagination is surely a projection into the visible order of creation of our eternal destiny, an image of the countless myriads of God's elect, each one of whom is a universe, who form the body of Christ and who are plunged into the fathomless and impenetrable abyss of God. We shall surely fly without stopping like eagles to the God whom we are seeking and always finding. We shall surely continue to be limited, because we shall still be creatures, even when we have become "gods" by participation, but those limitations will not be an obstacle to our joy, nor will they prevent our ascent. Just as Abraham was commanded to "go out," so too shall we be called on again and again to go out and our limitations will be overcome so that a new fullness can be revealed. The appeal of the prophet Isaiah: "Arise, shine out, Jerusalem, for your light has come and the glory of Yahweh is rising on you" (Isa. 60. 1–2) will never cease to be heard. Thus everything that will be brought about by total peace and all the happiness that will result from unshakeable stability will be made one in the eternity of paradise with this continuous movement forward into the infinity of God. And, as Gregory of Nyssa said, the Word will say again and again: "Arise" to the soul that has already risen and "Come" to the soul that has already come. In fact, it is necessary for the one who is running toward the Lord not to miss the wide space. The one who goes up should never stop, going from beginning to new beginning in a series of beginnings that has no end.[5]

NOTES

1. Father Valentin Breton said in his book *Saint Bonaventure* (Paris, 1943): "Holiness is not violent. It is not a heterogeneous element forcing its way into a nature that eludes it. On the contrary, it is a restoration or unravelling of already existing abilities that have become accidentally paralyzed. It is similar to the healing of a man who has been crippled by a nervous shock, but who has recovered the use of his limbs . . . The whole task of sanctification consists, in fact, of restoring in man his original similarity to God. This similarity certainly exists. It is not imposed from above. To be more precise, it subsists and waits for grace to operate and man to cooperate. . . . It is not a question of overcoming a rebellious enemy, but rather of setting free a friend who has been held captive."

2. This is the title of the last chapter of Hans Urs von Balthasar's book, *The Heart of the World.*

3. Saint John of the Cross, *The Ascent of Mount Carmel,* I, Chapter 13.

4. J. de Caussade, *De l'état d'abandon,* Chapter 5.

5. Gregory of Nyssa, *Commentary on the Song of Songs, PG* XLIV, Column 896.

8

The Presence of the Spirit

In the infinite abundance of its unity, the divine life is Father, Son and Holy Spirit, the three faces of God in which his nature opens out, is contemplated and is loved. God is therefore three times a person, in such a transcendent way that our own idea of what a "person" is cannot approach it, however elevated it may be. It is the mystery of mysteries, inaccessible in its great depth and yet open to us. It is true that we are separated from this mystery by infinity, but it is also true that we bear its imprint in the most intimate sphere of our being and that it is at the beginning of our creation and our recreation by grace and at the end of the opening out of our creation in glory. It is a mystery that we must worship and try to penetrate—not only with our mind, but also with our whole heart and all our power to know and love—to its innermost depths by being wide open to the Lord's promise (John 14.23).

This royal family of three consubstantial persons must, in its sovereign transcendence and infinite condescendence, become our own family—the family in which we live and breathe in an inexpressibly friendly atmosphere, despite the inviolable secret of its virginity, for as Gregory Nazianzen said, "the first virgin is the Holy Trinity."[1] It is so much a virgin—in God, since there is nothing that is outside God—that it is possible for it to come to us and, through us, to the lowliest parts of creation without being debased in any way. This is precisely what God wants and what he in fact does—

he goes beyond himself in creation until he is "all in all" (1 Cor. 15. 28) in a dazzling manifestation of grace and glory.

But who will take us to that end? Only the Spirit can do that as the breath of God or a great bird spreading its wings over the chaos to make it fruitful and transform it into cosmos. The same Spirit also sheltered the immaculate one under his shadow in order to let her conceive the man-God. He also bore witness with the Father to the Son of God when the latter was baptized, drove him into the desert of temptation, led him to his suffering and death and finally filled the risen one who had become a living Spirit with light. He was also left behind by Jesus as another Paraclete (John 14. 16) to spread himself over the Church and, in the upper room, to give that Church its final form, take it out of its swaddling clothes and launch it, like a beautiful ship, on waters of the ocean of space and time.

In the unity of their nature, which is the principle governing their function, the three persons of the Trinity act together. They are inseparable in the work of our creation and in the act of our re-creation by grace. It is, however, also true that each person, living in us to lead us to deification, retains the special character that is given to him, within the divine life, by his relationship with the other two. The "brazen law of appropriation," as Father Gardeil has called it, should not conceal from us the fact that the soul of the just man may be in contact with the divine persons, not simply as a whole, but also as three distinct persons in the distinction that forms the opposition between their relationship to each other and makes them persons. Each of us is able to be in touch with this inexpressible reality that springs from the most intimate depths of the divine life and makes it Father, Son, Holy Spirit.

Some deeply contemplative souls, such as Mary of the Incarnation, have been aware of this reality at particular moments of their lives in union with God. We may not be able to claim that we have ever reached such peaks of experience, but we are certainly allowed to move in that direction and to enter his royal sanctuary and, if it pleases God, to welcome, as the greatest joy that we can experience in this world, the mystery of divine privacy. In that case, does it matter if God leaves us on the plain? Surely the heavens, whose beauty we admire so much, and the sun, which shines down on us to fill us with its heat and light, are the same as the sky and the sun experienced by those who have climbed the mountain? God makes marks in every man who abandons himself to his activity. These marks are not always identical, but they are all signs of his being and life. Each of them has its own special effect, even if the soul is not clearly conscious of this. Finally, they are God's way of seizing hold of man.

We can therefore consider these three persons, pray to them, join them and hand ourselves over to their activity, both as inseparably one in nature and as separate persons. In our attempt to perceive their presence, we shall try to distinguish their beneficent activity without losing sight of their close solidarity. Here, we shall begin with the Holy Spirit and in the first place we shall give our reasons for this point of departure.

According to Saint Irenaeus, the divine life, which spreads itself out in itself and communicates itself to us by coming down from the Father, through the Son and in the Holy Spirit, follows the opposite order when it goes up from us to the Father, who is the last point of our ascending process, through the Son, under the movement, which is in a sense the first movement, of the Spirit (*Demonstration of the Apostolic Preaching,* Chapter 7).

The Father, who is the principle without a principle and was called by the early theologians[2] the "fontal deity," has never been sent. He has the initiative of a plan of salvation which he carries out with his two hands—the Word—the Son and the Spirit. The incarnation and the Pentecost are two missions that are united by moving from the Uncreated One to the creature. Both come from God and fulfill their task outside God. In this way, they are an extension of an eternal process. They both come down to us without leaving God and act in the most intimate part of our being to raise us up to God. This is the great mystery of the Church that lives in each one of its children, whom it makes members of Christ in possession of the Spirit.

Christ's mission preceded the mission of the Spirit because Jesus, as he himself tells us (John 16. 7), had to be glorified in order to be able to send the Spirit, which he breathed in the same breath of love with the Father. It is, however, the Spirit, the other Paraclete, that is, the one who supports, defends and consoles us, who is first in the task of making us holy, because he enables us to recall Jesus' teaching and to make Jesus present in our innermost soul. It is the Spirit who takes us back, as a great number of sons incorporated into Jesus, the one Son, to the bosom of the Father. It is possible to say, from the human point of view, that the Spirit, who closes the cycle of life in the Trinity, a life that has neither beginning nor end, the Spirit from whom no divine person proceeds, has a kind of revenge in the world. He develops and spreads the fertility that he does not use in the bosom of God in finite creation by making that creation infinite, in other words, by making it, in its spiritual aspect of angel and man, go beyond its own limits.

The Spirit, then is entirely gift and giving and we shall never be able to come to the end of examination of what this special privilege means. In God, the Spirit gives to God, the Father to the Son and the Son to the Father. Then he gives God to men and men to God and men to men in God. Finally, at the end of his mission, he gives God to God through men and a universe that has become absolutely transparent to his light and warmth.

In order to reach this end, God the Spirit, who has the secret of humble beginnings—creation as chaos shaken by the wind, the incarnation as a child sleeping in a crib and the Church as a handful of men still fearful and only roughly shaped—has first to reveal to us the ocean of his divine and infinite life without minimizing the distance—which is no less infinite—between himself, the creator, and us, his creatures. Penetrating to the most intimate part of our soul, as only he, who is love itself, can, he had to deepen in that soul, which is by nature the image of God, the ability to receive divine life and to be more and more open to be filled as he, the Spirit, is poured out. As he is also the movement in God which makes the Father and the Son both circulate and rest in each other and together in God, the Spirit has finally to be for us both the gentle, almost imperceptible breeze and the high wind on the open sea. He is, in other words, the breath that raises us up and lets us enter God.

But how very difficult it is to speak about this Spirit from whom comes the charity that we need in order to overcome all our obstacles! (Rom. 5. 5). The images used in Scripture to express the Spirit—wind, tongues of fire or living water—are mobile, fleeting and intangible. The Spirit seems to hide behind them and to be concealing a personality that, because it is above all gift and giving, does not want to retain anything for itself, but prefers to turn entirely toward the Father and the Son, of whom he is the nodal point, and to aspire exclusively to make them happy and glorious.

It is because he is the outpouring of God's goodness that he is also, within God's transcendence, the unlimited condescendence of God toward us. That is why he looks for us here below, as poor children taken out of nothingness, born in the mud of sin and yet looking forward to a sublime destiny. He comes down to us to seize hold of us and take us into the blessed sanctuary of the Trinity. He wants above all to fashion us so that we can live easily in that royal family, where everything is so vast, so rich and so beautiful that, without him, we would be in danger of losing confidence and of ceasing to believe in his wonderful promises.

One theologian[3] has spoken in a charming yet profound way about the "maternal rôle of the Holy Spirit" and indeed the Spirit is really our mother—the mother with whom the Church and Our Lady ought to be filled in order to be truly mothers. As a mother, the Holy Spirit represents love in its most disinterested, most devoted and most indulgent form. The Holy Spirit, our mother, is wasteful in giving us the kind of love that little children receive from their mother—being washed, fed at the breast, comforted and protected from the hostility of the world outside so that they can thrive and grow.

> Wash what is soiled,
> irrigate what is dry,
> cure what is sick
> (from the sequence *Veni Sancte Spiritus*).

He is not discouraged by our slowness, our mistakes and our failures to respond. He wishes us well. He knows the clay of which we are made and how difficult it is for us, wounded as we are by sin, not to turn inward on ourselves and not to think of ourselves as God, to make for ourselves a god outside God and not to succumb to the temptations of the world of our senses. He knows only too well that it is hard for us to transcend ourselves and give ourselves with all our soul to be led by our Father in heaven. He is our mother and will continue to be our mother to the very end—until the consummation of our spiritual life, so long as we do not, as the apostle Paul says, grieve or suppress him (Eph. 4. 30; 1 Thess. 5. 19).

At every turning point on our way, he sheds his light on us, urges us forward, points out our direction, illuminates our faith, gives wings to our hope and fills our love with holy audacity. He allows us in the end to enter an eternal home that is all on the same level. In this way, he does what only a mother can do, taking us to our elder brother Christ Jesus and putting him forward as our model. Even more than this, he fashions us in the likeness of that model and teaches us to say, with him, "Abba, Father" to his and our Father and to pray with inexpressible groans (Rom. 8. 26).

We have already seen how, with the help of his seven gifts, he has set the theological virtues free from subjection to our cool reason and has encouraged them to flourish and open out so that we can, through them, cling directly to God. He gives us ease, self-con-

trol and freedom so that we can move in the supernatural sphere
where God's thoughts, however far removed they may be from ours,
and his ways, however different they are from ours, become our
own.

Because he is gift and giving, the Spirit is also revelation. He is
present with us and penetrates us with his light and warmth especially when we read Scripture, that rich storehouse entrusted to the
Church. The Spirit chose the authors of the sacred books as the human instruments by which the texts were written and he is always
behind them, continuously inspiring them. As our creed says, "He
has spoken through the prophets."

What would the Bible be without the Holy Spirit? It would be
a series of stories, often apparently lacking coherence and telling us
the history of a people who were not particularly talented or creative
in themselves, who were morally undeveloped and who seemed to
lack any metaphysical instinct or any desire to achieve the purity of
spirit that would seem to have been necessary for a nation that was
destined to become the religious leaven of mankind as a whole.

Yet, by the intervention of the Holy Spirit, the Bible is made
as translucent for us as it was for the apostles after Pentecost, the
Fathers of the Church, from Justin Martyr and Origen to Saint Bernard, and the mystics and exegetes who have tried to go beyond
mere technical skill and to reach the spiritual meaning and full significance under the bark of the letter. Through Scripture, it is not
so much they who go toward God as God who comes to them, like
a Father speaking to his children and revealing his eternal thoughts
and his loftiest truths to them.

As the Spirit going to meet the Spirit,[4] Scripture becomes clear
to us by taking us into the depths of love where everything is harmony and unity because everything recalls Christ, refers to Christ
and expresses Christ. From the book of Genesis to the last cry of the
Spouse inspired by the Spirit: "Come, Lord Jesus!" (Apoc. 22. 20),
the mystery revealed by the apostle, that is to say, the mystery of
the eternal Christ and his eternal bride, the Church, the mystery at
which the angels long to gaze because it is the central and unique
mystery toward which everything moves and within which everything is enlightened—this mystery is gradually unfolded in a continuous process of spiritual development. It is the working out of a
plan of tenderness, salvation and wisdom which begins humbly in
the shadow of a reality that took place quite late in human history.

Gradually, however, it evolves and becomes explicit. The Bible presents us with this process in a series of preparations, promises, covenants, figures, symbols, prophecies, providential events and purifying ascents. These events culminate in the expectation of Christ's second coming in glory and majesty. We look forward to this event in which the wedding of the Lamb will be consummated.

Touched by the Spirit, the Christian knows at once that, if he is to plunge into the depths that lie concealed under the letter, the only thing that he can do is kneel down. The more deeply he goes into the text in the light of the Spirit, the more he is bound to admire the simplicity—which is in itself a challenge to all human rhetoric and a sign of transcendence—of a word that only the most humble souls can understand and that the most learned scholars will never fully comprehend. That word speaks with the same austerity and the same absence of emotion about creation, the giving of the law in thunder and lightning, the drama of Calvary on the one hand and the most ordinary and apparently unimportant details of everyday life on the other, such as the color of Laban's sheep or the happiness of Tobit's dog.[5]

The whole of Scripture is filled with the infinite holiness of God. Confronted with that holiness, man sometimes seems great, but more often he is presented with his wrongness and weakness and his exposure to the power of evil. In contrast to this, we see in Scripture the cross, placed in the heart of the world by the one who is himself the center, the reason and the end of the universe and the history of man.

The Spirit continues to speak to us in Scripture. Sometimes he speaks to us in prophecies, sometimes in parables and sometimes in plain realities. Always, however, he speaks with the same serenity. He addresses us as he would address children, teaching us with the patience, care and authority of a Father. The word of Scripture is illuminated by the Spirit and comes to each one of us. Like manna in the desert, its flavor is suitable to every appetite and taste. It provides us with an answer to the greatest human problems and to the most intimate needs of the human heart. According to the apostle Paul, "Everything that was written long ago in the Scriptures was meant to teach us something about hope from the examples Scripture gives who did not give up were helped by God" (Rom. 15. 4).

The Spirit, who is both in the Bible and in us, is also both God's presence and a movement toward God. He is at the same time a Spirit of fear and joy. When we hear or read the sacred words of Scripture, we inevitably experience a deep feeling of reverence. Origen insisted that:

> As we go further in our reading, the mysteries pile up in front of us. If we sail close to the coast in a fragile little vessel, we are not afraid. As soon as we venture into the high seas, however, and are tossed up and down on rising and falling waves, an immense fear seizes hold of our soul and we tremble with terror at the thought of having entrusted such a small craft to the immensity of the waves. This is very much the feeling that we, whose spirit is so weak, have after having dared to voyage on such a vast ocean of mysteries. . . . Everything that happens there happens as a mystery.[6]

In his *Confessions* (12. 14), Augustine declared: "O admirable depths of your revelations. They only give us their most outward aspects. They smile at us like children. But what admirable depths! We cannot consider them without a certain sacred fear, a feeling of respect, awe and love."

This fear, which is the very breathing of Scripture, is very different from what may be called fright. The latter is destructive, whereas the former is close to adoration and is expansive. It causes us to tremble because of the proximity of God's majesty. It also comes from the atmosphere of intense life that surrounds the divine throne, as though Isaiah's vision (Isa. 6), that great peak rising between other peaks in the Bible, were still present. That is why this fear is nourished by an immense joy, which is undoubtedly the same joy that the psalmist hoped to experience when he said to his God: "Make me single-hearted in fearing your name" (Ps. 86. 11).

This joy is compatible with the bruising of the contemplative's soul caused by sharp contact with Scripture. This is really a wound of love caused by a wound of love, since all the wealth of Scripture is communicated to us by the mystical and bodily death of Jesus. They have come to us in the unveiling of their secret, through the side pierced by the lance and the pouring out of the Spirit, who has to open our hearts so that they can receive the blood shed by Jesus. The divine life-blood that circulates in the Scriptures is the spiritual blood of Christ, whose cup circulates and comes to us in a magnificent banquet, the earliest Fathers of the Church have assured us.[7] To this banquet, the Spirit invites us by making the bridegroom of the Canticle of Canticles speak to us and lead us into the garden where his bride, the Church, lives: "Drink my wine and my milk; eat, friends, and drink, drink deep, my dearest friends" (5. 1).

How is it possible for us not to be wounded by the witness borne throughout the Bible by this "too great love" in the heart of the apostle? The divine economy reached its end, the culmination of this love, in the incarnation, death and resurrection of Christ and thanks to the communication of the Spirit, in the fullness of God's mysterious marriage with mankind.

Throughout the Old and New Testaments, we experience, and, as it were, "suffer" the affirmation expressed in the epistle to the Hebrews: "The word of God is something alive and active; it cuts like any double-edged sword, but more finely. It can slip through the place where the soul is divided from the spirit, or joints from the marrow; it can judge the secret emotions and thoughts" (Heb. 4. 12). This sword would be really terrible if the Spirit were not there, joining his activity to that of the Word. The word of Scripture is certainly a separation, but the Spirit unites. The Spirit is like oil, penetrating and impregnating imperceptibly. He is the oil of happiness flowing from Christ and uniting us to Christ. That oil flows into the wound described above, making it sweet and soothing it. Through that wound the Word, the Son, can pass into the soul and grow there like a child growing to maturity.

Scripture is not, it is true, an incarnation of the Word, the Son, but it is like the flesh of Jesus who concealed the fire of God himself who was consuming him within. The Spirit enables us, as we have already seen, to penetrate beneath the bark of the letter. By opening to us the spiritual significance of our life and letting us enter the abyss of the mystery of God and Christ, the Spirit enables us to be one spirit with Jesus. The Spirit shows us that same Jesus in the Old Testament, living, as it were, before he was alive. He then shows us Jesus in the New Testament as the eternal Word who assumed our flesh and then went up to heaven while still remaining with us, thanks to his Spirit, and preparing us from that time onward for his glorious second coming. Finally, it is through the Spirit that we are able to come into contact with that great reality, the Church of Christ, which, although it is distinct from him, is also inseparable from him.

The Church is inseparable not only from Christ, but also from the Spirit. Is the Spirit not, after all, the uncreated soul of the Church and the principle of unity and love that unites the members to the Head, the bride to the bridegroom? It was thanks to the action of the Spirit that the Church was born, in a twofold mystery of pain and triumphant joy, both in the side of the dying Jesus, like Eve being born from the sleeping Adam, and in the burning flames of Pentecost.

The Spirit dwells in the Church, animates it and leads it by his powerful and delicate breath, which is impossible to resist and yet respects us as human beings, toward its eternal destiny, as the Church continues on its pilgrim path throughout time. He plumbs the depths both of the Church and of God, acting as the Spirit of love and penetrating everything, and in this way he reveals those depths to us.

He has the task of making us understand, more by a kind of intuition in which the heart plays an important part than by speculative thought, the point at which the life of the three consubstantial persons of the Trinity flows in the Church, through the missions in which the Father takes the initiative. The Spirit does this in such a way that there is a real descent in the Church from the invisible reality of God into the visible reality that is brought about. He also has the task of making sure that this interaction between heaven and earth, described so pathetically and so magnificently in the book of Revelation, continues to take place in time.

Finally, the Spirit shows us that the Church, which is made in the image of the man-God and is both divine and human, is identical in a sense with its Head, of whom it is, as Möhler said, the "permanent incarnation." In this way, as Bossuet pointed out, the Church is "not simply the assembly of the children of God, the army of the living God, his kingdom, his city, his temple, his throne, his sanctuary and his tabernacle. We may go much deeper and say that the Church is Jesus Christ himself, but Jesus Christ scattered and communicated."

However gifted they may be and however much religious experience they may have had, men cannot form a healthy or balanced judgment about the Church as the bride of Christ without the light of the Holy Spirit. Despite his wonderful perspicacity, Newman thought with the prejudices of an Anglican Protestant and therefore termed the Church the great prostitute and a Babylon just as did the visionary of Patmos. For Simone Weil, it was the "great totalitarian animal." Although they do not go as far as this, too many Catholics remain deceived by the Church's appearance here on earth and the faults of its members who, as sinners, are often subject to error and one-sided passions. Others admire the Church, but also remain too firmly on the human level, praising the hierarchy, order and disci-

pline in the Church and the Church's moral stance and teaching office, without going any further.

The Spirit, however, leads us much further—far beyond this
necessary, but very external aspect. In the Spirit, we are able to penetrate to the essence of the Catholica, the Church rooted in God and
with immense dimensions in time—from the time of Abel down to
that of the last one chosen—and in space—the universe filled with
the power of God. The Spirit lets us see the reality of the Church
conceived by God from all eternity, the Church for which he created and ordered all things and that is permeated with his satisfac-
tions and his creative and redeeming love.

Through the Spirit, we can see beyond appearances and catch
a glimpse of a personality living the life of God and filled with the
wealth of its three elements—humanity, Christ himself and the
Holy Spirit. These three elements "call and support each other and
act like the mass, the movement, the heat and the light of a planet."[9] This personality cannot be conceived without a visible head.
That head is the pope who is uniquely inspired by the Holy Spirit
and is the voice and expression of Christ who is invisibly present in
the Church with his truth and his infinite care.

The Church has often been compared with our Lady and, in the
line of predestination and grace, with woman as such, as pure as a
virgin and as loving as a mother, as Clement of Alexandria said, and
as a mother because a virgin. The Church is the very old woman
whom Hermas saw and of whom he said: "She was established before all things and the world was created for her." At the same time,
however, she is also the young bride without spot or wrinkle (Eph.
5. 27), perfect because she is continually washed by the blood of the
bridegroom. He poured out his blood and gives his sacraments for·
her and her children. She is also a virgin by virtue of the truth of
which she is the storehouse and the unity that she enjoys. She is also a bride by virtue of her love and faithfulness.

The Church is a pilgrim here on earth and suffers in her members, who are separate and, although saved, not yet purified. At the
same time, however, she is the same as the heavenly Church toward
which she is always moving and which is also inclined toward her,
making her more beautiful and strong. Paul Claudel described the
Church in his *Five Great Odes* in the following way:

Jerusalem and Zion have embraced each other like two
    sisters—

the heavenly sister and the exile, washing the sacrificial-linen
in the Khobar river.
The Church on earth raises up her head crowned with towers
to her royal consort.
I greet you, world that is new to my eyes, world that is   now
complete!

The glory of the Church is more heavenly than earthly, since
the risen and divine Lord penetrates to the depths of her being with
his rays. The Church is also possessed of a sovereign beauty. This
is not only because of her wedding, which is, here on earth, more
properly only a betrothal with her royal "bridegroom of blood"
(Exod. 4. 25), but also because she is so fully developed as a mother.

The same Spirit who enables us to understand the mystery of
the Church also hovered over creation like a great bird and later
overshadowed Mary so that she would conceive Jesus. He continues
to fertilize her in order to enable Jesus to be the Christ who is quite
perfected in his fullness, his pleroma, and will be until the end of
time (Eph. 4. 13). He is above all the Spirit who communicates life
because he is the love of the one who is life itself and who came to
give us life and to give it abundantly (John 10. 10). His activity
makes it possible for faith to be born in men's souls and for the bap-
tismal font to be a pure womb from which a new race is born. This
race is the *sanctum* that was promised to the Virgin Mary (Luke 1.
35), the race that is gradually gathered into the Church and will in
the end be one, total Christ.

Yes, it is true that the Church is our mother. We still need,
however, the Spirit who has made the Church as it is so that we can
understand how tender and demanding is the love of that mother
who has so much anxiety for those whom she loves and who are so
exposed to so many dangers in this world that is plunged in sin. It
is from this mother that we have learned everything that we know,
kneeling, as Claudel has said, like children beside her. She is also a
strong and generous mother who brings us in from outside to beget
us in her own womb, in this way differing from our earthly mothers
who conceive us in their wombs in order to give birth to us outside
of themselves. She is our foster-mother, nourishing us continuously
with her own life and with that of her bridegroom and spouse by
means of the sacraments and above all by the body and blood of Jesus placed in her. This body and blood prepare our bodies for the
resurrection that arises from death.

In the Church, thanks to the presence of the Spirit who unites the members as Christ is united to his Father—"that they may be one as we are one" (John 17. 22)—there is a deep and mysterious solidarity between those members which gives to each one the treasures of grace and merit that are stored in the mother's bosom.

What is more, the Spirit also helps us to share in the contemplative life of the church by inviting us to take part in the divine liturgy which, with its praise and intercession, surrounds the sacrifice of the altar. It is the Spirit who inspires the liturgy, as he inspires Scripture and, in this homage of adoration, everything is love and wisdom. It is in fact only in the light and warmth of the Spirit that we are able to enter this great movement of prayer which, as Pope Paul VI told us,

> aims to make every Christian a living and active member of the mystical body and to raise him up so that he will personally participate in the most sublime, beautiful, effective and mysterious action that man, who is still a pilgrim here on earth, can perform—the action in which he is introduced into the process of his destiny as it develops and intercedes between the world and God.[10]

This divine liturgy, which is so dependent on the Spirit, gradually unfolds and at the same time rises up like a great spiral, beginning each year, for man who is on the way to perfection, at a higher stage and closer to the peak, which is paradise. It enables us to enter all the different conditions of Christ and plunges us into the great mystery of that admirable interchange of the incarnation of the man-God. It gives us more and more intimate access into the great family of the Trinity that forms the center, the *Sanctus, Sanctus, Sanctus,* as well as the beginning and the end of all our praise.

Because they were filled with the Holy Spirit, the Fathers of the Church, from Ignatius the Martyr to Saint Bernard and Bossuet, loved the Church with holy enthusiasm and spoke in language that was both forceful and persuasive. Indeed, they spoke so well that, even though it was centuries ago, their words seem still to spring from a most pure scource and continue to echo deeply in our hearts. Their statements are scattered here and there in works dealing with various subjects and they lack the strictness of sytematization and the methodical elaboration of patient reflection covering many centuries of the kind carried out by Cardinal Journet in his *Eglise du Verbe incarné.*[11] On the other hand, however, they are full of warmth and light and they impart to the reader in a very vivid way that *sensus Ecclesiae* that plays such an important part in his faith. What an impression of openness and exaltation we gain from Irenaeus's *Adversus Haereses* and very many passages and chapters in Clement of Alexandria (especially his *Pedagogus*), Origen, Saint Ambrose, Saint Augustine, Saint Gregory the Great and Saint Leo the Great! They all put us in touch with the love that is present in the unfathomable depths of the heart of our mother, the Church.

It is through such testimonies of admiration, love and trust that we are able to understand how it is possible for men not only to suffer for the Church by shedding their blood for her if God so desires it, but also at the hand of the Church. Acting as prudently as a mother, the Church can, after all, make severe demands on her children, who are required to suffer patiently if they are to become mature and come to grasp what the Church values most in the world—truth.

Saint Augustine has said that to have the Holy Spirit in oneself is the same as loving the Church.[12] Moreover, if we recognize ourselves as being moved by the Spirit and desiring intimacy with the Lord, we shall also be conscious of the opening out of the mystery of the Church within us. The soul is filled with grace and lives, together with other souls, in the one bridegroom. It therefore shares the same life that flows from the Head into the body, with the result that everything in the Church belongs to Christ (see 1 Cor. 3. 22–23). For Christ, in faithfulness to his word, every believer is a mother, a sister and a brother (see Luke 8. 21), a place of rest so deep that nothing can disturb it and so impetuous that nothing can stop it and a little temple in the great temple of the universe.

The Church, as revealed to us by the Spirit, is fullness and unity. It is also both heavenly and earthly. Saint Augustine looked forward to dwelling in that Church, which had given rise to such unforgettable thoughts in him, expressed toward the end of his *Confessions* (12. 15):

During my exile, I will my memory and the affections of my heart to Jerusalem, my homeland and my mother—to Jerusalem and you, its king, Father, guardian, bridegroom and pure and powerful delights, its lasting joy and unique and inexpressible happiness, to you who are everything to her. I shall never again turn away from you, until, in the peace of that dear mother, who bears the first-fruits of my spirit, you have finally and completely received me.

Although the Church is so immense and is, moreover, related to everything, it is not the universe. Everything is, as we know, not yet subjected to Christ. It is only when "God is all in all" (1 Cor. 15. 28) that everything will become the body of Christ. It is then that there will be a palingenesis, which is at present a mystery to us, but in which we are able here and now, thanks to what Paul and the author of the Apocalypse have told us, to believe.

The Church is the center and the highest peak of the cosmos. At the same time, it is also moving toward a triumphant universality through the presence of the bridegroom, the Lord of the cosmos, the first-born of all creatures and through the Spirit of love and unity, whose breath leads it to its end. This Spirit has, even here and now, to attract us so that we also move in the direction of that universe. Its most perfect expression is found in the book of Revelation. This book, more than any other in the Bible, forms the framework of our existence here on earth. It is both obscure and magnificent and we cannot penetrate into its mystery without the help of the Spirit. What would the universe be for us and all its many forms and colors, if we did not have the light of the creative Spirit?

The universe is a beautiful countryside, groups of villages and towns, technology, noise, bustling activity and the restless movement of men, many of whom do not know that they have an immortal soul that reflects the Holy Trinity and, breathing above time, is a reality for which God shed his blood. This universe is both friendly and hostile. It is ambiguous and disturbing.

For us, the Spirit transfigures this world, which he leads back to his truth—a truth that goes beyond the centuries. This transfiguration, however, usually takes place by means of a purification and a testing. When we are tested in this way by the Spirit, we experience one of the effects of the gift of knowledge which will eventually become a gift of the Spirit.

Through this gift of knowledge, we become painfully conscious of the great vanity of the universe and at the same time of the inaccessible transcendence of the only reality that matters—God. In this way, we are torn between two poles—between God who is infinitely distant from us by the absolute nature of his holy being and this nothing built on nothingness, this created reality, this frail and broken dust destined to be scattered. We are exiled in this chasm which separates God, whom we do not see, from this universe, which we can only see in its disappointing autonomy. We lack the strength to look at the one who lies beyond, infinitely beyond everything and the whole of creation that is hastening toward death. We experience a great loneliness and a painful sense of emptiness and, sustained by grace, we suffer in silence, because there are no words to express or relieve that feeling. It is the hour for prayer to which the Spirit responds and which he has himself inspired. He does not, however, change the reality of the two poles. God, who is too great and too distant, and the things of the world, which are too lowly—these are the two poles, which the Spirit does not alter, but which he brings together in their extreme opposition.

There is, then, a strong attraction, even a mutual embrace between God, who is so transcendent that he is like air that cannot be breathed because it is too hard for our chests, and these realities that are too bound to this earth to be able to seduce us. The Spirit reveals to us in the depths of our being that God is love and unity and that everything proceeds from his goodness and bears the imprint of his uncreated beauty, which fills all being and order with this immense manifestation of existence. As though through a mysterious prism, the invisible presence works through the visible world to break down the undefined reality by his bright light. It is true, of course, that we have always known in theory that God is everywhere, that the great mystery of the man-God has united heaven and earth with indissoluble bonds and that, behind the veil of a disappearance beyond space and time, the risen Lord has summed up everything in himself in a great act of recapitulation and has prepared for his creation an eternity of life. This view of our faith and our thinking, however, was hidden in the depths of our spirit and could be brought to light only in an experience that had a powerful effect on our senses, almost distracting them.

The Spirit is the gentle yet blazing clarity that displays to eyes illuminated by the heart a world bathed in love and already containing, in embryo, its eschatological glory. A world, springing from the eternal thought of a creator and Father, that, in the single moment of its life, contemplates him in his Word and breathes him in his Spirit. A world that goes beyond the sphere of evil, sin and death and which is, in spite of so much suffering and conflict, filled with divine mercy. A world destined to go through death but, in order to live an indestructible life in eternity, projecting into him the infinite perfections of an unfathomable wisdom. A world that is entirely an epiphany of God and in which matter is the channel of the Spirit and will one day be transformed by the Spirit into the flesh of those whom God has chosen. Finally, the world revealed by the Spirit is a world that is wonderfully fraternal and young with the very youth of God himself, who creates it at every moment of time—a world in which everything gives rise to life and communion and which already bears within itself the shining first-fruits of what it will be when it is ultimately transfigured.

Now, however, it is not by reasoning or intellect, but by a mysterious intuition that arises from the depths of the soul that the latter is able to know that God, who is completely different, is never without the world and that the world is never without God. This friendly universe which is so open to God was glimpsed by Saint Francis of Assisi when he spoke of "sister water and brother fire" and by other saints in their own way—Saints John and Paul of the Cross, for example.

The Spirit uses the gift of wisdom to make us contemplate the illumination of creation in the splendor of God's essence. He is also in us what he is in the Holy Trinity—the one who "reaches the depths of everything, even the depths of God" (1 Cor. 2. 10) and, in this light, uncovers every depth in creation for us.

This privilege of the Spirit—to know the depths of all things, even of God himself—will never be exhausted. Thomas Aquinas has commented on this statement of Saint Paul in the following way:

> The one who loves is not satisfied with a superficial outline of the object that he loves. He tries to examine all the intimate details of the object and penetrates so deeply into its inner reality that it is said of the Holy Spirit, the love of God, that he even looks into the depths of God.

> The Spirit gives us access to these depths of light and love, within a faith that is both splendor and night, in order to take us down to even greater depths. He begins by stripping us of ourselves, by opening us to God while at the same time opening God to us, by making us deeper to receive God and by giving us to God so that we can give in return. He wants us to be stripped, naked, ultimately free, so that we can be drowned in the ocean of love. If we can really give ourselves completely to his activity, he will not let go of us until he has transformed us entirely and deified us to the point that we have ourselves become love. With him, it is the love that does not return to itself that goes forward to encounter the Love that is flowing in us from the Father and from the heart of the Son in order to unite us to the Father in the Son. It is the Love breathed by the Father

and the Son that is also breathed into us who are the brothers and co-heirs of Christ and lets us enter the endless cycle of the circumincession of the three divine persons.

The Spirit in us, then, is both movement and rest, since it is the special attribute of the Spirit to reconcile and fulfill everything in unity. It is in this way that he allows us to experience God as the *tremendum* and the *fascinens*, the one who is fearful and yet is irresistably attractive, the Father of immense majesty, whose tenderness is inexhaustible, Christ who is cosmic and immeasurable and at the same time infinitely lovable in the humility of his heart, the deity who burns with ardor and yet is so gentle in his power to invade our souls. As wisdom, he penetrates into the deepest recesses of our being because of his purity (Wis. 7. 24).

Having in this way been made love, we also become a gift, given not only to God, but also to others in God. We no longer belong to ourselves in the one who lives only for the Father and the Son and is their mutual embrace, their glory and their happiness. The man who is possessed by the Spirit does not recognize what is his and what belongs to the other and, because nothing is owing to him, he is without the bitterness and bad feelings that come from a sense of ingratitude, injustice and indifference. He has no enemies and the sinfulness and suffering of his fellow-men and of all creatures fill him with great compassion. Nothing that lives is excluded from this sense of pity and tenderness that makes him, like his God, all in all. He sees everything—animals, plants, the earth and everything in it—as coming, like himself, from God and at one with the body of Christ. He is conscious of the need to share with them the divine goodness that holds them, as it also holds him, up above the void by a golden thread that is very slender but very strong. He will be able to say with the angelic dying man in Dostoyevsky's novel: "Do not cry, mother! Life is paradise and we are all in paradise, although we do not want to recognize it. If we were to recognize it, the whole world would from that moment become a paradise."[13]

If we are to find living examples of men and women who have been nothing but a pouring out of love in humility and renunciation of self, we have to turn to those saints whom the Holy Spirit invaded and transfigured. We have already mentioned Francis of Assisi, Saint Paul of the Cross and Saint John of the Cross. These are great saints, but surely their holiness is equalled by that of many of the great Christians of distant Russia! Sergius of Radonezh, Seraphim of Sarov and Sylvanus of Mount Athos—these saints were wonderfully evangelical in their complete simplicity and entirely filled by the deific light that was reflected even in their bodies. For them, as for the angelic brother Karamazov, everything was joy and the world was a paradise bathed in the light of the risen Christ, whose cross was at the center of creation. They were really the meek to whom Jesus promised the earth (Matt. 5. 5). They were not conscious of any tension between the active and the contemplative life, the life of love for one's neighbor and the life of love for God. There are indeed no barriers in the infinity of God in which they lived and everything in that life is one, because everything is filled with God. They received everything in superabundance in their divine home and were therefore able to give everything in their words and actions without losing anything.

The early Christians affirmed their great tenderness for the Christ whom they loved, for example, in hymns and canticles of great purity and beauty, such as those preserved in the collection known as the *Odes of Solomon*. Their souls were deeply rooted in a gratitude that, moved by the Spirit, bore fruit in praise which rose from their hearts to their lips. If these early believers were made present by the love of God to all things and all men, it was because their whole being had been invaded by the presence of God in the Holy Spirit. Divo Barsotti has said, in his book on Russian Christianity:

Sylvanus' complaint is the expression of a longing for heaven, a desire to enter God's presence and to feel that he is submerged and drowned in the peace of God. He felt an immense pity for men and an insatiable longing for God. He did not move from the one feeling to the other, because the pity was longing in him and the longing was pity. Everything in him was simple and pure. Everything was reduced to the unity of a life that was a presence with God and men. Every thought, every dream, every memory—all lost their sustenance and fell slowly from his heart. His life descended and entered the silence of God.

Saint Ignatius, the tender and impetuous bishop of Antioch and the disciple of those two great heralds of love, Saint Paul and Saint John, was clearly also filled with the Spirit. It must have been the Spirit whispering in the depths of his being like living water when

he was close to his passion: "Come to the Father." This call to come
to the Father is undoubtedly the last word of the Spirit in us, his
unmistakable inner groaning and his supreme attempt to raise our
hearts up to God. In this all-consuming activity, the Spirit, in unity
with the Son who is entirely related to the Father and is his perfect
image, takes us irresistibly to the Father and we are swallowed up
in his glory.

Ought it not to be possible for our old Western civilization, after such a long period in which Christian thinking has become more
and more mature, to be renewed and enriched as the divine life is
poured out and to return to the pure sources of a religion of the Spirit which is Christocentric in its sovereign perfection? There would
be no need for the West to give up its great treasury of knowledge
and culture or its deposit of doctrines enunciated throughout the
centuries by the Church's teaching office, theologians, exegetes,
thinkers and historians. We would, however, derive enormous benefit in the West if we were also to approach the writings of these simple and truly evangelical men who went beyond the speculative
thought of pure intelligence and became wonderful channels of the
Spirit. Reading their works, we are profoundly conscious of the
grace, the innocence and great joy that proceed from them, since
these saints dissociated themselves from worldly possessions in order to be totally open to God, men and the whole of nature. Such
saints have also arisen in the West and even relatively recently.
Does the pure message left behind by the Curé d'Ars, Charles de
Foucauld or Thérèse of Lisieux, to name only three, not invite us to
follow their example of light and humble fervor?

Night is falling and we do not really know where mankind is
going with its heady conquests, its immeasurable ambitions and its
exaltation of man at the expense of God. Surely the only answer to
the apparently supreme reign of matter is the rule of the Spirit? Who
can enable us to transcend the power of worldly wisdom but the
Spirit of love? He can reveal to us the "mystery" of human possessions—that they are no more than dust and ashes. We dream and
long for life and in this our dreaming and longing are the same as
God's (see John 10. 10).

But where can we find that life, the life of which Saint Irenaeus said: "The glory of God is living man" (*Adv. haer.*, 4. 20.7)?
The answer to this question can be found in the Sermon on the
Mount: "How happy are the poor in spirit . . . the gentle . . . those
who hunger and thirst for what is right . . . the merciful . . . the pure
in heart . . . the peacemakers . . . those who are persecuted in the

cause of right" (Matt. 5. 1–10). These are authentically alive. They are in possession of a treasure that will not be destroyed or taken away. They have already been taken by Christ and the Holy Spirit to the kingdom of the Father, the living God. They are no longer in search of themselves or preoccupied with themselves. They have in a very real sense become love.

NOTES

1. Gregory Nazianzen, *PG* 37. 523.

2. Pseudo-Dionysius, *The Divine Names, PG* 3. 645.

3. A. Lemonnyer, "Le rôle maternel du Saint-Esprit dans notre vie surnaturelle," *La Vie Spirituelle,* January 1921.

4. It is interesting to note that Saint Augustine had no taste for the first chapters of the book of Isaiah when, as a catechumen, he was advised by Saint Ambrose to read them. The saint, who was later to show such a deep understanding of scripture, was originally not inclined, either naturally or supernaturally, to examine the meaning of the divine words; see *Confessions,* 10. 5.

5. Origen, *De Principiis,* 4, said: "There are certain things whose meaning cannot be expressed in human words. Much more light is thrown on them by a simple look than by the roundabout way of words. This law also applies to our knowledge of scripture and this is why the norm of the value that we place on scripture should be based not on the humility of the details mentioned in the various stories, but on the divinity of the Holy Spirit inspiring the whole."

6. Origen, quoted by Hans Urs von Balthasar, in *Esprit et feu,* II, p. 44, note 167. Henri de Lubac has shown to what extent scripture is unfathomable in his *L'Exégèse médiévale,* II, Chapter X, pp. 533–654, in which he relies on the Fathers of the Church in general and in particular on Gregory the Great (Seventh Homily on Ezechiel, a commentary on the prophet's first vision): "It is the same God who gives us scripture and enables us to understand it . . . What seems to be two separate actions, one following the other, is therefore really only one action. God has not in fact submitted himself to our external, historical actions. There is therefore a mutual priority or causality between the objective meaning and the interpretation of it every time the interpretation comes from the Spirit. There is nothing in this that bears any resemblance to the idea of new dogmas held in reserve, since the Spirit was given to the Church for a kind of revelation to come. We should not think of the sacred text as concealing a number of meanings that are already formed and ready to be discovered. The Spirit communicates an unlimited virtuality to scripture, which therefore includes depths which have possibilities that cannot be defined. Like the world, scripture—that other world—was not created once and for all time. The Spirit created it and continues to create it every day as it, so to speak, opens it. By means of a wonderful and strict agreement, he expands scripture as he expands the understanding of the one who receives it. As Origen says, *extenditur anima nostra, quae prius fuerat contracta, ut poss it capax esse sapientiae Dei.* The

volatus of the contemplative soul, however deeply he leads it into the depths of the heaven of scripture, will never encounter any barrier, since the space and the flight are both measured. . . .This is a very bold view, but, if we understand it correctly, the boldness is the boldness of faith."

7. Hans Urs von Balthasar, *Parole et mystère chez Origène*, p. 130, note 25.

8. Saint Ambrose, *In Ps. 1*, 33.

9. Father Clérissac, *Le Mystère de L'Eglise*, p. 68. The author goes on to say that "the Mass is the assembly of those who are baptized; the light and heat are the life-giving action of Christ the redeemer and revealer and the movement is the Holy Spirit."

10. General audience given on 13 January, reported in the *Osservatore Romano*, 22 January 1965.

11. One of the most important Patristic texts in this context is Cyprian's treatise *De unitate ecclesiae*.

12. "We also receive the Holy Spirit if we love the Church, if we are one in charity and if our joy is in the name and faith of Catholic. We should believe this, breathren: a person has the Holy Spirit in him to the degree that he loves the Church . . . If you love unity, whoever possesses some good or some grace in unity, it is for you that he possesses them" (*In Io.*, *tract.* 32, 8).

13. We may also recall in this context, with the Staretz Zozimus, the memory of the angelic brother Alyosha (in Dostoyevsky's *Brothers Karamazov*): "His room overlooked the garden with its old trees. The buds had opened, the birds had arrived and were singing beneath his window. He took pleasure in watching them and he even began to ask them to forgive him: 'Birds who belong to God, happy birds, forgive me! I have sinned against you!' We could not understand him. He was crying with happiness. 'Yes, the glory of God surrounded me. The birds, the trees, the fields and the heavens were glorious and only I was living in shame, depriving creation of its honor. I did not see its beauty or its glory . . . You are responsible for many sins, our mother sometimes used to sigh . . . Dear mother, I am crying not for grief, but for joy. I want to be guilty of sin against them. I cannot explain why, but I do not know how to love them. If I have sinned against them all, they will forgive me. That is paradise. Am I not there already?' " (This passage is quoted by Romano Guardini in his *L'Univers religieux de Dostoievski*.)

9

Jesus Christ— Eternally Present

Habit, alas, blurs the outline of the most astonishing realities. The most astonishing reality of all, the one that ought to make us melt away with joy, thankfulness and adoration, is the incarnation. If we were really conscious of the inexpressible greatness of God— "I am the one who am"—and of our lowly status as his creatures, we would, confronted by this mystery, undoubtedly experience something of the unpronounceable emotion that seized hold of Saint John when he wrote that sentence, the content of which flashes like lightning across the created universe, the history of man and the existence of each one of us: "The Word was made flesh, he lived [literally: he pitched his tent] among us." The evangelist is describing how the two furthest limits met to bring about our salvation and our deification. God and our flesh—there is an infinite distance between them. At the same time, however, there are harmonies between these two extreme poles that respond to each other and that are created by love.

The Father has placed the deepest secret of his being in the Son whom he has begotten by a flash of light. He also contemplates himself and possesses himself in the Son in order to give of himself. Man, and with him the whole of creation, place in the Son, the humanity of Jesus, their original nothingness, their poverty, their sin and their mortality. The whole of God's fatherhood is exhausted in the Word. The whole motherhood of the earth, in producing the second Adam, man who is both heavenly and earthly, is exhausted in the humanity of Jesus. The Son is the unique and substantial Word that expresses the whole of God and all the creatures in God. Jesus' response to this eternal Word is the crying of a little child in a crib and later the cry of anguish in the garden and the cry of abandonment on Calvary. Looking at the infinite distance that love has spanned, we are tempted to say with Saint John of the Cross, on Christmas Day: "My sweet and gentle Jesus, if love is to kill me, now is the moment!"

It is only infinite love that can do that. If it is to develop freely, love needs unlimited spaces that it can fill and overcome with its unifying power. The two extremes are brought together as completely and as intimately as it is possible for them to be in Jesus of Bethlehem. It is hardly possible to imagine a more perfect union than that in which two centers are touching and embracing each other in the oneness of the same person and in the bosom of an unfathomable love springing from the heart of the Trinity itself and penetrating into the heart of the world to return to its origin.

The Word, the Son who is at the center of the life of the three consubstantial persons of the Trinity, joins the center of creation. That center is man, who is placed between the angels and the animals—the world in miniature, the microcosm, as the ancient Greeks said. The eternal Word became the *Verbum abbreviatum*[1] in that being that is at the same time so great and so small. In our own flesh he accomplishes the marriage bond between divinity and humanity.

This, then, is the mystery proclaimed by the apostle Paul (Eph. 1, 2 and 3). It is both concealed and revealed. In its humility, it contains a seed so powerful that, at the end of a process of unlimited expansion, it will project a transfigured universe into the immensities of God.

There was, therefore, some two thousand years ago, a visible presence in the flesh of God on earth, united to the invisible presence of the one who never ceases to embrace with his being all places and and all centuries. What is more, inexhaustible sources of grace that are capable of making the world holy and raising it up to God spring from that visible presence that culminated in sacrifice and death.

But how disturbing at the human level this earthly presence of Christ was! Jesus lived on earth for only thirty or so years and, although he had the gigantic task of redeeming the world from sin, he began apparently by wasting his time. For the first thirty years of his short life he remained hidden in the depths of a carpenter's workshop. And even when he finally decided to show himself to men, he did not travel through the world as a pilgrim or a missionary, but remained confined within the narrow strip of land known as Palestine, going from Judea into Galilee and back from Galilee into Judea, revealing his Father, sowing the seed of the word of life, preparing the way for his Church and proving the value of his message by his miracles. Finally, he was rejected by his people and condemned to an immense death, one that seemed to be without a future.

We are therefore bound to ask: What relationship is there between this existence, which ended in failure, and the omnipotence of this heroic God who came down from the heights of heaven to save men and take them into the realm of glory?

If we approach this question from a different direction and meditate on the gospel story with an open, loving heart, receiving the inexpressible power that comes from it, we are in danger of being seized by a kind of longing for the tangible presence of the one who was both divinely human and humanly divine. Like Péguy's Joan of Arc,[2] we cannot be consoled because we are not among those who have, as people who were close to Jesus, contemplated him with their eyes, touched him with their hands, heard him with their ears and had among them the living Word (1 John 1. 2). What suffering it is not to have been there! "When I think, my God, that it only happened once . . . and that the last people of those times and of that country had what the first among us, the most holy, the greatest saints among us will never have in eternity. . . . What a mystery that is, God!"

If, however, we thirst for truth and depth of experience, we are bound to recognize that this attitude of heart and emotion must be transcended. We must go further and higher—to the Christ revealed to us by the Spirit of Pentecost in the fullness of his infinite holiness. The Spirit, after all, prepares in us a deep and wide inner space within us, a space that is, moreover, always able to become even deeper and wider and in which we can receive Christ himself. Jesus has assured us, as he assured Mary Magdalene, "Do not cling to me, because I have not yet ascended to the Father . . . to my Father and your Father, to my God and your God" (John 20. 17).

We must therefore look for Jesus now in his glory, as the one who has overcome sin and death and has returned to the Father who has placed all his satisfaction in him and has achieved his eternal plans through him.

We must say at once that this Jesus has no spatial and temporal dimensions. He is the cosmic Christ, great in his reality and lordly universality. He is the one whom Paul met on the road to Damascus in blinding light, the one who made the persecutor of Christians into the most obedient of converts and the most excellent apostle. He is the same Jesus who, during his mortal life, affirmed his unity of being and activity with his Father and boldly stated, to the scandal of the Jews, but to illuminate our way: "I tell you most solemnly, before Abraham ever was, I am" (John 8. 58).

In his letter to the Colossians, Saint Paul comments on this word of the Lord with exceptional precision and energy. It is in the clarity of these lines, quoted below, that we should look for and shall find the transcendent presence of the man-God, the beloved Son into whose kingdom the Father, thanks to the blood that the Son shed for us, has taken us, tearing us away from the power of darkness:

> He is the image of the unseen God
> and the first-born of all creation,
> for in him were created
> all things in heaven and on earth:
> everything visible and everything invisible,
> Thrones, Dominations, Sovereignties, Powers—
> all things were created through him and for him.
> Before anything was created, he existed,
> and he holds all things in unity.
> As he is the Beginning,
> he was first to be born from the dead,
> so that he should be first in every way;
> because God wanted all perfection
> to be found in him
> and all things to be reconciled through him and for him,
> everything in heaven and everything on earth,
> when he made peace
> by his death on the cross.
>
> (Col. 1. 15–20)

We do not intend to analyze this text in detail here. We would, however, like to support the view of certain modern exegetes, such

as Father Durwell,[3] that this passage should not be regarded as a
kind of diptych, the first tablet being concerned with creation and
the Word and the second tablet with the redemption achieved by
the incarnate Word. Everything would be clear and simple if we
were to accept this interpretation. But are the most transparent so-
lutions always the most true? There can be no doubt—if we are to
interpret the apostle's thought faithfully, we must recognize that
the "he" repeated so many times in this text refers only to Jesus
Christ established in the glory of his resurrection and thus made the
perfect image of the unseen God.[4] Everything, then—his primacy
over every creature that comes from him as its effective cause, his
cosmic lordship, his being the head of the Church, his perfection of
pleroma and the universal reconciliation that he brings about—everything relates to the person of Jesus and his mission and everything takes place in the unity of an immense creative and
redemptive plan. In possessing these two prerogatives, Jesus "existed
before anything was created and holds all things in unity" or, to
translate this verse more simply, "he is before all things and all
things subsisted in him" (Col. 1. 17).

But there is, of course, a possible objection. Is it not extravagant
to claim for the glorified Christ, who was born, died and rose again
in time, an activity and therefore a prior existence before he came
into this world? We cannot refute this objection if we stay within
the confines of time. And how are we to go beyond those confines
if we are—as we are—plunged into time and living always with it?
And surely Christ himself, the eternal Word, put on time, achieved
his plans in time and came to introduce eternity into time by coming to us centuries after the act of creation that marked the beginning of time.

But God, who created time with the universe, is outside time
and his thought and his will are, like his being, eternal. There is
therefore a perspective that is different from that of time and this
is the perspective that we must look for if we are to understand this
teaching. One word that Saint Paul uses in the text would seem to
be the key to introduce us to God's point of view—the point of view
that dominates and throws a clear light on all history.

That word is *pleroma.* In Colossians 1. 19 above, we read: "Because God wanted all perfection to be found in him"—and here
"perfection" can be more simply translated as "fullness" *(pleroma).*
The Father, then, concentrated in the triumphant and glorious
Christ all the divine energies of creation and sanctification. Every
virtue that creates, saves and deifies the universe is contained in the

body of the risen Christ and is at the root of his being. All things are created and recreated by sharing in that fullness of Christ. Outside it, there is no being. That *pleroma* was already there before it was historically realized in time. It is also from this fullness that all nature, grace and life and everything that unites man with God derive their cause, their model, their *raison d'être*, their movement toward their end, their destiny and their ultimate consummation.

We ought not therefore to take the origin of the world as our point of departure in tracing the line of time. On the contrary, we should proceed in the opposite direction, beginning at the eschatological peak where Christ, who is both the summit and the center of creation, dominates time and makes flow over the world, which emanates from his creative love and power, in and through the Spirit everything that causes being and deifies.

Christ therefore appears to us in the full extent of his eschatological lordship that is both paschal and cosmic. In this status, he attracts everything toward him and at the same time gives himself to all men and gives everything with himself. Everything comes from him and everything flows toward him. He is the transcendent reality. He is the body before which is thrown the immensity of a shadow that extends as far as the beginning of creation and would not exist without the sovereign presence of that body.

In this perspective, everything can be seen as depending on Christ, subjected to Christ and reconciled and recapitulated in him. This presence of Christ has infinite breadth and majesty. It is a presence in which we see God bring about his creation in Christ as it were within the act of redemption in which everything is consummated in the achievement of a single plan of salvation and love and in which sovereign and radical unity exists, beyond the very real difference between the world of darkness and the world of light, in Christ who is both alpha and omega and the first because he is the last.

We may ask at this point: Does this view of Jesus in his supreme greatness not hide from us or even banish the vision of Jesus that is presented by the gospel—the Jesus who is gentle and humble even in the affirmation of his divinity?

It does not. The two presences of Christ are the same. They are in perfect harmony. They are one. The Christ who is triumphant and radiates light in the Apocalypse is the Christ who is presented as the Lamb that is slaughtered in the same book. He is the same as the master on whose breast Saint John laid his head at the Last Supper. Did the disciple whom Jesus loved not contemplate these two presences in the same heavenly clarity when he recollected his undying memories?

Saint Paul knew only the risen Christ in his glory and yet he spoke of the suffering of Christ on the cross, which he did not witness, in tones of inexpressible emotion. The fact that he did not see Christ "according to the flesh" did not prevent him from describing the image of Christ crucified to the Galatians (Gal. 3. 1). Are his letters not the best commentary on the gospel that it is possible to imagine and the completion of the story of Jesus—if it were possible for such a story ever to be completed?

As for Jesus himself, the gospel is eternal. The words and gestures of the one who is the Word without a beginning and who works unceasingly with his Father (John 5. 17) must be extended into eternity. They must have an eternal meaning even if he wanted to be subject to time in the development of his humanity and the events of his earthly existence when he emptied himself and became for a little while lower than the angels (Heb. 2. 9) and to express, in time, his total orientation toward his Father. In this way, then, we see how the two presences of Christ, the universal and royal presence and the earthly presence that was divinely and simply human, penetrate each other and merge into each other.

It is possible for us to appreciate the regretful feelings of Péguy's little Joan of Arc, but we have nonetheless to overcome them in ourselves in the light of a mature faith. We know that all true Christians, from the apostles to those living in the twentieth century with its problems, doubts, hopes and despair, are Jesus' contemporaries.[5]

As believers, we live here on earth at a level at which the passing of time, which only carries itself along with it on its unceasing course, adds nothing and takes nothing away because it is the level of unshakeable eternity. That eternity is one and cannot be moved. Christ is eternal, and we are grafted by grace onto our living stock, who is Christ himself living at the heart of the mystery of the incarnation that was completed in his death and resurrection. For this reason, we cannot experience the aging of time. By entering more and more profoundly into the unique act of God who became man and from whom springs the source of life which comes from the eternal now of God and which gives us living water, we are always moving toward a perpetual rejuvenation. There, at that point, there is no more history and no more progress.

"If only you would listen to him today; do not harden your

hearts" (Ps. 93. 7). The author of the letter to the Hebrews used this text from the Old Testament to open a very wide perspective to us. We have therefore to live authentically at the heart of this "today" without a beginning and an end as the generation of the eternal Word. If we live in this "today," listening to the word that gives birth to and nourishes our faith, we shall continue moving forward and away from the evil world, buying back time so that it becomes an instrument of our redemption.[6]

Entering the eternity of God and his Christ is what constitutes our greatness and our dignity. The "today" is the reality that establishes us in the truth of our being and our relationship with God. It is a vertical, not a horizontal relationship, hanging over the line of time and forming a cross with it. It is both the trophy of the man-God and the lever of our salvation.

In this perspective of an eternity that absorbs the time of Christ himself and makes us Jesus' contemporaries, we ought perhaps, with Romano Guardini, to think of the mysterious period of forty days that separated the resurrection from the ascension as having a very deep meaning. What happend then? The Lord came and went. He appeared and disappeared. He belonged to time and to eternity. As Guardini said, silently and with discretion "the years that have passed enter eternity, the events of long ago are strengthened and the reality of our previous life is taken into the hereafter. The days of which we are speaking are the days that take us to eternity."[7]

The eternal Christ is omnipotent. He is the *pleroma*, fullness in his beginning that makes him creative and in his end that makes him the judge of the living and the dead. He also blesses us and came to serve us and save us and to die for us. The whole past of his life on earth has entered an eternal present, where it remains with us. It has been present in this way in a very precise sense since the ascension and, although time continues to pass, there is no more history. In the fullness of the creative and redemptive incarnation, everything becomes deeper until the perfect man, Christ, is completed in his mystical body—"a single Christ loving himself," as Saint Augustine said. At this point, all who turn toward him and live in him, even if they are not conscious of it, are his contemporaries. Jesus is for them the way, the truth and the life.

If we are to be more precise, we are bound to say that this presence, of which we are aware when the Spirit, who opens us to God and gives him to us, is poured out on us, is only possible thanks to the Church, the body of Christ.[8] The Church is the fullness of the one who is fullness itself and who fills all his fullness (Eph. 1. 22–23) and assures us of the sacramental presence of Jesus, a presence that is also secret and invisible. Jesus has placed in that presence the communication of his life, his word, his grace and his person. The relationship between time and eternity is achieved in it by the very act of the incarnation, which is also at the same time the act of the suffering and resurrection of Christ present in the mystery of faith at the center of our worship of him: "This is my body; this is my blood."

The presence of the only beloved Son continues to be heard here and now in these words. It is the unchanging presence of the enduring "today." May we never be blinded to this mystery by any vagueness in its manifestation—today Christ is born . . . today the Church is united to her heavenly bridgegroom . . . this is the today that the Lord has made . . . today all the days of Pentecost are accomplished. All these "todays" are one single "today"—the one that radiates from the person of Jesus and contains in itself both the past and the future: "Jesus Christ, the same today as he was yesterday and as he will be for ever" (Heb. 13. 8). He is the Lord who is the Spirit (2 Cor. 3. 17), because, in his risen state, he has the fullness of the Spirit and has therefore become a "life-giving spirit" (1 Cor. 15. 45). For this reason, he is the one in whom, through whom and toward whom everything is created, fulfilled and taken to its end.

As we write these lines, however, we feel, with a certain regret, obliged to admit that the great vision of the apostle, especially as it is presented in the epistles of the captivity, is very far from having been fulfilled. As we learn from the epistle to the Hebrews (2. 8), "we are not yet able to see that everything has been put under the command" of the one whom the Father has made the universal Lord. There are so many disorders, conflicts and struggles here on earth, surely, because we are not yet perfectly open to the fullness of Christ. What is more, the apostle has assured us that Christ will not be in total command until the last day. Only then will his reign over all the created powers be complete—when he has finally and forever destroyed death (1 Cor. 15. 24–26).

Although we have already touched on this mystery, it is worthwhile considering it again for a moment. It is precisely this mystery of freedom that forms the basis of our relationship with Jesus Christ and is the most personal, profound, intimate and holy aspect of that relationship. It is a relationship that can best be compared with that of marriage and which makes Christ's presence in us wonderfully effective and alive, a presence that can change and deify us.

Christ's love for us is so real that it inevitably elicits a response from us. In the love of that heart which so loved men there can be no difference between *eros* and *agape*. The depth of that love and the intensity of that desire flowing from it are impossible to separate. The thirst that Jesus has to be loved is also infinite and inexhaustible. The *agape* that rises up from the depths of the life of the Trinity and flows into his soul is not simply a necessity that urges him on or a mere need for pouring out that does not require any return. It is more than this. Jesus wants us for himself. He is a beggar, calling out unceasingly for us. To obtain our love as well as to prove his love for us, he died on the cross, with his arms outstretched in a great gesture of welcome.

How, then, should we, who are so weak and so ready to be swallowed up in the world of the senses, respond to that love that comes from the depth of eternity to open our human hearts? We may not be able to respond with the whole of our being, raising ourselves without reservation up to God, but we may be able to utter the simple word "yes." This would be both opening ourselves to his invasion and giving the full consent of our hearts and minds, all our intelligence and all our most tender emotions rooted in faith. But our dignity and greatness as human beings are shown with great clarity in this opening of ourselves, this "yes" that we say in response to God's love, because this response is above all the fruit of our freedom, which is kept imprisoned because of sin, but which is gradually delivered by grace.

We should be very conscious of this double reality. On the one hand, there is everything that God has done and still does without us, before us and once and for all time, in obedience to the eternal counsel of his Trinity of love, wisdom and power. This includes above all the incarnation, the first end of which is the death and resurrection of Jesus Christ. On the other hand, there is everything that God has continued to achieve in us and with us throughout time and will continue to do until the completion of his mystical body and his second and glorious coming. This is the Church, the assembly of those whom he has called, and, within the collective reality of that Church, the sanctification of each one of the countless members. There is the hypostatic union, there is the Church and there are the many souls who are in the Church and who are the Church itself. These three realities are only one single mystery. As we have hinted earlier in this work, this is a single nuptial mystery based on the covenant between the Word and Jesus' human nature and extending to the limits of creation as far as the Church which is its peak and at the same time throughout history, opening out in the soul in whom the mystery of the Church, the bride of Christ, lives. There are therefore three levels that can be distinguished, but which are closely united and which flow into each other, the first embracing the second, which is rooted in it, and the second inside which the third unfolds its infinite virtues.

The bridgeroom is first of all the Word of God in his pure divinity of second person of the holy Trinity and assuming our humanity in Jesus, the most beautiful virginal fruit of that humanity. Then he is the same Word, but incarnate and marrying on his cross the Church born from the opening of his heart pierced by the lance as Eve was born from the side of Adam, her sleeping bridegroom. Finally, he is the same man-God making a covenant with each soul who, in the Church, consents to live and experience the mystery of his divine betrothal.

The act of the incarnation in which everything originates does not depend on us, but on the great generosity of eternal love. The incarnation was above all a marriage act, of the kind described, according to certain commentators, in the Song of Songs.[9] For this reason, it calls on us not only to cling to the Word of God, the one who is absolute freedom, but also to the changed human character of the Savior's thirst, since the suffering and the hunger of God originate in God himself: "Oh, that you would tear the heavens open and come down!" (Isa. 64. 1).

When the angel Gabriel announced to Mary, the eternal woman, that she would give birth to the Savior, she responded for all of us. The nuptial consent of creation was given above the noise of time and space, in the silence of Nazareth: "I am the handmaid of the Lord, let what you have said be done to me" (Luke 1. 38). Thanks to this "yes" pronounced by the woman, the eternal presence has been married to earth and everything is saved, at least by implication.

Implicitly everyone is saved, but for the explicit salvation of all men, what is required is the individual consent of countless souls— as many as the number of the predestined since the beginning of the world in the one bridegroom, Christ Jesus (see Eph. 1). We are led to this sum total of countless words of consent by the one of the whole Church that is both the bride of the Word made flesh and the mother of all those who have been redeemed. The immaculate bride of God, who is also the mother of the Church and who represents what is most holy and most perfect in that Church, accepts those words of consent in his name.

On Christmas Day, it was not simply and solely Jesus as an individual who came from his mother's womb. He came, as the liturgy of the day reminds us, "out of his pavilion like a bridegroom" (Ps. 19. 5), but already holding, in his infant's arms, his bride, for, as Saint Gregory the Great said, "the birth of the head is also the birth of the members." The *sanctum*—a meaningful neuter—promised by the angel consisted of both Head and members. The Church was, in other words, there at the annunciation and the nativity, even before the one who is the eternal Word began to preach and before Peter, on whom the Church was founded, confessed his faith at Caesarea and declared his love for Jesus three times on the shores of Lake Tiberias. Even though it had not been born from Jesus' side with the water and the blood of the redemption and the sacraments and had not been thrust out of the upper room by the fire of the Spirit, the Church was already there with the bridegroom in the womb of the *Theotokos,* as it had already been present at the origin of the world, united to the first-born of all creation.

In pronouncing her *fiat,* then, Mary was replying for the whole of creation in the name of the Church that she represented. This mystery of marriage is celebrated in the Song of Songs, Psalm 45, which is on the theme of a royal wedding, and several of the prophetic books, especially Hosea and Ezekiel. Although this scriptural celebration takes many forms—it is sometimes fiery, sometimes gentle, sometimes strikingly realistic and sometimes concealed—it is always lyrical. John the Baptist, who stands as it were between the Old and the New Testaments, presents himself as the paranymph, the bridegroom's friend whose task was to prepare the wedding, declaring that the one who has the bride is the bridegroom. His greatest joy is finally to hear the bridegroom's voice, to efface himself and eventually disappear until the bridegroom occupies his place entirely (John 3. 29).

It is remarkable how many cases there are in the New Testament when Jesus does not indulge in explanations. Examples of this are his revelation of himself as the bridegroom in speaking of the kingdom of heaven as a king giving a feast for his son's wedding (Matt. 22. 2), his protestation: "Surely you cannot make the bridegroom's attendants fast while the bridegroom is still with them?" (Luke 5. 34) and his parable about the ten virgins waiting for the bridegroom in the middle of the night (Matt. 25. 1–13). In these and other cases, he refers to realities that do not have to be justified because they are so self-evident. We should therefore not be surprised to hear Saint Paul, that other paranymph and friend of the divine bridegroom who had died and had risen again, say to his Christians at Corinth: "The jealousy that I feel for you is God's own jealousy: I arranged for you to marry Christ so that I might give you away as a chaste virgin to this one husband" (2 Cor. 11. 2).

For the apostle Paul, the Church united to Christ is the "mystery," the bride and the body. Although "bride" and "body" are two realities that are only one reality, these two terms imply elements that appeal to each other, are in harmony with each other and complement each other. And, although it is concealed, the "mystery"— of the one Christ who fills everything with his presence and his activity, God who is "all in all" (1 Cor. 15. 28)—is at the beginning of everything just as he will be at the end of all things in a final and complete revelation.

Let us try for a moment to fathom the shades of meaning contained in these two words "bride" and "body." The first calls to mind a fundamental idea of love and choice: "You did not choose me; no, I chose you" (John 15. 16). It also expresses the idea of a search on the part of the bridegroom who, although he remains in his own country, makes his beloved come, by the Spirit from an idolatrous nation. This was done by Isaac in the Old Testament story. On the initiative of his father Abraham, he received, through the agency of Eliezer, the beautiful Rebekah as his bride. The word also expresses the idea of promise and commitment and of the bride's sharing in all the bridegroom's privileges—his truth, his holiness, the inexhaustible treasure of his infinite merits, his power over all flesh and, on the negative side, the lack of understanding and hostility of a world sunk in evil. Like the first Eve for the first Adam, the Church, strengthened by all this wealth, is a second Eve for the second Adam and a "helpmate like himself" (Gen. 2. 18). As she was taken from him, so too can she turn back to him as a fruitful bride and the mother of the living.

Called on to express herself, the bride, who had been freely chosen, also chooses her beloved in preference to all idols and all ideals that belong exclusively to this world and are so remote from the living and personal God that they are really no more than abstract illusions.[10] From the very beginning of Christianity, the Church has given blood for blood and sacrifice for sacrifice in martyrdom. Its confessors have always been quite intrepid. By abandoning their own will to the will of God and by giving up all their worldy goods, they were consecrated to God and in that state were called to the perfect life. All that was present in the Virgin's *fiat* has throughout the Christian centuries been lived in the Church and through the Church, and this will be so until the end of time, since the Church is really the bride who gives love for love.

Let us consider now the word "body." What strikes us at once is that the reality of perfect membership is to be found in it. It points to a fulfillment in giving oneself and unity in the most complete, the most intimate and the most concrete fulfillment. Jesus will not appear in his definitive form as the Son of God to whom the Father has given all things until he forms, with all those who have been redeemed, one single and organic reality, one single Christ, Head and body, one single vine in which the same living sap circulates through the stock and the branches. In the meantime, he waits and continues to grow and become formed through, in and with the Church. They are not two presences one confronting the other; they are two, but one within the other, one embracing the other and one extending the other. Each is the *pleroma*, the fullness of the other. This is so much so that the Church never ceases to plunge itself into the depth and the immensity of the one who has an ever-increasing abundance of members of his body.

The close bond that unites the bridegroom, Christ, to the bride, the Church, and makes them one flesh and one spirit is the Holy Spirit. He is entirely present in each and he makes each one penetrate into the other with the same intensity and the same tenderness with which he unites the Father and the Son within the Trinity and the person of the Word and the manhood of Jesus in the womb of the Virgin. In this way, the unity that makes Christ and his Church one body is the last seal that proves and confirms the title of bride. Thanks to the Holy Spirit who begot the Head in the womb of the immaculate Virgin and the members in the waters of baptism, this unity is the mark of an irrevocable reality of love that only separates in order to unite in a mutual interiority and an inexpressible satisfaction, the fruit of which is the calling into existence of the children of the second Adam, the father of the future age (Isa. 9. 5).

In this way, the mother of loving children acquires her real personality as a free, strong woman. Far from being merged into the bridegroom, she remains distinct. She returns to her bridegroom washed in the waters of baptism and nourished by the Eucharist.

The marks of her personality are known to us. They are unity, holiness, Catholicity or universality, and apostolicity. These four marks are, however, no more than aspects of the unity created in the Church by the lasting presence of the one Christ. What, after all, is the holiness of the Church but the unity of teaching and morality? What is Catholicity but unity spread everywhere? What is apostolicity but the continuation of a single mission given by the Father to the Son and the Spirit and transmitted to the apostles and their successors: "As the Father sent me, so am I sending you" (John 20. 21).

Jesus promised that he would be with the Church until the end of time. That is why the bride, moved by the same Spirit who made her bridegroom a "life-giving spirit," goes through the many vicissitudes of human life and the imperfections of her members who are still on the way toward the radiant transfiguration of purity, beauty, and brilliance described in the final pages of the book of Revelation. Compared with this consummation of her heavenly wedding with the Lamb, the great mystery of marriage here on earth, however astonishing it may seem to us, is really no more than a preparation or a betrothal.

The personality of the Church and the mystery of the marriage between the Church and Christ are together a reality which is far more intense and goes further than anything comparable in the world as we know it. But where does this mystery make itself felt if not in the souls of those who belong to their mother the Church and are therefore the living members of Christ? Those souls are spiritual universes, that "greater than all" (John 10. 29) entrusted by the Father to Jesus. It is in them that the great drama of marriage, which will never come to an end and which is so exalted that it has been discussed throughout the history of Christianity, takes place at different levels and in various ways. Following the Church Fathers who, from Origen to Saint Bernard, commented on the Song of Songs, a disciple of Saint Thomas Aquinas also stressed this marriage bond between Christ and his Church. This commentator wrote:

Just as the reality is far greater than the sign that it represents, so too does God's union with the soul go far beyond the love of a bridegroom for his bride. . . . We find there a much more inviolable faith, a much greater indissolubility and a much more useful posterity. . . . It is true that the soul united to God is not God's only bride, but does the bridegroom not love his

bride exclusively because he loves her head, her hands, her feet
and all the members of her body? Is the species in any way less-
ened in the individual because it consists of many? Oh my soul,
God is united to you in a very wonderful way. With his whole
being he loves you entirely without reducing his love for you
by loving others. . . . Human bonds are broken by death, but between you and God, oh my soul, the marriage which was concluded in baptism, confirmed by a holy life and consummated
in heaven is indissoluble.[11]

Because he wanted to be the bridegroom, God who is transcendent became, in and through Christ, like us. In order to make us
conscious of the reality of his wedding with us, he invites us to look
deeply into the fundamental mystery of his hypostatic union. What
kind of stripping away and what invasion of himself did the Word
of God bring about when he allowed the human nature that he had
assumed to be exempt from all human personality and put in its
place his own divine personality? Is it possible to imagine a closer
union as the root and model of the one that he wants to achieve
with each of us?

Once again we have to stress the twofold nuptial character of
freedom and membership. Each one of us is a person, that is, a free
being, confronted with the one who is sovereign freedom and, although, as we shall see, he has conquered us by force, he has not
used and will not use violence. He wants us to come of our own free
will to him in the lucidity and limpidity of our hearts and minds.

Here, the word "freedom" means something much deeper than
the ability to choose between good and evil or between various values, or goods of unequal value. True freedom is above all the ability
to obey, without reservation, the call of God, the infinite good who
is our end, our destiny and our happiness. Because of our sin, however, this freedom which is our joy, and our nobility is in chains and
its flight is prevented by our propensity for the flesh. Saint Paul,
who was invaded by the love of Christ in his militant and triumphant writings, is quite pathetic in his description of the pain suffered by man who does not do the good that he wants to do and does
the evil that he does not want, wavering between the law of the inner man, the law of reason, on the one hand, and the law of sin on
the other. "What a wretched man I am!" he cries out, "Who will
rescue me from this body doomed to death?" (Rom. 8. 24). But at
once he is conscious of grace: "Thanks be to God through Jesus
Christ our Lord!" (Rom. 8. 25). It is Jesus Christ who releases our

captive freedom. He sets free, at the most intimate level of our being, the power to move toward God, to choose him beyond all created being and to go beyond ourselves and find ourselves finally in
him alone. He leads us to the point where we can lose everything
and gain everything in him.

It is in the heart of our royal bridegroom who, from his cross,
"draws all men to himself" (John 12. 32) that our freedom is made
a living reality. Free among the dead and more living than ever, he
waits for us and calls us. He is the truth that delivers us and the love
that sets us free. What he loves above all else in us is what he loved
in Saint Gertrude—the freedom of heart and spirit that makes us
open to receive his grace and, in the unity of both wills, makes our
created freedom enter his eternal freedom: "Where the Spirit of the
Lord is, there is freedom" (2 Cor. 3. 17). Enjoying the fullness of the
fruits of the Spirit (Gal. 5. 22–24), the soul cannot be in a state of
conflict. In that peace and serenity, there is a continuous conversation between God and man: "The Spirit and the bride say, 'Come'
. . . I shall indeed be with you. Amen; come, Lord Jesus" (Apoc. 22.
17–20). The one who is always there is always coming and the more
the soul possesses him, the more it desires him. It is risking nothing
in following the advice of Saint Augustine: "Love and do what you
want." The bridegroom's will and that of the bride coincide perfectly.

Our clear and total response to Christ's call has immense con-
sequences. By the mystery of the incarnation, our human nature has
been assumed and implicitly saved by the Word of God. We give our
consent to this, echoing and extending the *fiat* of the Virgin and the
whole Church, and the Word made flesh therefore assumes our person. He as it were accepts responsibility for the whole of our being
and our entire destiny. They are in his hands and in his heart. Our
consent is individual and irreplaceable. For each of us, it is as though
we were alone in the world as the object of his care and satisfaction.
There is no longer anything that belongs exclusively to me or to
him. All his wealth is ours and our poverty becomes wealth in him.

Both the hero and the saint are his and indeed we all belong to
him. As Saint Paul said: "The love of Christ overwhelms us when
we reflect that if one man has died for all, then all men should be
dead; and the reason he died for all was so that living men should
live no longer for themselves, but for him who died and was raised
to life for them" (2 Cor. 5. 14–15).

But ought we not to overcome it ourselves, co-operating with
the grace of his presence in us and deriving the strength to do it

from the infinite merits of the full possession of the whole of our being that he has gained for us through his sacrifice and death? With the freedom that is conferred upon us by the influence of his absolute freedom on ours, we can make our choice and enter, within the simplest but most open forms of our daily life, open, that is, to the depths from which life itself springs, the great nuptial mystery. The soul is like a bride who is always ready to give and to receive and to be conscious of a love that is demanding only because it is too real, too strong and too generous. It is also a love that is always revealing itself from the slightest breeze that refreshes the face in the heat to the most divine of pleasures tasted in the intimate depths of solitude and total austerity.

What else is this love? It is as spontaneous as a fountain springing from the depths of the heart and yet it is clear and reflecting at the highest point of the spirit. It lives, without returning to itself, in the soul that also ceases to want itself because God wants himself in that soul. It goes beyond what is felt and what is not felt and finds its refuge in the depths of faith where Christ, who is both silent and speaking, active and dormant, dwells in us and in that refuge it is able to open out. It is like a field sown with seed and irrigated by water from the most pure sources of revelation, with the result that it is protected from anything that can injure its delicate nature, impair its strength or divert it from its aim. It is also the most simple and unconditional form of obedience. This is because the Lord's commandments and precepts express his will and are always in accordance with the aim toward which our real freedom is directed. Those commandments also favor the victory and the triumph of our freedom. Is our submission to everything that God asks of us not, after all, proof of our love for him? "If you love me you will keep my commandments" (John 14. 15). "Anyone who receives my commandments and keeps them will be one who loves me" (John 14. 21). And finally there is the wonderful assurance of Jesus himself: "If anyone loves me he will keep my word and my Father will love him and we shall come to him and make our home with him" (John 14. 23).

So, for the attentive, calm and ardent soul, the life of love will be like that described by the Lord in his message to the visionary of Patmos: "Look, I am standing at the door, knocking. If one of you hears me calling and opens the door, I will come in to share his meal, side by side with him" (Apoc. 3. 20). It is an adventure of love of such a quality that we cannot have any idea of it from our experience of human adventures. Although it begins here on earth, it prepares us for eternity and is itself already eternal, despite the painful and troubled appearance that it may have.

The soul does not, however, experience the presence of the bridegroom and his heavenly family as an inhabiting. How could God, who is infinite, be contained within my finite self? The experience is more like a loss of herself and at the same time an opening of her person by being plunged into God who is three times one person—this is how the bride enjoys the presence of the one who is more intimate than her own intimate self. The invading wave of love goes beyond all limits and takes the soul to the point where it can do no more than simply close its eyes and abandon itself entirely.

It would be foolish to claim that this examination of the subject is exhaustive—the matter is, after all, so wide and deep—but even in such a cursory study it is important to point at least to the way in which the fullness of this nuptial love is clarified by the two great apostles of love, Saint John, the "sun of thunder," and Saint Paul, the herald of that charity that is one of the higher gifts and a more perfect way (1 Cor. 12. 31; 13 *passim*).

The first spoke of an ecstatic, illuminating love that is rooted in peace and unites each one of us to Christ himself. The second sees love as recreative and expansive, as making the whole Church into one single body and as being expressed in us in a militant and triumphant form. It is obvious that everything that the apostle says of all the faithful can be applied to each individual soul. Each soul is a "church" within the Church and we would not be overlooking the great vision of the epistles of Saint Paul and their connection with the impressive understanding of the visionary of Patmos if we were to say that everything that the apostle says about the relationship between Christ and the whole body of believers can be almost identified with his teaching about Christ's relationship with each one of us.[12]

The soul experiences this double and single message alone with the one Christ in silence and solitude. In this situation, the love of the bridegroom sets the soul, the bride, apart from everthing in a mystical experience that cannot be described in words. The bridegroom pours out his love in this experience on what he loves and the soul is transfigured in the beloved. Very gradually, the bride is transformed into the bridegroom. This transformation takes place in a process of imitation. This imitative process cannot occur outside the relationship between Christ and the soul and it would become artificial, absurd and improper if it did, since Christ is and must always be unique. It is also a process of participation, assimilation and integration coming from the deepest level of the soul.

In this process, the soul is like melted wax open to receive the impression of the seal of the man-God. The more deeply the soul experiences God, the more clearly he is recognized as the one who is completely different and the more conscious the soul therefore becomes that it is quite unlike God. At the same time, however, it is also conscious of the nearness of the bridegroom—there is not the slightest distance between them. The soul is united to the Word in a close embrace in the most intimate part of its being, in a zone that is both deep and open to the infinite nature of an experience of which it can, as the bride, have only the most superficial inkling during the initial period of the betrothal.[13]

In any consideration of our marital relationship with Jesus, the bridegroom, we ought not to forget the part played by the human relationship that is summarized in the words "brother," "sister" and "child," although this is raised by the infinite dignity of its object to a higher than human level. Was this not, after all, the case with the Virgin Mary in the mystery of her divine motherhood? It is interesting in this context to note that the first three evangelists all recall Jesus' reply to those who informed him that his mother and brothers were looking for him as: "Here are my mother and my brothers. Anyone who does the will of my Father in heaven, he is my brother, sister and mother" (Matt. 12. 49–50; Mark 3. 32–35). Luke adds to this: "My mother and my brothers are those who hear the word of God and put it into practice" (Luke 8. 21).

Jesus is our brother. He not only became one of us in order to make us his own—he also gives us the grace to do the will of the Father who is his Father and ours and, what is more, the grace to hunger after that will and to regard it as the object of our greatest delight. We, moreover, are his mother, since he enables us to share in the motherhood of the Virgin by giving us a humble but living faith. What is more, he makes this increase in us in a growth that accompanies our growth in him and culminates in the fullness of unity with him.

We may perhaps be tempted to smile when we read these words of advice written by Saint Jerome to his beloved Saint Julia Eustochium, but we should pause for a while and recognize the profound truth that they contain:

Apply the example of the blessed Virgin Mary to your own life. In her admirable purity, she deserved to be called the mother of God. You too can also become the mother of God. Yes, you are the mother of the one whose image you have conceived in your heart that is made open by love and whose name you have inscribed with a stylet in your soul. He will grow in you and, when he has stripped off the hostile powers and fixed them on to the cross, by a new miracle, you will become his bride.[14]

We are not considering an extraordinary mystical experience here, of the kind described by Saint Bridget when she became conscious of an admirable movement in her, as though a living infant was turning round in her heart. It is rather the normal process in which the soul receives, in the light and warmth of the Spirit, the seed of the divine word that comes from him who is the eternal Word of the Father and continues to be nourished by the flesh of the soul with whom he is in this way united.

It is certainly possible to see this mystery of divine motherhood as being both at the beginning and at the end of the mystery of marriage. It is at the beginning of this mystery because the begetting of a child destined to become the immensity and the wholeness of the universe is creation's response to the perfect act of begetting the Word performed by the Father who wanted the incarnation to take place. This great desire entered the immaculate Virgin, who conceived Jesus in her mind and her flesh, but it was not confined to the Virgin. It flowed into the Church in an act of great fertility that has continued to be a source of greatness and holiness, an act that embraces the whole of history: "This is my body. . . ." As Divo Barsotti has pointed out, the priest makes a maternal gesture and bends like a mother over her child when he says the words of consecration.[15]

We may not, of course, be priests, but the mystery of divine motherhood still continues to live in our soul and the Word is still begotten there by our faith. As our spiritual life grows, we give birth to the Word who has been conceived in our soul. This, at least, is what Saint Bernard said in his commentary on the Song of Songs.[16]

Jesus is therefore, in our most intimate depths, the child of a divine motherhood that shares in the motherhood of the Virgin

Mary and at the same time he is also the bridegroom, the active principle of the soul which bears fruit because it dwells in Jesus and Jesus dwells in it (see John 15. 5). The soul allows the Word to spread
throughout its being and its whole life. It also takes the Word to
others in many different forms of charity and self-giving, in an apostolate that may be silent and invisible or may be active and visible,
like the mission of the eternal woman from the time of the annunciation and the visitation to the culmination at Calvary and in the
assumption.

This remarkable flourishing of virtues and good works, which
is seen more by the angels than by men, reveals the nuptial nature
of the union between the soul and the Word from whom it lives and
who directs it. As Saint Bernard says in his sermon on the Song of
Songs:

> If we were to see a soul leave everything and cling with all its
> being to the Word, live in a state of total giving and abandon-
> ment to the Word and give birth from the Word to what is be-
> gotten by the Word, to such an extent that it could truthfully
> say: "Life to me is Christ, but death would bring me something
> more" (Phil. 1. 21), then we would believe that it was the bride
> of the Word.[17]

Thérèse of Lisieux saw very clearly that the only thing that the
soul is called to do is to love, and we have good reason to think that
this poem, which deals with the soul's wedding with Christ, is perhaps the most sublime that has ever been written:

> In the secret cellar
> I drank of my beloved. When I left
> I knew nothing more
> of the fields around me.
> There he opened his heart to me.
> There he taught me his delectable knowledge,
> and I handed over to him
> my whole person and kept nothing back.
> There, where my promise is,
> I will be his bride.
> I have given up my soul
> and all my estate to his cause.
> I have no more sheep to feed.

I have only one task now—
henceforth I only have to love.
If, then, no one sees me
or finds me in the meadow,
you can say: I am lost.
I belong entirely to love,
I have resolved to lose and I have won![18]

Christ, then, is everything for us. The one whom we can and must love with a love that includes all loves that deserve the name of love, and with an exalted love that is as transcendent as his own person, is capable of taking us into the heaven where he is king and into the heaven that our soul will become when he dwells in us.

But what is the greatest work that he can achieve in us? What is the final end of his union with us? Surely it is to lead us to the Father! If the Father draws us to the Son, as he himself has assured us (John 6. 44), then he also draws us irresistibly to the Father, whom he came to reveal: "To have seen me is to have seen the Father," he told Philip (John 14. 9). He is the glory of the Father. He is translucent and behind him the soul perceives a mysterious and silent abyss, an inexpressible ocean from which attitudes, words and miracles—everything—emerge. An unfathomable and luminous reality is there and on it the whole biblical revelation is placed. Everything is given meaning within that reality. Hans Urs von Balthasar has spoken of

an experience of faith in which we are conscious of the breath of infinity coming from the inaccessible depths of the Father. In this experience, we know that all the words—both exterior and interior—all the gestures and all the actions of Christ are not only surrounded by silence, but are also permeated by an inexpressible reality, have come from silence and can at any moment be broken away from their deep roots. These roots are not seen, but without them what is seen outside would very soon lose all meaning, density and value.[19]

Should we, perhaps, try to say something about this inaccessible reality?

NOTES

1. For this term *verbum abbreviatum* (Rom. 9. 28), see Henri de Lubac, *Histoire et Esprit*, p. 445, and the interesting text of the Abbé Guerric, *Sermo 5, In nativitate Domini*, note 260; see also Henri de Lubac, *L'Exégèse médiévale*, Part 2, Vol. I, p. 180 and especially pp. 190ff. This author has said, for example: "There is a twofold *abbreviatio:* that of time and that of eternity. These are united to form only one *abbreviatio* and time and eternity are similarly united—and indissolubly so—in this abbreviated Word. This Word is certainly abbreviated and indeed very abbreviated, to the extent of being *brevissimum*, but it is above all also substantial. It is the abbreviated Word, but it is greater than what it abbreviates. It is a unity of fullness and a concentration of light. It is the abbreviated Word that is always inexpressible in itself, but at the same time it expresses everything. It is the fulfilled Word, summing everything up, fulfilling everything, refining everything and unifying everything."

2. See his *Le mystère de la charité de Jeanne d'Arc*, pp. 49ff.

3. See his article "Le Christ premier et dernier," in *Bible et Vie chrétienne*, 54, November–December 1963. We are indebted to what this author has said in this article, which completes his valuable book: *La Résurrection de Jésus, mystère de salut.*

4. L. Cerfaux has given this translation in his *Le Christ dans la théologie de saint Paul*, p. 327: "And we all, who contemplate as in a mirror, with face uncovered, the glory of the Lord, the Image par excellence, are transfigured. . . ." (2 Cor. 3. 18).

5. In his *School of Christianity*, p. 80, Kierkegaard said: "True Christians of every generation are Christ's contemporaries. They may have nothing to do with Christians of the previous generation, but they are closely related to the contemporary Christ ... Christ's life is permanently contemporary here on this earth."

6. Hebrews 3. 7–4. 10.

7. *The Lord*, Vol. II, p. 135.

8. Joseph Huby has said, in his *Mystique paulinienne et johannique*, p. 30: "The Church as a society has priority in the intention of God. It is true that it does not exist without the subjects of whom it is formed. Among them, however, there are those who may individually miss their vocation. But, as the body of Christ, the Church will never cease to exist." The same author has also said, *ibid.*, p. 169: "For both Saint John and Saint Paul, baptism is not a purely individual act. It placed the baptized person within a society which goes beyond him and which transmits to him every supernatural gift."

9. Especially Rupert de Deutz.

10. It is worthwhile recalling what Claudel has written in this context:

"Bless you, my God, for you have set me free from idols
and have made me worship only you, not Isis or Osiris,
Justice or Progress, Truth, Divinity or Humanity,
the laws of Nature, Art or Beauty
and you have not allowed all things that do not exist to exist
and you have not let me worship the Void, where you are absent."
(From the *Magnificat* in his *Cinq Grandes Odes.*)

11. This text, which has often been attributed to Saint Thomas Aquinas, was in fact written by Helvicus of Erfurt, a fourteenth-century Dominican, who was also the author of an abridgement of the book of *Sententiae*. This passage is taken from his short treatise 61, Chapter 13.

12. In this context, we can point especially to the frequent repetition of the terms *In Christo Jesu* and *in Domino*, with their meaning in each case subtly shaded, made more precise and clarified by the context. These terms are also emphasized in the whole of Saint Paul's teaching—on the one hand, for example, there is the sense in which they point to Christ as the first-born of a new life, while, on the other, there is the emphasis that they give to a living relationship with Christ and the things of Christ. Saint Paul also makes astonishing use of certain verbs with the prefix *syn- (con-)*, which, as Father Louis Bouyer has pointed out, "imply the idea of an action of which we are the subjects, but which is in the first place performed by another" (see his *Sens de la vie monastique*). There are also many adjectives compounded with *syn-* in Saint Paul's writings, such as *summorphous* ("conformed," Rom. 8. 29) and *sumphutos (complantatus*, Rom. 6. 5), which calls to mind an insertion into Christ resulting in his and our becoming one plant. The life of the one whom the apostle has called our wisdom, our justice and our peace and whom he has shown to be our all, by describing him not only with a noun, but also with a verb, has really entered us like sap. The verb that the apostle uses to express what is essential in this activity is the verb "to live": "To me, to live is Christ" (Phil. 1. 21).

13. Saint Ambrose, *Cant.* 1, *PL* 15. 1854ff.

14. *Epistola 22 ad Eustochium, PL* 22. 394.

15. "The liturgical gesture of the priest when pronouncing the words of consecration is an act of love and is maternal. His bending over the host and pronouncing the words is an imitation of the mother's gesture as she leans tenderly over the cradle of her new-born child," *Vie mystique et Mystère liturgique*, p. 374.

16. Saint Bernard, *In Canticum, Sermo* 85.

17. Saint Bernard, *op. cit.*, 85, 12.

18. Saint John of the Cross, *Spiritual Canticle*, 17–20.

19. Hans Urs von Balthasar, *Dieu et l'homme d'aujourd'hui*, p. 225.

10

The Presence of the Father

The terms "the Word, the Son" and "Holy Spirit" call to mind invisible realities that, in order to penetrate into our hearts and understanding, go beyond the images that are transmitted by revelation. They point to God—not only to the hidden God, wrapped in the mystery of his divinity, but also to God made manifest. These two titles point to the God who, in this world that has been created by his omnipotent love, raises us up from visible things to the most secret realities.

The Word, the Son, is God's eternal word, an explosion of light and knowledge within the Trinity. He is also God with a human face like our own. He is the Son of man, not only in his majesty and glory as Lord—the splendor that was glimpsed by the prophet Daniel and the visionary of Patmos—but also in the familiarity, humility and gentleness of Jesus of Nazareth, the Lamb of God.

The Holy Spirit is the stream of living water that flows from the depths of God and the heart of Jesus and never dries up. He is the breath, at times strong and at others hardly perceptible, whose sound we hear, but do not know "where it somes from or where it is going" (John 3. 8), and which enables us to be reborn into a higher world where we are children of God. He is also the flame that purifies, sets fire to and consumes us.

What image can we have of the Father? He is beyond all our powers to represent him. No one here on earth has ever seen him. We know, it is true, that all fatherhood in heaven and on earth is named after him (Eph. 3. 14) and that there is an element of sacred mystery in all fatherhood, in its aspect of begetting. The word "father" also calls many religious images to mind in ancient religious thought, in which the greatest gods were regarded as fathers, as were kings. The whole concept of paternity in fact implies a manifestation of divinity.

But what form should we employ to suggest the idea of the one who, coming from himself alone, is beyond everything and invisible? If it is possible for us to say that there is, in the family of the three consubstantial persons of the Trinity, one reality that is less accessible and more fully concealed, then we may certainly say that it is the Father. He is not begotten, the *anarchos* or beginning without a beginning, the source from which come all being and life outside, originating in the intimacy of his pure essence, the end in which everything culminates and is recapitulated and in which everything rests in unity and finally the fathomless and silent depths.

His voice was heard three times during the life of Christ Jesus on earth (Matt. 3. 17; 17. 5; John 12. 28). These fleeting revelations were made to give authority to the mission of the Son. The Father remained outside that mission, although he originated it. He sent, but was not sent himself. Saint Irenaeus taught that the Father took the initiative and ordered, while the other two consubstantial persons carried out his commands. For this reason, no one on earth has ever seen the adorable face from which came the voice that charmed the innocent Adam when the evening breeze was blowing in paradise. No one has ever seen the face before which Abraham went unhesitatingly toward his mysterious destiny as the head of a people without number. No one has ever seen the face that Moses, the psalmist and so many righteous men living under the old covenant so longed to see as the most desirable good of all. It was believed that the experience was so intensely charged with life that one could not contemplate the Father's face without dying.

Following so many saints, who have themselves followed the revelation of Christ himself, we too long for the Father as the deer longs for living water. We feel that the one who has created us and who has given us everything when he gave us his own Son (Rom. 8. 32) is also the end and the climax of our anxious and trusting expectation as children of God who have been called to share in his eternal glory.

Before we go too far in our affirmation of God as our Father and in order to avoid confusion, we should make a distinction. In one sense, God is our Father as the Trinity, the creator, ruler and Lord of the universe, as providence and as the effective cause of everything both in the natural order and in the order of grace. This brings us into contact with the abyss that separates us, as the adopted sons of God, from the only Son of God, the natural Son to whom he has given the whole of his substance and without whom he would not be God. God is, after all, the one who, both spontaneously and of necessity, has begotten a Word, a Son, who is his perfect image, the radiance of his glory and the object of his infinite satisfaction. We poor human creatures, on the other hand, are not necessary to God and we add nothing to the fullness of his perfection.

The Son's and the Spirit's proceeding from the Father is only barely outlined in the Old Testament and does not emerge clearly until the full revelation of the New Testament. Despite this, however, the fatherhood of God nonetheless appears in the history of Israel, to whom God presented himself as transcendent, all-powerful and inspired with exceptional love for the people who contained within themselves the destiny of the whole of mankind. That fatherhood is, for example, affirmed impressively in the book of Deuteronomy: "Is it not your father who gave you being, who made you, by whom you subsist?" (32. 6). The same is expressed in more tender and even lyrical language by the Third Isaiah on the day of distress: "Where is your ardour, your might, the yearning of your inmost heart? Do not let your compassion go unmoved, for you are our Father. For Abraham does not own us and Israel (Jacob) does not acknowledge us; you, Yahweh, yourself are our Father; our redeemer is your ancient name" (Isa. 63. 16).

The whole of the Trinity, then, is my creator and Father. If I am brought back by grace to the deepest root of my being, I am in contact with the Father. In a mysterious initiative of grace, he, who was not begotten, thought of me when he begot his Son and wanted me in their unique breath of love, the Spirit. The image of the Trinity is inscribed in my innermost depths and I am a person because of the Trinity—I come from a God who is three times one person.

At the same time, the three basic elements of my fragile, fortuitious and scattered being—power, eternity and unity—are represented for me in the person of the Father. In the image that rests in the depths of my soul and cannot be lost, the Trinity corresponds to the latent memory of the goodness and power of my God on to whom my knowledge and will are grafted. I dimly recognize that, in the least accessible depths of my being, I can encounter the depths of God himself, the inaccessible Father, and that it is there that I am able to worship him, thank him and beseech him. The two

sources—the source of my created life and that of the life of God
that is displayed in the three persons—have to be united. When I
came into existence, they were separated, but only to enable the
Spirit to fill me with that fullness of sonship that I can cry, together
with Christ: "Abba, Father" (Rom. 8. 15).

It is from this identification with Christ that the second meaning of God's fatherhood comes. The first person of the Trinity is
really our Father, the one whom Jesus, on the morning of his resurrection, called "my Father and your Father, my God and your
God" (John 20. 17), because of the grace of our adoption as sons in
the one Son who, through the incarnation, became our brother, the
first-born of many brothers (Rom. 8. 29; Heb. 2. 11).

We should never forget that we are not only children of the Father because he gives us the name of sons, but also Christ's brothers
because, of his own free will, the Father begot us by the word of
truth to be the first-fruits of his creation (James 1. 18). We are certainly not sons by nature, but what we have here is an adoption that
goes far beyond the legal and moral significance of that word.

Let us try to leap ahead here. We want to understand precisely
where the Father receives us in his Son, where we are inseparably
united to him. We have therefore to appreciate the continuity that
exists between the fact that the Word, the Son, and the Holy Spirit
have proceeded from the Father on the one hand and the visible or
invisible missions of these two divine persons on the other.

Saint Thomas Aquinas has emphasized this doctrine in a very
striking way and it is only within this great perspective that we can
really understand this mystery of love which, in the unity of the one
uncreated and created life, shows us that everything that comes
from God, in the order both of nature and of grace, is taken back
by him to its divine origin. The best that we can do in this context
is to quote Father Chardon:

There are two ways in which the divine persons proceed—the
first is eternal and the second is temporal. The second has a beginning, the first has none. The second is immanent, the first
is outside the world. The first is called a generation or a production, while the second is called a sending or mission. Both the
one and the other form the perfection of the will and
understanding, the first those of God and the second those of
man.   .

The first is the eternal reason for the production of creatures and for their emergence from their cause, God, while the second is the model for their return. In the one we worship God as the source of our being and in the other we see him as our end. The first has effects within the gifts of nature and is a presence that is common to all things, both good and bad. The second is always in communion only with supernatural gifts and graces and with these it closes the circle of love and providence that the other began in God in order to come to us, while the latter begins in us and ends in God. Eternal production is the origin of the second, or rather the second is simply an extension of the first.

This can perhaps be expressed better in the following way: eternal and temporal production is only one single production. The condition of time adds nothing new to God, who is unchangeable and the fullness of perfection. It is only in the creature who is enabled to share, by means of a new change that takes place in it, in what God has always been from eternity. In other words, God begins to produce in the soul the persons who proceed in his bosom before all eternity.[1]

We should therefore see, looking at eternity and time in the same shaft of light, the divine persons proceeding from the Father. We should also see, in creation, their extension in their mission outside that aims to bring everything back to the Father. In seeing this, we should not separate our sonship as humble creatures who are called to share in God's nature from the natural sonship of the eternal Son. We should also recognize that, by virtue of his mission, only this one Son was able to reveal to us our sonship—a sonship that is ours by grace—and the greatness and tenderness of the Father who has placed all his satisfaction in the Son. In this way, we should be able to see what our relationship with him should be.

Jesus wanted his apostle, Saint John, to hand down to us the story of his conversation with the pharisee Nicodemus, so that the mystery of our heavenly begetting might be revealed to us. The Lord tells us that we have to be born again and indeed, born from above, if we are to enter the kingdom of God (John 3. 3). Our first birth is according to the flesh and what is born of the flesh is flesh and tends toward the flesh. Our new birth, of the water of baptism and the Spirit, is spiritual and tends toward higher things (John 3. 5). These two births are therefore at the origin of two lives, each of which points in a different direction. The first points to an earthly and broken world, while the second fits us for a heavenly and eternal world. This second, supernatural birth is really a rebirth, making us children of the Father who is in heaven. The foundation, the heart and the end of all true Christianity is there.

The living God, then, is the one who, in the extension of his begetting within the Trinity, begets living images of his one substantial image, the Word, and calls them to a life that is so sublime and so powerful that death here on earth can only be, for them, a passing, even an accident, since that life is made to be lived forever. We ought, however, to recognize that we are not, as we are when we are begotten on earth, begotten once and for all time when we are baptized. The character that we receive at baptism is indelible. In God, however, although we do not leave his bosom, which is both a father's and a mother's, we are, at each moment of time that coincides vertically with eternity, both conceived and begotten. Unless we ourselves refuse to remain, we never leave the home of that Father, on whom we are always dependent, especially for the reception of his grace. We are always nourished and given life by him and in this way are similar to the one Son who was begotten and whose person is simply a reception of the Father and a reference to the Father. We are therefore the newborn children of whom Saint Peter speaks (1 Pet. 2. 2). We are all the more children because, through the grace that we receive, we are all the more deeply conscious of everything that the Father is for us and of our being so rooted in his great tenderness. And how is it possible for us therefore not to be determined to be like our Father? "Be perfect just as your heavenly Father is perfect" (Matt. 5. 48)—this evangelical commandment is echoed by Saint Paul: "Try, then, to imitate God, as children of his that he loves" (Eph. 5. 1).

The Son of God tells us, then, that we should be born again of God with a heavenly life in view. He also speaks of the Father in terms that we should study and consider deeply in the wonderful aura of purity and love that surrounds the Sermon on the Mount. The Father who rules the world is concerned with each one of us. The one who sees us all and provides for us all regards us as infinitely more precious than the birds which "do not sow or reap or gather into barns," but whose "heavenly Father feeds them" (Matt. 6. 26). He also values us much more than "the flowers growing in the fields," which "never have to work or spin," but which are robed by him more beautifully than "Solomon in all his regalia" (Matt. 6. 28–29). We should therefore not "worry about tomorrow" (Matt. 6. 34). God is providence and, because he is our Father, he will never abandon us.

What can we say about this? Should we take this teaching of the Lord Jesus seriously? Is it not perhaps a pious idyll, something that can relieve us from anxiety and lull us into idleness, making us hope for a miracle in urgent cases? No, it is none of these things. It is too sublime, too divine and too wise to be opposed to all human prudence. If we are to understand the full scope and meaning of Saint Matthew's text, however, we should look more closely at the whole of it: "Set your hearts on his kingdom first and on his righteousness and all these other things will be given you as well" (Matt. 6. 33). It is on this condition that the Father guarantees to be our Father and our providence.

Let us try to understand what this means. It means that we should look for the kingdom of God, put this activity before everything else and put the best and the most essential aspect of ourselves into it. We should do this in the complete trust that our Father will always take care of each one of us as though each one were his only child and will give us our daily bread and the clothing that we need. Saint Francis of Assisi must have experienced something of the immense joy of this total placing of the whole of his being into the hands of his heavenly Father when he gave up everything in order to enter the kingdom. He did this by stripping off the fine clothes that he had received from his all too prosaic father, Pietro di Bernardone, and by forcing his bishop to cover him with his cloak to avoid the scandal of his nakedness.

Looking for the kingdom and seeing in everything only the generosity of the Father—this is a superhuman ideal that at once transfers us to the level of the absolute God. It is a call to free collaboration with God's plan and at the same time a tearing away from our all too earthly attachments. When our eyes meet those of the Father, we see a transfigured universe, where the apparent chaos and absurdity that are subjected to the interplay of mechanical forces and hide from our gaze the activity of the sovereign first cause is stripped away and the truth is revealed. Looking at the world in the clarity of God's providence is tearing everything away from the evil one and returning everything to God. It is also sufficient to convince us that God sees everything, and is active and alive as he was with his servant Hagar in the loneliness and distress of the desert (Gen. 16.13), not only in the history of those peoples and races in which the eternal struggle between the city of God and the earthly city has taken place, but also in the existence of each one of us.

Seeing the world in this way in the light of God's providence is always collaborating with him and, as children of the light, showing ourselves to be infinitely more far-seeing than those who think of nothing but amassing treasures and storing their grain in barns. It is never allowing ourselves to be discouraged by what seems to us to be contrary to our humanity—failure, temptation, sin, ingratitude or scorn of our fellow human beings. We are, after all, sure—indeed, convinced in faith—that everything contributes to the good of those who love God and that "nothing can come between us and the love of Christ" (Rom. 8. 28 and 35). It is also an imitation of the patience and long-suffering of the Father "who causes his sun to rise on bad men as well as good and his rain to fall on honest and dishonest men alike" (Matt. 5. 45). Finally, it is loving all the Father's children and in this way sharing in all the feelings of his heart.

We are therefore able to say the sublime prayer to the Father, *Pater noster* (Matt. 6. 9–13), which came directly from Jesus' heart and enters our heart or from his lips to our lips. It is a prayer that is so deep and full in its power of intercession that none of those who have studied it in the history of the Church—Tertullian, Origen, Romano Guardini or St. Paul of the Cross—have ever been able to penetrate to its ultimate depths.

It is not difficult to understand what greatness can be added to our life by abandoning ourselves totally to the Father's providence in an attitude of faith and dynamism and by allowing the spirit of docility, flexibility and adaptation to grow in ourselves so that we truly become children of God. This attitude is not only sublime; it is also prophetic and eschatological. It is directed toward the end of this world which is passing, but which is at the same time moving toward an eternal stability.

The man who really listens to providence is already living in a universe that will not be manifested in its full dimensions until the end of time. He is already the new man, going toward the new heaven and the new earth, a world which is finally completed and given by the Son back to the Father so that he should be all in all (1 Cor. 15. 28).

What part does chance, which is always present in our life and which is sometimes catastrophic in its effects, play in this vision? Chance, it has been said, is only the unknown aspect of providence and, for the man whose true life goes beyond the appearances from which the absurd and the disordered elements are derived, there is a state of peace and harmony between his soul and the events of the world. Whatever they may be, these events come to him as friends and he welcomes them as friends. As one wise author has said:

> My body is one with my soul and is made for it, but chance events lie in wait for me and the external circumstances surrounding my existence are always present, like an additional body imposed on my soul. Even the least predictable contingencies are mysteriously adapted to my nature and gather around it like the organs and members of a nucleus . . . Every man's destiny and all its apparently vain, meaningless and contradictory elements are of the same nature as his soul.[2]

Through our everyday, concrete experience, then, we are united to the Father, from whom both the most exalted and the most humble gifts come. There is nothing that is base in this view. On the contrary, everything is noble in this perspective that brings us into contact with the goodness, power and majesty of God, whose wisdom stretches from one end to the other of the universe of space and time. This goodness is the goodness of the Father who holds in his hands the number of hairs on our heads and the size of our bodies (see Matt. 6. 27; Luke 12. 25; Matt. 10. 30).

The Father's goodness is revealed not only in his providence, but also—and even more powerfully—in his expression of his omnipotence in forgiveness and mercy. We pray on the twenty-sixth Sunday of the year to God as the one who gives us the supreme proof of his power in being patient with us and never ceasing to show us mercy. Saint Luke is our guide here. He has finished the task begun by Saint Matthew in several parables included in his gospel. The most moving is undoubtedly the parable of the prodigal son.

Before we discuss the parable itself, we should, however, consider the mysterious reality of the Father's mercy. If we speak of mercy, we also speak in this context of compassion, pity and at the same time a state of sadness and suffering. We know, of course, that the Father does not suffer in his pure and essential nature and that he is infinite and unchangeably blessed. Yet, in our hearts, we have the inescapable feeling that the Father is not a God who is frozen in Olympian serenity even though he is unchanging. We cannot believe that the Father, who is presented in the Old Testament as so open to the trials of his people, so slow to punish and so quick to forgive, is not a God whose "bowels" are moved by mercy. We can be sure that the plan of a fallible creation and a redemption by the blood of Christ comes from the fathomless depths of this God.

God's mercy is no greater than his love. It is only one of the aspects of the eternal love to which our sinful condition makes us especially sensitive. It was necessary for the world to have emerged from the void and to be always inclined to return to it and for a painful incarnation to take place for full light to be thrown on God's love and the mercy that flows from it. It is our wretchedness that makes that mercy flow from God's love and thus gives the Father a glory that he would not have had if he had not created us.

In God, however, everything is eternal. The perfection that presupposes a tenderness that has no beginning and is capable of melting away in pity is therefore also eternal. We can only gain some idea of the Father's mercy when we consider Jesus weeping over Jerusalem his homeland or over his friend Lazarus, Jesus whose heart was torn with pain so that he sweated blood in the garden of his agony and finally Jesus who said to Philip: "To have seen me is to have seen the Father" (John 14. 9). It is therefore through Jesus and then through ourselves who are his body and to whom he said: "Be compassionate as your Father is compassionate" (Luke 6. 36) that we should contemplate the shattering possibility of the Father's suffering. El Greco suggested that possibility of suffering when he depicted the Ancient of Days holding his dead Son in his arms and gazing at him with a terrible yet gentle seriousness imprinted on his face.

The revolutionary newness of Christianity is to be found above all in this inexpressible compassion of God the Father. Because of it, the transcendent, absolute and holy God is also the being who is most near to us, living within us, not only through his immanence as our creator, but also because he is indissolubly one with his Son, the one in whom we are all saved and rehabilitated and who is sublimely generous. Origen said of that Son that, in him, "we accept God's way of life and he accepts ours." This text of Origen's is so remarkable that we cannot refrain from quoting it in its entirety:

> What is that suffering that Christ underwent for us? It is the suffering of love. But does the Father, he who is God of the universe and full of long-suffering, mercy and pity, not suffer in some way? Or are you unaware that, when he concerns himself with human things, he experiences a human suffering? "For the Lord your God has accepted your way of life, as one who takes his child on himself" (Deut. 1. 31). God, then, accepts our way of life as the Son of God accepts our suffering. The Father him-

self is therefore capable of suffering. If we pray to him, he has
pity and compassion on us. He suffers with the suffering of
love.[3]

The poet Paul Claudel has echoed these words: "Longinus's
lance did more than penetrate the heart of Christ. It entered the
very center of the Trinity".[4]

It is of this Father that the parable of the prodigal son speaks.
Because it expresses a deep pathos in its narration of many vicissitudes and of good and bad fortune, it contains a real element of drama. In its terseness and sobriety, however, it is even finer and more
moving. Certain suggestive details emerge from it and certain harmonies are sounded. These form the basis of a mystery that evokes realities of love, a love that is infinite, profoundly disturbing the
heart, because those realities are both too human and too divine.
The parable takes us to the very heart of the drama of man and into
the most intimate and essential center of his destiny. Opposite the
Father, who is the one who forgives us, there is the Son who is each
one of us, whatever may be the moment in our sinful life—our happiness—a wretched happiness—when we leave, our distress when
we fail, our conversion and our return to our Father's house.

The parable tells us nothing of the suffering, the anxiety or the
protestations of the father caused by his son's demands and then by
his running away. These aspects are of secondary importance and
the story keeps to what is eesential. But it may also be true to say
that the real Father is the one who never abandons his child, however ungrateful he may be. The son leaves the Father, but the Father
will never leave his son. He lets his son go and, drunk with a false
sense of freedom, pursue pleasure and adventure, and this is because
he is the omnipotent Father who is able to lead his son back to his
home whenever he wants to and using whatever means he wants to
use.

That Father is always present. He follows his son in his sin and
his unhappiness. He plumbs the depths of his heart. He watches
over his fate. His presence is invisible, but there in the most intimate part of the child's heart. We are reminded here of the poignant
desolation expressed in the painting by Puvis de Chavannes. It
shows the son, haggard, hungry, stripped, lonely and almost naked,
staring and miserable. We can imagine his eyes encountering the immense vanity of all things outside himself and the great wretchedness inside him. We can also imagine him recalling the freedom and

sweetness of his childhood home. The Father is present, aware of this first moment of regret and repentance that he has himself brought about in the son's heart. He is there too when the son eventually resolves to return along the long road that separates him from the home where he was, unknowingly, so happy.

We all have this longing for the home where we spent our earliest years in purity and simplicity. If we were to be touched by a mysterious grace, we might perhaps even be able to go back over the countless past centuries to the golden age, the lost paradise of tenderness and familiarity with God, where our first parents lived in early innocence. Baudelaire, Edgar Alan Poe and other authors have assured us that it is because poetry and art arouse in us an insatiable longing for lost happiness. . . . But this is a digression and we should not identify ourselves so much with the prodigal son of the parable that we lose sight of the presence of the Father.

Although the Father knows and directs everything, we see him in the story watching the road that his son had taken when he left home. How great is the poverty of our heavenly Father! How anxious and watchful the eternal, blessed and transcendent God is! The rest of the story is familiar to us. As soon as he sees his son approaching—"a long way off"—he runs toward him. He embraces him so warmly and so tightly that the prodigal son has no time to finish the words of contrition and humility that he had prepared. The Father's great joy over his son's return is expressed in hasty preparations for a feast. The finest robe is brought and the son is given a ring and sandals. The fattened calf is killed and friends are invited to banquet. We can imagine the music and all the trappings of a wedding feast served by angels obeying the orders of the Father and radiating inexpressible joy in heaven.

We should also note how wise the Father is in his mercy. He begins by touching the flesh of the one who had sinned in the flesh, but he does this in order to reach the son's soul and stimulate repentance. What a great thing repentance is! The Father wants only to forgive us, which is why, at least according to Saint Ambrose, he rested on the seventh day after creating man. The whole flood of divine *agape* is waiting to pour on us, but it has to be received by a deep valley. Repentance hollows out that valley by tearing open the heart, making a terrible yet sweet wound. In the depths of this wound is the bed along which the powerful stream of the Father's love flows.

Divo Barsotti believes that love is not obtained by a great effort of the will.

It is simply a question of receiving it. This love will live in you in order to make you go beyond yourself and work without ceasing. You have, however, simply to receive it, to open your heart. And your heart will be opened above all by repentance, by the recognition of your sinfulness and poverty. This will make you accept God's gift as mercy and forgiveness. God's love for you is the kiss of the one who forgives you. The more his forgiveness grows in your lively, spontaneous yet deep understanding of your own unworthiness, the greater will be the gift of his love.[5]

This grace is truly creative. What had been prostituted is made as pure as a virgin, thanks to this wound of repentance that shines in the very heart of our heart. The wound is healed, but it remains open and calls for the soothing presence of the one who is infinitely merciful. The Father makes the child who has come back to him into a new being. The son, on the other hand, goes down into the depths of his misery and nothingness and comes into contact with the goodness of the Father. Through Christ, how many men—from Saint Peter and Saint Augustine to Charles de Foucauld—and how many women—from Saint Mary Magdalen and Mary of Egypt to Eve Lavallère—have experienced that!

Our sin cannot be washed away until we repent in response to the Father's mercy and this, when it is poured out on us, leaves his justice intact. Our Father in heaven is in no sense a kindly, easygoing grandfather whose only desire is to give pleasure and who closes his eyes to the faults of his grandchildren. In his love, which is light, our Father is, on the contrary, all too anxious to educate us and fashion us for eternal life and to make us really divine for his love to be completely undemanding. We should recognize the paradox that is present in God's love for us. He is both infinitely merciful and infinitely vulnerable. He forgives everything, but he is conscious of the slightest lack of moral refinement and calls for everything in expiation.

The Father's justice, then, is inseparable from his love. If we love him as his children and are disinterested, we ought to be able to contemplate his justice, which, like his mercy, is an aspect of his love and holiness. There is no mercy without justice and no justice without mercy. Both are as pure as virgins, both are light and both are flames. The flame of justice, however, is inexorably and infallibly directed upward. It is "like the mountains of God" (Ps. 36. 6).

The flame of mercy on the other hand spreads out and penetrates everything. It fills the earth (Ps. 33. 5; 119. 64).

Both are quite pure, but one seems to be able to resist all attraction, while the other overcomes us with its inexpressible condescendence. The first is like an arrow coming from the depths and flying straight up in uninterrupted flight. The second is ready to follow every bend and turning in the path of our destiny. The effectiveness of God's justice is determined by the limits imposed on it by his creatures. His mercy, however, is boundless. Anyone who has really experienced the presence of the Father and the fullness of his love in Christ crucified is bound to love both equally and is as ready to die for the one as for the other. They are, after all, God himself, the living, holy God, whose perfect love is totally united with the absolute nature of his being. God examines each star in heaven and puts it in its proper place. He illuminates each with his own light— each one of the myriads of planets and stars in the heavenly galaxy.

In this way, the Father is, in the pouring out of his goodness, nothing by pity and forgiveness and, in the adorable intransigence of his justice and holiness, the one whom we cannot touch without being holy ourselves. In his mercy, however, he gives us the wonderful privilege of being able to judge ourselves in the light that he sheds on us. This is why repentance here on earth is so important as expiation and as causing the love of God that makes us righteous to flow from on high. After death, while we are still unworthy to see God face to face, our soul, that has been separated from God, is driven to seek the place of purification that he, in his goodness, wisdom and justice, has prepared for us. We shall spontaneously cry out: "Father, I no longer deserve to be called your son!" (Luke 15. 21), in the pain, joy and expectation of certain fulfillment, echoing the prodigal son.

If the Father is effectively to be our Father, we must for our part effectively be his children. We must also be perfectly identified with his Son and reflect in our being the old saying: "The Christian is another Christ."

But what is the essence of that Christ in whose image the Father wants to fashion us? As we have already seen, within the Holy Trinity, the Word is always in reference to the Father from whom he receives everything that he is, and to whom he relates all that he is. Each dwells within the other and each circulates within the other in a movement of infinite vitality, thanks to the breath of the Spirit of love.

At the time of his incarnation, when he entered our world and was still in lasting union with his Father, the Word, the Son, received in all its wonderful newness everything that the Father's will meant for him, in and through both the least and the most important events that took place during his life on earth. This accounts for the many spontaneous reactions, some expressing joy and others expressing sorrow, that are found scattered throughout the gospel story. Jesus reacted in this way to the words and deeds of those who surrounded him. He reacted to the apostles when they came back from their mission, to signs of trust and distrust, to miracles, to the pride and stubbornness of the pharisees and to the perspective of his passion. He always welcomed these events as the holy will of his Father, whose will was his food (John 4. 34) and who guided and upheld the whole of his life.

It has been said that "it may seem astonishing that what we have to imitate in Jesus Christ is the most sublime, the most intimate and the most mysterious element of all—the life of the Son of God in all the details of his human existence."[6] But is this expression on earth of the unique and eternal activity by which the Lord Jesus is related to the Father not our most certain way of joining, together with him, the Father in the depths of his holy will, of coming into contact with eternity in and through time and of becoming the worshipers in spirit and truth of the kind that the Father wants (John 4, 23)?

There is, then, what Father de Caussade called a "sacrament of the present moment" for every true child of God. Every moment of time is available to us and should be welcomed as a sacred reality. If we cling to this certain sign of God's will as united to our faith in his providence manifested in each event in our lives, we shall become his blood-relations: his "brother and sister and mother" (Mark 3. 35). As blood-relations, we are more closely related to him than we are to our natural blood-relations.[7] We are rooted in the Father's peace—the peace that Christ left to us. This peace goes beyond all personal affectation and selfishness and even beyond all feeling.

Does this attention to the present moment not help to make us really childlike, fresh and abandoned in our attitude? The child does not dwell on memories of the past and regret what has happened, nor does he try to predict the future and plan the shape of his life. He lives rather from day to day, in the present, adapting himself constantly to his concrete existence.

In the same way, the Christian should live in the present moment and not ask whether he is living in happiness or suffering, pleasure or sadness. He should live and indeed does live according to the will of the Father who sees him constantly. The grace that is poured into the most intimate and interior part of himself encounters in him the grace that each event brings to him from outside. The two merge together and everything is made easy because, identifying us with Jesus, the Spirit enables us to "do little things as though they were great, because of the majesty of Jesus Christ who does them in us and lives in us, and great things as though they were little and easy, because of his omnipotence."[8]

Is it possible for us to go even deeper in our search for the Father? Would we not find, in our innermost depths, another and more hidden aspect of his presence? Are there no stages in our spiritual life, as we go down into our own depths, or is there not perhaps one decisive stage where we are especially influenced by the Father? Is it not possible for us to have mysterious encounters with the Father, who might touch us in those inner depths with special tenderness? All this is certainly possible, but the reality is so deep and at the same time so delicate that one hardly dares to speak about it.

In this search for intimate union with God and our attempt to return to him, the Father is what Saint Thomas Aquinas called "the end toward which we are moving."[9] He draws us unceasingly to him, through his Son, the Word, and his Spirit of love, in order to welcome us into his deep rest. Again and again he comes to us to dwell in us with the two whom he sends, and again and again he fashions us, through them, in order to make us his children. At the same time, however, he continues to wait for us in order to welcome us into his bosom. We are the first-fruits of the universe that he will receive in its completed form at the end of time, when Christ, having subjected all things to his kingdom, will give them to him in a great offering so that he, the Father, will be all in all.

Along the whole path of our life, then, we have to seek entry into the Father as the supreme end to which our eternal predestination as children of God destines us and try to reach, in unity with Jesus and driven by the breath of the Spirit, the unfathomable depths of his paternal tenderness. There we shall lose ourselves forever and at the same time find our authentic self, which exists only in the self of God. But is that infinite self of God not already present in us, as the great Hindu thinker believed?

> At the center of the cave of the heart,
> the only one, he alone,

I supreme, self supreme,
he shines in himself.[10]

The Father is the source. How can we, who have been created
and recreated in his image, be united to him? We can do this only
by becoming more and more interior until we reach the point where
we are most naked and pure and where there is no beginning and
no end, no limit bordering on the infinity of the Father who bore
us in his bosom even before he created us.

Is it possible to go down into these depths without being separated from the created world outside us? We certainly have first to
go to God, who is already present in us simply because we exist, and
we can do this through his creation, of which we are aware through
our senses. So long as we are not spiritually blind, his creatures will
come between the visible and the invisible worlds like a veil and
then lead us from the first to the second. They reflect God's perfection. They are also signs of his presence and symbols of a kingdom
that has already begun to exist, but will one day burst out in all its
splendor when all creatures have disappeared and have been transformed.

Nonetheless, anyone who is drawn from within by the Father
and who longs for what is absolute and senses the presence of the
transcendent and completely different one calling him from the
depths of his truth, love and beauty ceases eventually to be attracted
by the universe. This state is necessary, at least for a while, until the
dawn of the fullness of existence that must come one day. When the
depths of man's soul and those of God come together and the *memoria sui* is united with the *memoria Dei,* the whole of creation will
be transfigured and everything will appear in the light of the creator
in which all is unity and harmony.

Until we reach this blessed state at the end, however, even innocent creatures strike us as strangers. We feel as aliens in their presence and are irresistibly drawn by the Father. We prefer the taste of
ashes that they leave behind for us and the gaping void that they
hollow out in front of us to the temptation and the rest that they
obtain for us. Paul Claudel wrote: "Things gradually leave me and
I leave them. We can only enter the counsels of love when we are
naked."[11]

It is then that we experience the great vanity of this world, even
though its night may be full of stars, for the universe calls out to
us! "I am not God! There is an infinite distance between him and
me!" We find ourselves in a state of loneliness without a name,

alone in the presence of God. This loneliness is something that we may feel more or less strongly and it may be more or less painful and austere. It is certainly near to us. God is so close in it that we can no longer speak to him or look at him. We no longer dare to call it love—it is as though we were encountering love for the first time—because the word "love" has become too profane or perhaps because we would prefer to find a word, if it exists, that might more fully express our having gone completely beyond ourselves in this experience. Is this, however, not the highest expression of love?

After we have experienced this, we can never again forget the God who is beyond everything, yet who is not enclosed within his own sovereign greatness, but gives himself to everyone and everything and is everywhere immanent. Even the incarnation, which is a mystery that is astonishing in its humility, cannot lessen this great and inexpressible depth, this abyss that throws such a clear light on an equally infinite dispensation of humility. Transcendence and immanence are opposite poles. They cannot be separated in our experience of God, but they do not contradict each other. They are united because they complement each other and the great majesty of the Father who is transcendent is at one with his unlimited condescendence and throws light on it. This heart of the Father is further from us than the heart of Christ and deeper than anything that exists. It includes all things. We are led into the heart of the Father where the heart of Jesus had its origin. We are taken back to the Father's heart by Jesus.

What part does the human spirit, with its need for concepts and images in the search for God, play in this journey and this encounter? It behaves rather like a swimmer trying to beat back the waves with every stroke in order to float on the surface of the boundless ocean of being. The further the soul advances on this ocean, the more clearly it sees God and the more spiritual its ideas about God become. As it moves forward, so does God remove himself further and further from it, going to the limits of its thought and beyond its embrace. He is always, as it were, in flight from the soul, since, if he allowed himself to be grasped, he would not be God. He would cease to be the mystery that he is if man could embrace him.

The soul therefore knows that its search for God can only end in one way. It has to let itself be swallowed up in the fathomless abyss. It has to give up the attempt to understand God. A suffering experience of God rather than any abstract knowledge should have taught the soul that God is incomprehensible and that something of his being can be perceived, but only in inner silence. Alone in the hollow of the rock, Elijah heard the still, small voice of God. It is in this way that the soul may, perhaps for the first time, be able to contemplate the ineffable mystery.

It is only in this divine silence, before all creation, that the soul can become conscious of the begetting of the Word from the silence of God the Father while the Spirit, who makes them one in love, proceeds silently. This is why, as Saint Gregory Nazianzen and, centuries later, Saint John of the Cross have assured us, it is only in silence that God can be honored and that the soul can hear and contemplate the pouring into each other of the three consubstantial persons and their return to unity. The images, forms and concepts that present themselves to our intellect have therefore of necessity to be renounced. The soul's reply to them can only be in the negative: "It is not this and it is not that; it is not like this and it is not like that." This is the negative description of God and the soul's experience of him given by the Hindus who have received the seeds of the Word by which all things in this world are illuminated and who will, we hope, one day help us to discover the full meaning of our inner life as Christians.

God, then, is always becoming greater, yet it becomes less and less possible to grasp him. His presence is fascinating and he draws us to him, yet he is always in flight from us. Since the very beginning of Christianity, contemplative souls have been conscious of this mystery. On his way to martyrdom, Saint Ignatius of Antioch declared, under the beautiful sky of Asia Minor, "Beauty is not to be found in what our eyes can see." In the third century, Novatian affirmed, at the beginning of his treatise on the Trinity, that "God is the one with whom nothing can be compared."[12] A century later, the Cappadocian Fathers, Gregory of Nyssa and Gregory Nazianzen, and after them the Pseudo-Dionysius and Saint Maximus the Confessor appealed to the negative theology, according to which nothing here on earth can give us an adequate idea of God. He is completely different, inaccessible and mysterious. The hymn to God written by the great theologian of Nazianze is an unparalleled testimony to the glory of the one who transcends everything.[13] A little later and under different skies, the ninth-century Indian mystic Śankara also celebrated this mystery.[14] Later still, Saint Bernard spoke in his commentary on the Song of Songs of a "death of angels," which is more than a human death. It is a divine death setting us free not only from every desire of the flesh, but also from our images of bodily things. Contemplation is precisely this kind of death. Saint Bernard illustrates his spiritual teaching by quoting a verse from Psalm 55 and saying: "Blessed is the man who can say: 'How far I would take my flight and make a new home in the desert.' That man is not satisfied with merely going out—he seeks flight in order to find rest in solitude."[15]

Following both Saint Bernard and Saint Augustine, very many spiritual writers have testified to the deep meaning of God's incomprehensible nature. We may mention Saint Thomas Aquinas, especially in his commentary on Boethius, Master Eckhart, John Tauler, John Ruysbroeck and Nicholas of Cusa in this context. We should not hesitate to follow them at God's invitation and, while we are still here on earth, enter what appears to be the nothingness of God, his desert, in comparison with the being that is shared by the billions of creatures that inhabit this world. However conscious we may be of its frightening solitude, we know that this desert is really a fullness of being that goes far beyond us. We, who are poor and nothing and who have become strangers to ourselves, can only be filled to overflowing with this apparent nothingness of God.

If we enter the nothingness of God, it is not so much that God dwells in us as that we, who have become dispossessed, enter him who is everything. From that time onward, we shall be truly lost, but there will be no more limits in us. Our soul will be translucent to the light in which it is bathed and it will go forward into this clear ocean and the further we go, the more its boundaries will disappear. In this state, there is no more dualism, no more tension and no more scattering. There is only a great unity, a sovereign peace, a spontaneous and irreversible obedience and a lack of all desire to see, to know and even to give. "I do not know" says the soul with the bride in the Song of Songs. And if the Father were to question the soul, it could only say: "You, my Lord, you know," as the visionary of Patmos said to the angel of the Apocalypse who questioned him on behalf of God. It is alive and that is all.

The Father whom the soul worships in silence with a barely perceptible movement of the heart will not disturb its rest. He knows that if the soul does not speak, it is because love is inexpressible and because it has become nothing so that he may become everything. He is the Father whose providence is felt in the smallest details of life. Like the father of the prodigal son, he is ready to forgive and to console. He is, in his inaccessible transcendence, as far from me as he was before I looked for him, but he is also more intimate than the most intimate part of my being in his excessive tenderness.

But he is unlimited depth, a depth that is inexhaustible, and it is therefore necessary for me to go down into him with my eyes closed and my ears attuned only to the voice of the Spirit flowing in me like living water and whispering: "Come to the Father."[16]

NOTES

1. Father Louis Chardon in *La Croix de Jésus*, Third Theme, Chap. 5.
2. Gustave Thibon, *L'Echelle de Jacob*, pp. 121–122.
3. Quoted by Henri de Lubac in *Histoire et Esprit*, p. 241.
4. Paul Claudel, *L'Epée et le Miroir*, p. 256.
5. Divo Barsotti, *Vie mystique et Mystère liturgique*, p. 151.
6. See Father Paul Agësse, "La grace du moment présent," *Christus*, 45, especially pp. 73–75.
7. "When Jesus encounters someone who is doing the will of his God, his heart beats more quickly and his will is to his spirit what his blood is to his natural will. When I encounter someone in whom the blood of my own family flows, I feel that he is part of me. What unites us is more rudimentary than what unites me to other men. The will of God is for Jesus a vital spiritual principle. When he encounters someone who is subjected to that will, he feels related to him—more closely related than he is to his natural blood-relations."
8. Pascal, *Pensées*, Fragment 553.
9. Saint Thomas Aquinas, *Commentary on the Sentences*.
10. Ramana Maharishi.
11. Paul Claudel, *La Messelà-bas*, Introit, p. 20.
12. *PL* 3. 889–891.
13. *PG* 37. 507.
14. "The eyes that see me do not discern me; the ears that perceive are deaf to my silence; those who would name me are reduced to silence. I am infinite knowledge; I am the life that is hidden behind all life; I am the absolute one, infinite existence."
15. Saint Bernard, *Sermo 52 In Canticum Canticorum*.
16. Saint Ignatius of Antioch, *Epistola ad Romanos*, 7.

11

The Pure Presence—
Presence in Absence

Whatever our personal attitude may be toward God—whether we are saints or sinners, deeply and fervently convinced of his presence or totally alienated from him—he is always there. Here on earth, we may be without everything, but we are never without the presence of God, which is inseparable from his being and, like him, transcendent and sovereign.

At every moment of time the eternal God creates us, looks at us, loves us and waits for us. His presence is life. The prophet Elisha cried out: "As Yahweh lives, whom I serve" (2 Kings 3. 14; 5. 16, etc.). Surely we should also make this cry of admiration our own, by seeing it in the light that has been shed on us by the incarnation and by everything that has come to us from the Spirit of Pentecost since the resurrection of Jesus. If I consent to serve this living God, like so many saints, then not only will God be in me more than I am in myself, but it will no longer be I who live, but Christ—the Son of the living God—who lives in me (Gal. 2. 20).

Here on earth there are many realities that can communicate life to us, but they are transient. Art and music can, for example, give us an intense impression of life emanating from a divine world, but however deep the traces they leave on our souls may be, they are still fleeting and do not transform us totally. We cannot listen every day to Bach's Mass in B Minor or to Beethoven's Seventh Symphony, nor can we spend all our time uninterruptedly contemplating a Giotto or a Rembrandt. But we are given the presence of our God all the time and all that is required from us is the attention of our hearts illuminated by grace.

It is true, of course, that this presence can be revealed to us in many different ways. It may be like a flash of lightning, quite unexpected, coming to us as the result of an outside circumstance and entering the texture of what God in his providence has to offer us. This momentary grace can at times be so powerful that it leaves its imprint on our personality and for a long time determines the course of our life. The obvious example is, clearly, Saint Paul on the way to Damascus, confronted with the risen Christ, but there is another, more modest example—that of Dom Chautard, who had a similar experience of God's presence while he was still a child, in the splendor of the mountains. Yet perhaps each one of us can recall such a brief but ineradicable impression of this kind which has, in the course of time, become a less striking but solid certainty that God is, though transcendent, very close to us.

Because it is in itself indestructible, however, this presence will always be—so long as we treasure it as the fundamental mystical experience in our inner life—the unmoving backcloth against which everything in our existence takes place. Our being as creatures, our spiritual pilgrimage, all the events, both small and great, in our passage from the cradle to the grave, our view of the created universe, our sum of human knowledge and our relationships with our brothers and sisters—everything passes in front of this backcloth of God's presence.

Another comparison springs to mind—God's presence is like the whispering waters of Siloam heard by the prophet Isaiah in ancient times and still audible to the ear of the silent and attentive heart. This murmur is more meaningful and persuasive and more charged with the dynamism of truth than all the din of the nations, the noise of political, ideological and social dispute and the clash of cosmic catastrophes that plunge us into mourning. It is the gentle trickling of these waters that is heard by the silent and recollected soul living in a peace that is beyond time and space, a peace that existed at the beginning of creation. We can, in this silence, go beyond the created world and be in touch with the silence of the three consubstantial persons of the Trinity who rule the world.

The feeling that this continuous presence gives us cannot be expressed in words, yet we must try to express it. It is strong yet gentle. It is light yet shadow. It is a harmony, a wisdom and a unity of a kind that forms the entire poetry and music of life itself. It is a rest, a security and a peace, yet at the same time it is the mainspring of all the activity that God asks of us. It is also a great consolation in this valley of tears and, in its prudence, an inexpressible joy.

This presence has always played a dominant part in the lives of all the saints, however different the spirituality of each may have been. We have only to think, for example, of what God's presence meant to Saint Bernard, Saint Gertrude, the two Catherines of Siena and Genoa, Saint Dominic and Saint Ignatius, Saint Francis of Assisi, Saint John of the Cross and Saint Teresa. At the same time, however, it has been particularly important in the lives of those who experienced what may be called a spiritual childhood. By these we mean those men and women whose souls are translucent with rediscovered innocence. The soul of such a person is perfectly and completely given over, abandoned and sensitive. It is prudent, it is true, but with an amazing openness to every revelation and every sign of God's immanence. Such men and women are always present to their God who is always present. For them, the invisible world is always there and more real than the visible world. It is their real homeland, since where their heart is, there is their treasure.

Both for the saints and for us, poor mortals, there is, as long as we continue to look for God, an absence that is really a presence, but a hidden presence, a presence that is not felt, of the one who acts in secret in order to prepare us, through the void that is ourselves, for a presence that is more in accordance with the truth and the transcendence of his being.

A great deal could be said about this purifying absence of God, but this is not the place to say it, because it is a reality which is experienced in a unique way by each individual soul. The drama of the soul caught up in this absence is expressed in a most vivid and pathetic way in the book of Job, and such spiritual writers as Saint John of the Cross and Father Chardon[1] have spoken about it at great length.

We have called it a purifying absence and this is true. It is the means of purifying the soul that God uses on the one hand to deepen both our longing for him and our awareness of his infinity and his inaccessibility and, on the other, to raise us up to him by destroying the pious idols that we have created in our imagination and the all too human image that we have formed of his being. God is, after all, the holy mystery and he inevitably goes far beyond all our representations of him. These are always inadequate, even if they may seem to us to be sublime. But how can we continue to go beyond these ideas of God without becoming separated from those ideas and from God himself? We cannot do this without being plunged into a painful darkness where we will have no means of support, just when we may be ready to ascend again to God. He is, after all, the one who always avoids all our attempts to grasp him in order to give himself more fully to us if we really long to rest for a moment in his shadow.

This suffering experience of God's absence may be very extensive. Anyone who has this experience has to recognize that it points to a very unique absence of the kind that was experienced by the one who was forsaken on Good Friday and cried out: "Eli, Eli, lama sabachthani?" Ernest Hello did not hesitate to speak about the terror of this great absence in his book *Paroles de dieu*,[2] and it is clear that our redeemer's suffering in this respect was far greater than even the most painful of human experiences. When we stand in the light of his cross, we are also intimately united with him in his supreme sacrificial act.

But what a difference there is between our abandonment and his! However great our distress may be, we can never be so completely abandoned as Jesus was, since he had no one, that is, no human person, on whom he could, as we can, depend. What is more, however much man is able to suffer, he is always weak and easily distracted from the main course of his life. His power to receive is limited and, even if he lives very close to God and is conscious of painful separation from him in his absence, he is aware of this only within narrow limits. He is supported by his own human poverty and is therefore able to continue to live. But the one who is united to the Father in the mystery of the hypostatic union, and who lacks the human personality to avoid the full force of his abandonment and therefore suffered it in the pitiless brutality of the light of eternity, must have been plunged into an emptiness of frightening intensity. And this happened with the full consent of his redeeming will.

The infinite nature of his abandonment by the Father, however, corresponded to the infinite nature of another abandonment —a total handing over that was at the same time an acceptance and an unlimited consent: "Into your hands, Lord, I commit my spirit!" The author of Lamentations said: "It is good to wait in silence for Yahweh to save" (3. 26) and indeed silence always reigns, whether it is a question of an absence that is acutely experienced or whether it is a presence that cannot be perceived in the absence of silence.

Who knows whether this silence, which is the fruit of that queen of Christian virtues, patience, is not, despite its icy appearance, the result of the coming together of two fires—the fire of God and the fire of the soul that reflects God as his image? Is it not the intermingling of two fires that are consumed without destroying themselves or being destroyed? Is it perhaps not the silence of an unparalleled love within a redeeming suffering? Whatever it may be, it is certain that knowing how to suffer, be silent, wait and remain firm without seeking diversion is one of the most noble attitudes that the Christian can have and the best way of proving his faithfulness and love. It is also an attitude that releases grace and enables it to be poured out into the soul—a soul that has, in the practice of this virtue, become more completely stripped of itself, more translucent and more open to receive the beloved, who is only truth, love, spirit and flame.

We have described an absence of God that is above all sacred. But there is also an absence that is really demonic. This is the absence experienced by those who deliberately, knowingly and systematically reject God with passionate determination. These are the souls who are moved by the ambition of Lucifer and want to put man, as a superman, in the place of God. This is, of course, the great mystery of sin which is in contrast to the mystery of creative and redemptive love. Those who have been imprisoned behind the iron curtain or the bamboo curtain and have retained their faith know the evil that ideology is and how it is based on a hatred of God and the Church of his Son. They have learned that there is, beneath the surface of material progress, order, discipline and apparent prosperity, an organization that aims to conquer and at the same time to set men free, a kind of hell that the German poet Schiller describes in the verse: "Down there it is terrible."

Alongside a form of Marxism steeped in scientific theory that is fundamentally hard and incapable of reduction even if it at times seems to be less severe, there is also a deep lack of faith in God, who is absent from the hearts of these Marxists, who are able to exist as free men only by destroying God and putting themselves in his place. They would seem to fulfill the prophecy made by Goethe: "Since God became man, we must be careful not to let him become God again." It is a terrible truth that the mystery of supreme ingratitude corresponds to the mystery of love.

Nonetheless, this great rejection also contains a great promise. The God who has been so proudly and so violently banished can, after all, not be an abstraction. He must be *the* being—a being so fearful that man feels impelled to rise against him in his mad freedom:

> You—without a name, hidden, terrible!
> You—huntsman, veiled in clouds!
> I am struck down by you
> Scornful eye looking at me from the depth of a shadow,
> See me here, bent, prostrate, panting,
> Tortured by eternal torments,
> Smitten by you, most cruel huntsman,
> You—the unknown God!
> Go away!
> And he went off
> My only and my last companion,
> My great enemy,
> My unknown one,
> My executioner,
> God!

The combat is tragic—it is not against a phantom, but against a terrible rival. The living God sends thunderbolts and lightning down on the man who has pronounced him dead and has declared: "From now on there is no truth. I am free and give my full consent to life." God strikes this prophet of the superman down and transforms him into a little, almost unknowing child who stammers: "Mother, how stupid I am."

Sartre's revolt was also an expression of madness. He rejected the experience of sublime effacement in the presence of God and preferred to exalt man's freedom. With Orestes, the criminal who refused the forgiveness offered to him by Jupiter, he cried out: "I am my freedom. You had barely created me before I ceased to belong to you" (*The Flies*). This is the beginning of the terrible dialogue between man, tracing out his own course, and God, made impotent in his presence—the dialogue between God who does good and man who invents evil, God who is silent, absent and dead and man who alone constructs the rule of men on this death of God and for love of them becomes their executioner (*Le Diable et le Bon Dieu*).

God, then, continues to obsess those who have most vehemently rejected him. His presence in our innermost depths is indestructible. He is the rock against which every proud attempt to oppose or replace him is broken. He is our creator and without him we would not be. He alone possesses the secret of a freedom that can be open to infinity only in him and which will eventually make us one with him.

Between these two extremes of an absence of God that is fruitful and coincides with his nearness and a destructive and deliberately atheistic absence there is a vast zone of absence that is uncertain and ambiguous. It is in this vague zone that the world as we know it finds itself, constantly moving between good and evil and thinking more or less of God without being openly opposed to him. It is an icy pond enclosing both believers and nonbelievers. This world is welded to matter and enjoyment and yet it is, more or less without knowing it, longing for God. It is a world inhabited by desperate souls for whom everything is chaotic and absurd. It is also a world that is besotted with its conquest of space, its prestigious technical progress and its attempts to make this earth a new paradise.

In this vast intermediate zone, then, we have, on the one hand, an overwhelming pessimism, a consciousness of disorder and an obsession with the idea of suicide—we have discovered the scientific means for our planet to destroy itself—and the hope of entirely human success and happiness on the other. In this situation, we are confronted with a serious question: Is this absence of God really a form of atheism? It would at first sight seem to be so. But the problem is very complex and it is worth going a little deeper into it to find the real solution.

It is clear to us, whether we believe or whether we do not believe, that the world is not God. It is not possible to confuse God and nature as many of the romantics did in the nineteenth century. Nowadays we call for truth both in the sphere of positive science and in that of the supernatural reality. We are longing for something that is less alluring and florid and more austere and supraterrestrial than anything that can be provided by the earlier poetry of feeling and the senses. We are, as it were, in a desert and are waiting anxiously. The world is there with its pleasures and its attractions, but we are unable to forget the eternal Word that has, in the history of Christianity, impelled so many souls to follow the path of holiness: "What, then, will a man gain if he wins the whole world and ruins his life?"[3] The evangelist here speaks of "losing one's soul" and we feel that it is everything not to have received our soul in vain.

What does this soul, which God made for himself and which cannot rest, as Saint Augustine said, until it rests in him, enable us to see? We can see this: As we grow, so too does our creator grow greater. He seems to come closer to what he really is, becoming greater by raising himself up in our thoughts to a much higher and less accessible level. Confronted with this God who seems to us to be so far away that he is a problem, we should ask ourselves this question: Should God be less great because he put everything into the world when he created it—everything that it needed for its own evolution and movement in time toward its glorious destiny? Should God be less great because he gave man an intelligence that enabled him to explore the universe and use it for his own benefit and to extend his knowledge of the hidden forces of that universe? Should God be less great because he has introduced into this rich and beautiful cosmos the seeds that will, at the end of time, transform it into a new heaven and a new earth?[4] Would God be more holy and more powerful or more overflowing with goodness if he were to intervene every time beings changed? In his infinite wisdom, he has, after all, resolved to carry out his eternal plan of love by means of a harmonious process in which causes are connected in sequence with other causes and everything is ultimately directed toward Christ. This great Christ is made of all of us and, in and through us, of the whole universe and, at the end of time, he will glorify his Father in the unity of the Spirit.

No, the Christian, who knows that the Bible was not written to explain the phenomena of the physical world and that it is not possible to refute any scientific system with arguments drawn from Scripture, will not be influenced by the determinism of the created universe. If we could go back along the chain, whether it consists of a few links or is uninterrupted, we would find that the secondary causes do not automatically lead back to the first cause, which is God. God is not simply the point of departure and arrival inside the world—he is abolutely transcendent and therefore outside and above the world.

We must therefore distinguish the so-called atheism of the world from the determined, organized and demonic atheism of a handful of leaders who unfortunately bring great numbers in their wake. We ought rather to ask ourselves seriously whether the absence of God from the society of man today is not really a situation that challenges us believers to purify our faith and especially to consider more profoundly the notion of God's inexpressible exaltation above everything that he has created or even thought of. This idea of God's transcendence has, after all, always been present in the faith of Christians and it was solemnly proclaimed by the First Vatican Council. This vague atheism of the modern world may also be providential in the sense that it invites us to think in a more exalted and less inadequate way about God. We should accept the rough blow that it gives us without indignation, bitterness or offense and regard it as a stimulus to respond to the challenge by changing the world into a place that is full of light and peace.[5]

This absence of God should therefore be a call to man, who grows greater as his knowledge increases and he becomes more open to the world of visible realities, to transcend all his conquests and achievements and raise himself up to God. After all, this God is greater than he is and yet is capable, in the sovereign freedom of his love, of lowering himself and penetrating man with his most intimate presence. It should also invite him not to stop short at an easy illusion of infinity, but to go forward to what is higher, eternal and really infinite, to God who alone can give life. If man were to reach the farthest star in the Milky Way and so overcome pain and the decline of physical and mental powers with old age that he was able to live for centuries, he would have achieved very little. Nothing at all, in fact, when we think that his soul was not made for the immensity of the starry heavens, but for infinity and not created for extensions of time that might succeed only in producing in man a state of ultimate boredom, but for eternity.

Will spiritual man eventually come to understand that these many wonderful technical inventions have not been given to him to increase his material well-being and provide him with more enjoyment of a sensual kind? No, he has been permitted to make these discoveries so that he will have more leisure to think of God and the invisible realities, to worship God, give him thanks and contemplate the one who is the true end of his life. Now more than in any other century he ought to recognize that this life is a prelude to the beatific vision of God. Can we look forward to the eventual coming of such a man into the world, where the Church has, since the Second Vatican Council, raised itself so high that it can shed its light and the warmth of its love over the whole earth? Man's old sin is still there and behind it lies Satan. On the other hand, there has always been and will always be a selected number of spiritually gifted and holy men and women. Will they in the future form the leaven in the lump?

Whatever the future may hold, it is clear now that nothing will ever make our hunger and thirst for God disappear until the last day, when the presence of the one who is "all in all" with triumph in inexpressible glory. Whatever the obstacles may be, God always makes his presence known to men. The word of God will never cease to rouse men in a wonderful way, but it will also never again be possible to contrast it with constantly developing scientific knowledge or with materialistic ideas. As one great theologian noted,[6] the idea of God cannot be eradicated from men's minds because it is ultimately the presence of God in man who is created in his image.

No, man's idea of God is not, as has been suggested, the result of an intellectual, rational or imaginative effort on the part of man, nor is it the end-point of a religious evolution or revolution that has come about by a synthesis or an antithesis of all that man has ever worshiped in the question of gods, using the methods of integration or contrast. The idea of God is quite different and it comes from itself within man's consciousness. It begins to grow as soon as man's intellect comes to maturity. It exists before it is conceptualized and, as it were, goes forward to meet God, who in turn sees man, the living image of his own being and life and, through the veil of created things, beckons to him.

God is there even before he spoke to us through his prophets, those whom he sent and his beloved Son and even before we begin to look for him along straight or twisting paths. Like the bridegroom in the Song of Songs looking through the lattice of the window (2. 9), God watches and waits for us, ready to be discovered by us. Because his eyes are already on us, we want to go out to meet him and it is, as Father Poucel observed, true that we must be looked at if we are to be illuminated.

NOTES

1. Saint John of the Cross, *The Ascent of Mount Carmel* and the *Dark Night of the Soul;* see also Father Chardon, *La Croix de Jesus.*
2. Pp. 284ff.
3. This warning given by the Lord appears in all three synoptic gospels: Matthew 16. 26; Mark 8. 36; Luke 9. 25.
4. See Hans Urs von Balthasar, *Dieu et l'homme d'aujord'hui*, Part II, Chapter 1: "The material world contains indeterminate factors and these provide even stronger evidence of the freedom of the spirit, as though there were not two quite different phenomena there. Is it possible or impossible to derive life from matter? We ought to accept this as impossible only if the principles of life are not already contained in matter. Again, is it possible or impossible for the spirit to evolve from life at a lower level? It would certainly be impossible if the idea that governs the evolution of the spirit had not already been the idea of man himself. (In both cases, the evolutionary view is only one aspect of the total truth.) Nature's great leaps forward from

one stage to another may be fact, but it has not yet been proved that they require a supernatural cause to explain them."

5. *Ibid.*, p. 196. We are indebted to the German theologian Karl Rahner for this idea; see his "Wissenschaft oder Konfession?" *Wort und Wahrheit,* November 1954.

6. Henri de Lubac, "Réflexions sur l'idée de Dieu," *Cité Nouvelle,* 25 February 1942.

12

Other Forms of God's Presence

There are, as we have seen throughout this book, several ways in which the one God can be present in our lives. There are also modes of presence that are different from the presence of God. These are created modes that derive the whole of their value and importance from the presence of God and which similarly confer grace. God's goodness is transmitted to us through these other modes, which include the presence of the immaculate mother of God and the presence of the saints, the souls of the departed and our fellow human beings who also form part of the body of Christ or are destined to become so. These forms of God's presence constitute a universe of love and beauty that spreads out around us and penetrates to our innermost being with its mysterious influences.

THE PRESENCE OF THE IMMACULATE VIRGIN

We will not discuss the person or the special attributes of our Lady here, as there have been many books written about these and similar subjects relating to the mother of our Savior as well as about the ecclesiology that is inseparable from the question of Mariology.[1] All that we need to do in this context is to emphasize that the Virgin is above all the unique and eternal woman who fills the whole of time and space with her presence.

194

She is the first and absolutely translucent mirror of the Trinity and the first Virgin.[2] She is also in a very real sense the bride of the Trinity and was, from the very beginning, predestined and elected by God to be the mother of the incarnate Word. She was therefore included within the dispensation of the hypostatic union. She is also the bride of the Father, who has extended his eternal generation in her and to whom she is therefore able to say, with reference to Jesus: our child.[3] She is also the bride of the Son, the second Adam and eternal wisdom. She has been tied to him since long before the first dawn and before the first being came into existence. She is associated with him in a unique way in the act of redemption. She is the second Eve and even more than the second Eve—she is also the mother of the living. She is also the bride of the Holy Spirit and at the same time the sanctuary of the Holy Spirit who, when he overshadowed her at the time of the annunciation, fertilized her in a miraculous way.

She is above all the loving mother[4] and because of this motherhood she is present in a unique and solicitous way to mankind as a whole and to each of us in particular. She is also a mother at such great depths that it is difficult to define them. We have already seen that, even before the intimate part that she played in the mystery of our redemption which culminated in Calvary, she gave birth to us when she consented to conceive the Word of God in her womb so that he would receive her flesh. When she conceived the Head, she also conceived the spiritual body of all those who were to belong to Jesus.

It is worthwhile considering the words of the holy Pope Pius X in this context:

All of us who are united to Christ are, as the apostle Paul says, members of his body and we have come from his flesh and bones (Eph. 5. 30). We must therefore regard ourselves as originating from the womb of the Virgin, from which we emerged one day in the manner of a body attached to the head. That is why we have been called, in a spiritual and mystical sense, children of Mary and why she is, for her part, also the mother of all of us. Saint Augustine called her "mother according to the Spirit, but nonetheless a real mother of the members of Jesus Christ, which we are" (*De Virginitate*, 6).[5]

How is it possible for such a mother ever to be absent from her children? She is certainly present and her principal function is to intercede powerfully for us. She has traditionally been called the one who is *omipotentia supplex* and this undoubtedly points to the effectiveness of her prayer. Until the end of time she will be the one who is omnipotent in supplication, since men have great need of this. It would seem however, that her most important task is to prepare both the whole of mankind and each individual, by her presence, for the presence of Jesus wherever he is not present, that is, in human faith in his person and in his Church. It is in such circumstances that the Virgin of the annunciation and the visitation plays the part of precursor in a very discreet and hidden manner, preparing the way for the one who is himself the way.

Generation followed generation in Israel, preparing for the body and blood of Jesus, and the royal stem of Jesse, of which Jesus was to be the flower, grew among the thorns of sinful men. Like Jesus, Mary was alive even before she lived, living like a perfume that could already be smelled before its source had been revealed. She was already visible behind such fine and virtuous women as Rebekah, Rachel, Judith and Esther and through everything in the world of nature and art that is most gracious, most noble and most majestic.

When she came into the world, she came as the fulfillment of the true Israel, the Israel that was according to the heart of God himself. She was not simply a woman chosen from among all the rest of womankind so that the wedding between heaven and earth might take place in her womb. This was not her only destiny, although she had in fact been created only for that purpose. She was already full of grace and, as the faithful Virgin who passed from grace to grace, she understood that the Messiah would not be born exclusively for the Jewish people. Even more fully than the prophets of Israel, she recognized that he was to be born for the whole world. As such, then, she was the most perfect of all the spiritually developed Jews, the *anawim* or poor of Yahweh, who would cling in faith to her child and who would be the first-fruits of the Church of which she was to be the perfect and ideal type.

While Israel was still on the way toward the fullness of time, when the Virgin was to give birth to a Savior, a mysterious instinct made itself felt among the pagans. There too, the eternal woman was present in a premonition that a unique being would be born of a virgin. This is undoubtedly the meaning of Virgil's Fourth Eclogue and the statue dedicated to the "virgin who is to give birth." In China, there has always been a cult of the mother with very deep roots. Virgins who are both terrible and gentle, pitiless and yet compassionate and who present to man aspects of the *advaita* have always been worshiped in India.[6]. Is this not a popular conception in those countries of the Virgin herself, both "terrible as an army with banners" (Song of Songs 6. 10) and the enemy of the serpent (Gen. 3. 15) on the one hand and, to echo Léon Bloy, the "abyss of light and gentleness" from which an endless plea for mercy comes?

Christian missionaries are well aware today that Mary has always been present in the countries to which they are sent and which occupy a very similar position with regard to the Church of Christ as that occupied by the pagan nations with regard to Israel. She is there preparing the way for the rule of her Son, whose glory is her glory, and for the establishment of his Church, which is not yet present in its structures, hierarchy, sacraments and commandments, but which is already there as a desire and a power.

We should also recognize that what the Virgin is for the whole world she is also for each one of us, for, whether our soul is far or only moderately advanced along the way, it is always waiting for Jesus' coming. There can be no doubt—he is there. But he wants to possess us at depths that are always receding. He therefore comes to us with a grace that is always new. In perfect agreement with the Spirit of holiness and love who fills her and with whom she has a very special relationship, Mary gives birth to Jesus in us. Again and again, when she gives birth to him in this way, she enables him to grow to the maturity that the Father wants.

As we have already said, she enables us to share in her motherhood, so that, giving birth to him ourselves, we may also be not only the sister, the betrothed and the bride of our Savior, but also his mother. Where might she not lead us if we were to give ourselves up entirely to her influence, accept her as our unfailing model and listen attentively to her all the time? She, after all, knows so much better than we do what pleases her Son.

It is well known from the lives of the saints how much joy, light and grace her intervention has been able to bring into their souls. Five women in the history of the Church leap at once to mind—the three saints of the convent of Helfta,[7] Saint Catherine of Siena and, perhaps the most striking of all, Sister Mary of Saint Teresa.[8] The Virgin of Cana is always patiently listening and is always able to adapt herself to each one's needs. She entered the texture of God's providence discreetly and gently and continues to play her part in it unobtrusively and without ever violently forcing us, unless perhaps we sin as insanely as the Breton, Peter of Keriolet, when she has to reach down into the depths of hell to pull us out.

We should also never forget that, despite her cosmic dimensions, her immense heart and her eternal womanhood situated at the limits of God's divinity, which is reflected in all its glory in her, she is still a creature as we are. She possesses a supreme greatness because of her holiness and her mission and because she was predestined to be the mother of the Savior, but she is also so simple, so human and so completely within our reach! There is, it is true, only one mediator between God and men and that is Christ Jesus, who alone is holy. Nonetheless, he wanted this feminine presence to help us to bear the overwhelming weight of his graces and his demands, both of which formed too heavy a burden for us to carry. How fortunate for us it is that she is there, the woman who is blessed among all women and who enabled the Son of the most high God to be Emmanuel, "God-with-us," the meek one who was humble in his heart and the man whose friends could and can approach so easily, despite his dazzling majesty!

However dismayed we may be by the baseness of human behavior and however much we may be inclined to bitterness and disappointment, the Virgin, who understands and forgives our weakness as well as that of our neighbor and who is perfectly just and good, will prevent us from feelings of resentment. She is the mother who knows how to encourage us to keep an equilibrium between what is too great and what is too mediocre or low. Because she is so pure, she can include everything and everyone within her glance and her influence and obtain for us all those pristine graces that will allow us to concentrate on holiness without flinching and to be conscious of the depths of human misery.

Like God, she is all love and gift. There are also graces that are full of the scent of her presence and which are so discreet that the soul lacks the courage to grasp them for fear of checking its progress. These are the graces of the hidden life of the soul, of silence and self-forgetfulness and of recollection, tenderness and intimacy. Very few of us dare to or trouble ourselves to ask her for these very valuable attitudes, but she anticipates our unspoken desire and in this way behaves exactly like a mother. We know then that these graces that have come from the heart of God himself are the graces that she herself possesses.

In her sovereign simplicity, the Virgin revealed to us in the gospel teaches us also that action and contemplation complement each other and are in harmony with each other, and that there can be no action without contemplation for the soul that is open to God and therefore already made eternal. She also enables us to see that pure contemplation is the supreme form of action. We can also learn from her the true abandonment that she herself practiced with such total generosity. In abandoning herself completely to God, she did not try to know what lay beyond the immediate step that she had to make. She was content with the light that she received for that moment and with the grace that that light brought. We shall never know the sum total of her experience in this self-abandonment or how much, having become betrothed to Joseph and remaining quite silent after the revelation of the angel Gabriel and her miraculous conception, she, the Virgin who was eternally predestined, finally gave up to God when she entrusted to him alone the task of guiding everything toward the accomplishment of his plan of love!

She has been called the "faithful" Virgin by the Church. This title points not only to the depth of her faith, but also to the indelible character of what she did and of its effects. She prepared the world in a mysterious way for the coming of the Son of God into her womb and in the same mysterious way she also leads us, during our pilgrimage on this earth, which is an advent that is full of hope, filling us with longing for our heavenly home, to the parousia that each of us will experience at the hour of our death. She is in this way, then, the gate of heaven, and her permanent presence will be more effective than ever when eventually she hears that "now and at the hour of our death" that ends the prayer that she loves most of all.

She is also present at the heart of the Church militant, going resolutely toward the goal for which it is destined here on earth. She fills the period of Advent in this world that stretches from Pentecost to the time when her Son will return in glory with her gentle yet powerful presence, just as she filled, with the same presence, the time between the ascension of her Son and the pouring out of the Holy Spirit in the upper room.[9] She is, then, the Virgin who waits and who prepares and her task is to help to build the heavenly Jerusalem that she has always represented and of which she will, in the end, be the highest point.

Throughout the history of Christianity, her presence has been felt through the unending manifestation of her truth. Conciliar definitions and dogmas have proclaimed her greatness and her privileges. Scripture and the lives of the saints have gradually disclosed their treasures and have revealed her as the mother of love itself. The bride of eternal wisdom has emerged as one who has always been closely associated with God and who has never ceased to spread out over the whole earth, which she herself once trod, the protection and the light of her virgin motherhood. In the presence of God, she has become, not an object of adoration, but the one who above all obtains when we ask and whom we can contemplate without ever exhausting her possibilities.

According to Saint Louis Grignon de Montfort, the end of time will be filled with her presence. It would seem that we are already taking part in the fulfillment of that prophecy. As the Church becomes more and more fully conscious of itself, it seems to penetrate more and more profoundly into the depths of the mystery of the immaculate Virgin. There have also been more and more apparitions of the Virgin in the world—Lourdes, La Salette, Pontmain, the miraculous medal and Fatima. The Virgin is clearly present in this troubled world of pride and excessive pleasure. She is there to warn us that heaven is very close to earth and indeed leaning over it, that the true values are not worldly ones and that God wants us to be humble, chaste, penitent, prayerful and always ready to give ourselves to him and to our fellow-men.

There can be no doubt that our Lady was effectively present at a Council that was inspired by the Spirit to seek ways toward the unity of all Christians and to include in its care the whole of mankind redeemed by Christ. This Council also showed how great the heart of the bride of Christ is. The eternal, universal and cosmic woman wanted the leader of that great assembly, her "Christ on earth,"[10] to proclaim her officially as the "mother of the Church" and to call on her with this title as the one who has opened up and who continues to survey wonderful perspectives of light, joy and peace in union with the Spirit. For us, then, Mary will always be not only a being who is wonderfully familiar to us, but also the woman adorned with light and crowned with stars who was seen by the visionary of Patmos in a great vision in which her figure merges into that of the Church (Apoc. 12). Both Mary and the Church are mothers. Both continue to be present in the world, but are at the same time in God's desert, while the struggle takes place between Michael and his angels on the one side and the dragon on the other and we, who are already victorious, fight together with the Church militant in this vale of tears.

THE PRESENCE OF THE ANGELS

The mother of God and men is also the queen of innumerable pure spirits who form the crown of the bride, the Church.[11] These spirits, the angels, are simply intelligence and will, light and beauty and they are present with us in a very mysterious, but nonetheless real way. It may therefore be valuable—now, perhaps, more than at any other period in history—to consider their nature, activity and brotherhood here. We shall not do this because we are tempted, in our discovery of this world, to become preoccupied with that material world. We shall do it rather because the immense realities of the visible universe, which rightly astonish us, tend to obscure the realities of the invisible and spiritual universe, which are even more astonishing.

It is true that the limits of the visible order of creation recede into the invisible distance. Beyond the Milky Way, which we can see on fine summer nights and which calls to mind endless spaces, there are other galaxies that we shall probably never see. The universe of the stars seems to us to be constantly expanding. On the other hand, man first appeared on our old planet countless millions of years ago and, when we think of time as such, this does not seem to be exaggerated.

What, however, are these cosmic immensities compared with those of the world of angels who surround the throne of the most high God and exert an invisible, but gentle influence on our visible world? There must be countless myriads of these angelic beings looking at us in the light of the eternal Word. Their knowledge of us is spontaneous and intuitive and it does not depend on the things of creation. They are raised far above us and are spread out all around us, like a great and splendid tent. Their vitality, beauty and order go far beyond the limits of our imagination.

When we think of angels, we think first of all of a mystery of praise. We have become used to this understanding of the angels, which is, after all, extraordinary, from our reading of the Apocalypse, which is in turn derived from the great visions of Isaiah, Ezechiel and Daniel. God is, in other words, magnified and glorified by an incalculable number of pure spirits. It is not simply the task of these spirits to proclaim God's glory—they praise the God whom they contemplate face to face and adore in their very essence. The whole of their being is simply an echo, an impulse from God and a spiritual beating of wings that cry out their love of and gratitude to God. Their being is nothing but an echo of the praise that the Holy Trinity gives to itself, with the difference that their praise is one of creatures.

Their praise, however, is not simply confined to heaven. It comes down from the Church triumphant to the Church militant. At Mass we sing *Sanctus* three times after the preface to call for their presence. This is more than an echo of the choirs of angels. It is really the song of earth united to heaven, the song that makes the whole of creation, both visible and invisible, one. The mysteries of the incarnation and the redemption are made present in this *mysterium fidei* without any discontinuity between them, and heaven and earth are also united in the same sacrifice and the same act of adoration. They worship the same Lord, who is not the redeemer of the angels, but their God and their king.

How would it be possible for the angels not to be present as our brothers in this extraordinary heavenly liturgy that is completely at one with our own humble liturgy on earth? We are, after all, united with the angels to the same Head and, as Bossuet said, "it is not so much that we are incorporated into them as that they come to our unity, because of Jesus, our common head, who is more our head than theirs."[12] How too is it possible for them not to look at us with love, since we are destined to occupy in their desolate regions the places that have been left by the desertion of Satan and his accomplices? How, finally, is it possible for them not to respect and even envy in a sense those whose flesh Jesus wanted to assume and who, in their suffering and death, are partly able to share his great passion? Surely they must have these feelings about us, despite our moral and physical weakness!

This aspect of praise and liturgy is, however, not the only one that attracts our attention in our quest for the presence of angels. We should not forget that it was part of God's plan, when he created them, that they should be not only his ministers and messengers in the work of our salvation (see Heb. 1), but also those who governed the visible world. Their function in the cosmos is stressed in a very ancient Jewish tradition, and we know that Saint Paul reacted strongly against the excesses of a teaching that would, had it been allowed to persist, have led men away from true Christianity by relativizing the absolute primacy of Christ (Col. 2. 16–19).

The possible danger of a distortion of Christian doctrine should not, however, make us blind to the wonderful truth concerning these pure spirits. They are pure intelligence and knowledge, reflecting the light of the Word of God and going far beyond any of the laws of nature that scholars may be able to disclose to us. They are also at the source of everything that lives and moves in this world in order to enshrine the destiny of men and women and serve their good. Origen said of them that "they watch over all things on earth, in the air and in the fire, in other words, over all the elements. They are therefore the instruments used by the Logos in the management of all the animals and plants and of all the heavenly bodies."[13]

Cardinal Newman, who was exceptionally sensitive to everything concerned with the invisible world, asked himself what was the principle underlying the movements of the natural world. Why, he wondered, did the rivers flow, the winds blow and the rains fall? Why did the sun shine and warm us? According to Scripture, he concluded, the angels were apparently at the source of these mysterious harmonies, so that it was clear that nature had a soul and that its daily task reflected intelligence. Wherever we might look, everything reminded us of those beings who were full of grace and holiness. They were, he thought, the servants of the most high God who were also humble enough to place themselves at the service of those who inherited God's promise. He concluded that we were therefore able to touch the fringes of the robes of those who contemplate God face to face and to see their robes move with every breath of air, with every ray of light and heat and at every glimpse of the beauty of nature.[14]

These mysterious beings, then, are always present. They are raised high above us, yet they are also very close to us. They urge us to respect the world of nature that surrounds us—a world that they hold in their hands. At the same time, however, they never cease to praise God and they act as his instruments to pass on his providence to us.

The part that they played in the history of the Jewish people is well known to us from Scripture. They were initiators and teachers and then, under the new law, they surrounded Jesus from his birth to his ascension into heaven. Their mission is, however, as universal as that of God's providence and it is not difficult to imagine that they also had a mission to protect and enlighten in the pagan world with its demons encouraging men to worship false gods. Were they not present too in the lives of the great philosophers of ancient Greece, guiding their speculations, and in the work of the Greek poets and dramatists, inspiring their verses and their tragedies? Have they not also sown the seeds in other parts of the world and at other times that have germinated into wonderful fragments of metaphysical or moral teaching? We have only to think in this context of the work of Confucius, the Buddha, Zoroaster, Mahatma Gandhi and Rabindranath Tagore.

Christians also believe that a special angel is placed in charge of us from the moment that we enter this world. This is a very com-

forting dispensation on God's part and we should try to understand
it in a mature and adult way. It means that the invisible world is
able to emanate beauty and poetry without at the same time becoming unreal or fantastic, like a fairy story. The angels are vigorous and
masculine, yet at the same time very tender, upright, simple and
ready to serve us, although they do not have our senses. The poet
Rilke described them as representing the first stage of what is most
terrible, and we know that they did not hesitate to punish a saint
like Françoise Romaine physically or to beat the impious Heliodorus
on the one hand and, on the other, that they are ready to obtain
help for us, that they always respect our humble earthly state and
that they are full of zeal for the coming of the kingdom of God in
and around us.

As Cardinal Newman showed in his *Dream of Gerontius*, they
are waiting for us to die so that they can take us up to heaven or,
if they have to, to purgatory. But while we, for our part, also wait
for this final consummation of our relationship with them, we can
be sure that little could be more intimate, hidden and delightful
than this life with the heavenly companion, our guardian angel. It
is not possible for us to be separated from each other. We are always
together—the one for the other. What human relationship, even
that between a mother and her children or a husband and his wife,
can ever be like our relationship with our guardian angel? He is our
only one and we are similarly unique to him. He will never be replaced by another.

We may therefore regard the world of the angels as a sphere of
great attraction that exerts a divine influence on our mystical life.
That life ought to resemble that of these pure angelic intelligences
more and more as we ascend higher and higher to God. God, after
all, wanted to descend lower than the angels when he took human
flesh, and he passed through them when he ascended once more to
heaven after his death and resurrection. Like the Church, our soul
is a ladder. It is both Jacob's ladder, on which the angels came down
from and went up to heaven, and at the same time the subject of
a strange fight with the mysterious angel who allowed himself to be
beaten by the patriarch only in order to bless him and raise him
above this worldly reality. It is very clear that God wants us to be
men, not angels, and it is equally clear that, here on earth, we are
members of the Church militant clinging to God in faith, hope and
charity.

All the same, we are fully human only if we go beyond our-

selves every day of our lives. We have clearly to avoid going beyond
ourselves in this way by descending toward the angel of darkness
and nothingness. But go we must, and it must be by ascending to
the sphere of being and life, where we shall eventually come to the
realm of the angels of light and be included in the ranks of their hierarchy.

We may not be fully aware of it, but there are movements of
the spirit and the heart that are like signs of this kind of ascent into
the spiritual world. Our human senses may well be wounded by this
ascent, since they are not always able to follow us. This experience
can take several forms. In our longing to reach an absolutely pure
truth, untainted by anything human, we may feel a heartrending
pain. In tearing ourselves away from the good of this world that is
so infinitely small, we may be deeply bruised, but have to pursue absolute good. The call to leave behind all our prejudices, even those
which seem to be Christian, and to abandon the safety of cherished
views and to expose ourselves to the sharp light of God and to see
ourselves and others in it—this may cause us pain. We may similarly
be drawn to experience a deeper feeling of adoration and rapture in
the presence of the infinite holiness of the God who is justice and
love and this is costly. All these movements—including a liberation
of our consciousness and a sharper sense of the sacred character of
life and above all of what God loves in it, but the world despises,
namely poverty—are difficult, but they are influenced by the angels.
These pure, heavenly spirits do not, it is true, penetrate to the
depths of our soul in these movements, but they perceive on our
face the slightest signs of grace and help us to collaborate with it.

We are, then, too much at one with the angels, who are our
companions as well as Christ's, for us to be able to undertake our
spiritual ascent without them. We can only agree wholeheartedly
with the view expressed by Erik Peterson in his little book on the
angels. He insisted that it was important to remember that

the angel is not just something with regard to which our human
nature was constituted in the past—it is, on the contrary, something with regard to which that nature always continues to be
constituted here and now and in the future, which is why what
the angel teaches us about himself also teaches us something
about ourselves and why it is therefore very instructive to know
about the nature of the angels.[15]

Both the most obscure depths of our own souls and our highest aspirations become sharply and strikingly outlined in this light, which at the same time also provides us with a powerful stimulus to continue to go beyond and rise above ourselves, so that we may become the being that we are not yet—the being that will one day be revealed to us (1 John 3. 2). We have to go beyond ourselves in a metaphysical rather than a moral sense because it will enable us to join those spirits who are nearest to those who surround the throne of God and whose being echoes his glory.

This idea of echoing God's glory brings us back to the presence of the angels as above all a praising presence. This presence of God is really the consummation of everything. It is the revelation and the fulfillment of the praise that springs from our most intimate depths as creatures of God. When we come into contact with those most sublime creatures, the angels, whose vitality is both fearful and gentle and whose strength is combined with inexpressible sensitivity, we are attuned to the most noble and the most humble elements in creation and to the most elementary and the most profound.

We know, of course, that everything in creation, from the most fiery seraph to the smallest blade of grass, is praise of God. Man himself finds, the higher he ascends, that when he reaches the limit of his being, he is only a song of praise. When he ultimately discovers the essence of his being, in other words, that he is God's creature, he then discovers that everything is a brotherhood. Every created being and thing is his brother—the highest of the angels, whom he cannot see, as well as the water, air, fire and earth, the elements from which he lives.

He therefore adds his little voice to the great chorus and orchestra of the universe and his own humble planet and joins gladly in the great symphony in praise of God the creator. Everything is present for him and he is present for every being, as the stigmatized Saint Francis, who had reached a state of complete conformity in his soul and his body with the crucified Lord, was also present for creation. He already knows—and therefore possesses the first-fruits of heaven—the universal communion which, in the heart of Christ, will make his heart grow to the scale of God who is "all in all."

THE PRESENCE OF THE SAINTS IN GLORY

Every man is a unique being whose depths can never be fathomed and breathes, as it were, above time. His true personality is to be found in his relationship with God. If he is a true Christian—and therefore a true man—he will not be the plaything of time and history. On the contrary, because he has his roots beyond time and history, he will rise above them. That is why, exiled here on earth and not yet what he will be in his true country, he is already living, in the deepest part of himself, in heaven, of which he is already a citizen.

He feels already united, in the great charity of God, to all the blessed, however many centuries ago they lived on earth and whatever may be the differences between him and them in social state or place of work and home. We are all, whether we are conscious of it or not, really the contemporaries and the brothers of those glorious ones who have, like us, experienced the vicissitudes of human life and its joys, hopes and sufferings. They, however, unlike us, have already crossed the density of the created world and, victorious, have at last seen in the beatific vision of their God, the great wave of graces, which they did not receive in vain, disappear.

There is, then, a mysterious communion between the saints of the Church triumphant and those who are still on earth and belong to the Church militant. We live together in a unity that is fine, full and indestructible. This unity means that we have the inhabitants of paradise present among us and this presence is expressed in two ways. On the one hand it is expressed by the graces that their intercession can obtain for us—and indeed their interventions can at times be miraculous. On the other hand, however, it is also made manifest in a mysterious attraction that comes less from the supernatural affinities that we may have with the saints than from a choice that they themselves make and which forms part of the plan that God has, in his providence, elaborated for our sanctification and salvation.

It is because of this power of attraction and this initiative taken by the saints that we are not always able to account for our being attracted to one saint or another. Their influence on us is in perfect harmony with what God expects of us when he confers his grace on us. This harmony may persist throughout the whole of our existence and it may also be the reason why an intimacy may develop between certain saints and ourselves. This intimate relationship may in turn become a light in our lives, supporting and stimulating us.

It would seem, moreover, that the higher these saints are in glory, the closer they are to God and the more fully they play a part in the fulfillment of his great plan to make his truth shine in the world and to raise the world up by his love, the more fervent they were during their lives on earth in bringing about the kingdom of God then and the more powerfully they exercise their attraction on us now. What riches of a spiritual kind have been and still are dispensed, for example, by those remarkable vessels of grace, those pillars of the Church and those first apostles, Saint Peter and Saint Paul! And a similar spiritual wealth comes also from Saint John, the Fathers of the Church, the martyrs, confessors and virgins of Christ and from countless men and women whom the Church has declared saints. How comforting it is for us to have recourse to their presence and to know that we are their intimate friends!

A question arises here and it is a serious one. On the one hand, there are more and more saints in heaven. They are immensely loving and they have a deep knowledge of our needs. Our distress constantly urges them to come to our rescue in the Word of God. On the other hand, however, there is still so much disorder and so much evil on our humble planet. How does this happen?

This problem should not really trouble us. It should rather make us conscious of our own responsibility and act as a stimulus for us. After all, who can make that great flood of grace that is contained in heaven descend on our earth if we do not? The words of Father Rabussier, collected by the Abbess Cécile Bruyère, throw light on this question:

> There is in a single star enough heat to melt all the ice on earth, yet we have to endure winter and cold. There has to be a fulcrum for a lever to function. In just the same way, God wants every action in heaven to have a base on earth and that fulcrum, base or focal point is the saints, making their pilgrimage through this life.[16]

Because of God's base on earth, there is only one kingdom and only one life and there is also an effective pouring out of heavenly benefits onto earth within the presence of heaven on earth and of earth in heaven. The Church continues to go forward toward the parousia and the celebration and consummation of her wedding with the Lamb within this collaboration between the powers of heaven and the powers on earth, in other words, in the cooperation of glory with grace.

The saints do not simply want us to ask them trustingly for what we want. They want more than this—in order to fill us to overflowing, they want us to be totally committed with the whole of our being. If they are to be effective here on our poor earth, we in turn have to follow their light and walk in their footsteps. We do not have to imitate their work, their special virtues or their mode of being exactly, but we do have to love as they did and be as faithful as they were.

THE SOULS OF THE DEPARTED

Can there be any one of us who is not anxious to know what bonds united us to the souls of those who are dear to us, but from whom we have been separated by death? Do these bonds exist despite the veil that is placed between them and us by this world that we know through our senses? Are those souls present for us and are we present for them?

A great mystery that God has, in his wisdom, not disclosed to us, overshadows this subject. There is nothing in the Bible that can throw light on it. We can learn something about the state of these holy souls and about their great anxiety in the presence of God, whom they are not yet able to contemplate face to face, only from the teachings of theologians and certain mystics such as Saint Catherine of Genoa,[17] who experienced here on earth various forms of purification that were destined to set her free from the rust of sin and imperfection.

The souls of the departed are wonderfully alert and clear now that they have been released from their earthly wrapping. They are revealed in their original splendor now that they have been stripped of the covering of rust that has accumulated on them as the result of past sins. They believe in the God whose holiness they have seen in and through the infinitely lovable presence of Jesus. They are firmly rooted in hope and experience an intense longing for God. They live, moreover, in such a pure and perfect state of charity that they can no longer know the object of their expiation, because it is not possible for them to reflect about themselves.

We should respect the silence of holy Scripture with regard to the souls of the departed and the discretion of the mystics in what they have written about their own experience. It would be atrocious if anything were left to our imagination in this matter. What is certain, however, is that these souls look forward to the beatific vision in both suffering and joy of a kind that goes beyond our imagination. They also form an integral part of the Church to which we belong, so that the Church is right to offer the redeeming sacrifice of her bridegroom for them and to do this unceasingly. We also know with certainty that they share in the communion of the saints and are, because of this, at one with us. They drink at the same spring of divine life and are at peace. They cling to God's will, which is absolute for them.

There is no agreement among theologians—even among Thomists—about the question of our relationship with the souls of the faithful departed. In our prayer for them—which is generally recognized—may we communicate our wishes and intentions to them? Can they, who are firmly established in the immense charity of God, help us like good angels? Let us consider briefly the two main theories, which seem to be impossible to reconcile with each other. The first of these two theories is based on the principle that we should not pray to those who have need of our prayer. According to this theory too, these souls live in extreme solitude. They have no knowledge of what is happening here on earth because they are entirely absorbed in their longing for God and in the severe task of purification that they have to undertake if they are to rediscover their original innocence and purity. According to the second theory, the souls of the faithful departed are ready to listen to our requests and to grant us the grace that we ask for.

If, however, these holy souls in the Church suffering do not know anything about us on earth through themselves, why should they not have some knowledge of our needs, our adversities and our general condition? They may not learn this directly, but they should be able to know it from other souls who join them, from the angels or from God himself, whose sovereign good pleasure is always present. The Curé d'Ars believed that these souls can do nothing for themselves and this may be a reason for invoking their help.[18] His opinion seems to us to be completely in accordance with those reasons of the heart that reason does not know. It is also fully in accordance with the goodness of God, his plans for the unity of all Christians in the Church and finally in accordance with those interventions into the heart of the world of the hereafter, which have nothing in common with hell but the suffering that is experienced there[19] and of which we have some inkling from Scripture and the lives of some of the saints.

Cardinal Newman did not hesitate to turn his back on the Scholastic theologians and their subtle reasoning and to declare that the dead were very near to us. He asked, for example, what system had the right to impose a veto on our thoughts and memories in such a way? What layer of the earth's surface, he asked, is thick enough to prevent us from remaining united with our dead, finding out what they wanted, preserving their image and trying to imitate them? How could we be prevented from expressing our sympathy with the other world?[20] Elsewhere, he insisted that they were present with us like those who had lost their hands and their voices.[21]

We believe that all this is true. Because of this, we also believe that those souls suffering in solitude are nonetheless more than ever united to us in a unity of life in God and for God and in a charity that is more intense than any charity that they have experienced on earth.

Let us, however, be cautious in what we say. We may believe that these souls continue to be very close to us, despite the lonely desert in which they live and their lack of every means of communication with the senses. We should, however, not forget that their condition is a sacred one. They are firmly established in the good and filled with God's forgiveness. Because of this they are holy and call for the greatest respect. To address them in a familiar way and to distract them from their holy and religious silence would clearly be a kind of profanation. Our love for them should be tinged with reverence if it is to be really Christian. We ought to invoke them with reserve and discretion and we should never forget that they are preparing themselves, in the burning fire of God's jealous love, for eternity and for glory.

We may conclude, then, that the best way of staying with them, of being in constant touch with them and of proving to them how faithful our love for them is, every time that we are asked to do it by someone who is turned toward God, to direct toward him in turn the movement of a prayer or a thought, to live ourselves as the holy souls would want us to live now that they have glimpsed the infinite tenderness of their God and ours and to communicate with them in the presence of all beauty, truth and good.

THE PRESENCE OF OUR HUMAN BROTHERS

We are not monsters and we know that man is the crown of God's creation and therefore sacred. We also know that no other being here on earth is more worthy of our respect, love and devotion. Man is also a social being and was created to live with other men. This is so important a truth that those who have been driven by the Spirit to seek flight from the world and live in solitude have always been convinced that they were leaving their human brothers in order to find them again in a more perfect way in God and in order to serve them better by their prayer, contemplation and sacrifices.

Man is not an abstraction. Each man is an individual person and the product, within human freedom, of everything that has gone to make him what he is. This complex network that has formed each one of us includes heredity, race, country, education, culture and temperament. It is not difficult to see that the attempt to live in peace with all our brothers means that we live in a kind of crucible. This crucible is fearful and it is also a place of acceptance and disappointment. We would like to think of others as better than ourselves or else, in our ill-will, we are irritated by them as they really are. It is also a crucible in which we have again and again to deny ourselves. We are so often tempted to break through every obstacle and achieve greater scope for our own personality and, if we are frustrated, we are left in bitterness and hatred of our fellow-men.

The sovereign law of the Lord is, however, unequivocal. We can be his disciples and his friends only if we love. There is no greater demand made of us than this, yet there is also nothing more sublime or more in tune with the most rudimentary needs of our heart or with the deepest and most fervent desires of our soul.

But who is this man, my brother? Do I really know him? What do I see in him? Do I only see a weak, chance being who is as limited, faulty, base, dark and devious as I am? Yes, he is all these things, but if we penetrate beneath the surface to the intimate depths of his soul, we also find something mysterious that makes him shine in glory. He is, even when he is most wretched and low, the image of God his creator. He is, of course, disfigured by sin, but he is also able to regain his original splendor when he is recreated by God's grace.

It is for this reason that God himself became man and chose to live among men as a man. Jesus the man embraces and penetrates all his brothers with his presence and he does this in the Spirit, whom he came to spread over the earth. If we cling to Christ in faith, we shall never be able to see our human brother, however degraded he may be, outside and apart from the one who died on the cross for his salvation. The more disfigured, suffering and wretched he is, the more we are bound to see in him the sacred imprint of that unique man who entered the impressive mystery of self-emptying for our sakes.

It is therefore the God-man whom I encounter in my fellow-man. I may not even know that I am doing it and indeed I do not need to know, but it is to him that I give food and drink when he is hungry and thirsty, him whom I welcome when he is a stranger, him whom I clothe when he is naked and him whom I visit when he is sick or in prison (Matt. 25. 31–46).

No, it is not possible to be present for our human brother or to make him fully present for ourselves, especially with regard to his universal and particular needs, unless we put ourselves on the level of Christ. If we do that, we shall see the Head in the least important member of the body. We shall also see ourselves as a member of that body, receiving from the Head the life that flows within us like sap in a tree. Living at the level of Christ, we shall also see the adorable face of the one who died and rose again for all of us in the face of every human being that we meet.[22] At this level, there are no more distances and no more friends or enemies. There is only our neighbor in Christ, even if he persists in treating us as an enemy. That neighbor is everywhere and he is not a colorless or an ideal being. He is, on the contrary, a living being with difficulties and faults. Our task is to love him and help him on his way from Jerusalem to Jericho, the road that leads from within to without, from the intimacy of our being, which is pure faith, hope and prayer, to the realities outside, which are illuminated by our faithful prayer.

Where does this love come from—this love that transcends all our selfishness, all contradictions and everything that may serve as a foil and make us consider ourselves alone? It clearly does not come from our own heart, since that is too small. It is a great love and comes from that great heart that is made deeper by grace and is therefore able to expand until it corresponds to the limitless heart of God. God is in us and we are in him. The flood of *agape* that comes from the infinite depths of God, flowing through the Son from the Father and returning to the Father from the Son in the pouring out of the Spirit, is a love that led directly to the creation of the universe, its redemption by the incarnate Son and the new heaven and new earth of a creation of glory. What is more, that great love is in us.

This love goes far beyond all our own possibilities and limits. Going from the infinite to the infinite, it encloses in its unity the countless myriads of souls that the Father sees and knows by name in his Word. What could divert or stop this love? What power exists that can prevent this great river of love from flooding and irrigating all around it and making it bear fruit before returning to the ocean from which it came? This love is both light and heat and we should try to understand how we should react to its clarity and warmth.

Everyone who has flown in an aircraft has observed how, from the point of view of heaven, the earth seems very small and difficult to see with detail. With this detached perspective in a parallel sense there seems no longer to be men on the right or the left wing politically and no more ethnic or social differences. Having overcome the force of the earth's gravity, we are raised to a level in flight where everything is governed by what might separate us. If we apply the experience of love to the spiritual sphere, we see that everything is united in the pure light of love by a mutually shared presence that transcends all passion. What comes about is a mutual understanding between men who have come together in a shared encounter that goes beyond themselves and yet takes place in their most intimate depths. It is a flowing of love in light and warmth that sets them free. The encounter between men in this experience enables the subterranean flow to reach the surface.

God sometimes allows this kind of encounter to take place between two souls who have become quite open and receptive to each other. It may occur quite suddenly either in conversation or in silence. The protective covering is removed and all darkness recedes. We confront each other: "It is you!" Instinctively we make a religious gesture and fall on our knees. It is from this holy presence that love is born, a deep friendship that no physical absence can ever diminish. Absence may indeed even make this friendship stronger. We express it in prayer.

Undoubtedly this is an exceptional occurrence, but an experience at this level that is revealed to the senses in a sudden flash of grace from heaven must surely exist, perhaps at a different level, but nonetheless substantially, in all our encounters with our human brothers. Concealed beneath a covering of flesh is the sanctuary of an immortal soul looking, perhaps without knowing it, at its creator who is looking at it and at himself in it. Love does not suppress this covering, but passes through it in a secret movement of the heart. The result may be, as it was for Father Peyriguère while he was caring for the suffering members of Christ's body, pure contemplation.

Seen in this light, there is clearly much more to this love than anything that can be suggested merely by human reasons or natural affinities. It is undoubtedly correct to say that this presence of love is essentially an expression of the reality of the Church. The Church is, after all, the great focal point of light and heat which hopes to spread those elements over the cold, dark world. It is not, however, outside the world, nor is it enclosed in a contemplation of itself. It is the *Catholica*. What does this mean?

It means that the Church is not simply a well-organized society with a hierarchy, sacraments and laws, a necessary structure in the world in which it had to take its place after the departure of Christ Jesus. In its pure and original essence, it is also and above all the bride of Christ and the kingdom of God. As such, the Church has no frontiers. It is at home everywhere and especially where there are naturally Christian souls. This means, of course, that it is at home with all men, for whom Christ shed his blood. The true Christian, then, is in the Church and is himself the Church. He is in the Church only by being the Church. He is therefore universal man and everything is universally present for him. Because of love and like the Trinity and Christ himself whom he carries within him, he has no enemies. Nothing is excluded from his presence. Everything is present for him, with the exception of sin, which is the absence of being and the essence of refusal and negation. The secret of his presence for all things and all men is the openness that the love and presence of God, who is "all in all," creates in him.

In God's providence, this openness is found in different forms and at different levels. At the one extreme, there is the great human love that exists between married couples, whose physical union makes them one body, but is at the same time really an expression of the tenderness which makes them one soul. At the other extreme, there is the love that I feel for the stranger, the poor and needy person whom I may be seeing for the first and perhaps the only time. I may not trust him, but God has placed him on my path and has secretly advised me to help him. The openness that I have toward him is brought about purely by God's power. Because of his power, I can welcome this stranger and give myself totally to him. It is a power that makes me, who am so small, very great.

Everything is reconciled in this great and translucent love and everything merges together into unity. A presence is there which encourages all the others. Loving, it has been said, is not looking at each other—it is looking together in the same direction. My neighbor may not know in which direction to look. Has God not prompted me, then, to point it out to him? And if I cannot do this, can I not make up for this failure by a mysterious communion that is based on and opens out within the unique presence of God?

We are right to expect love to be reciprocated within the presence of the one who is himself love. The rightness of this expectation is borne out by every invitation to the apostolate. But we have to begin to love ourselves and to make ourselves present. If we cannot achieve a reciprocal relationship, then we have simply to give love where there is no love, in the confidence that love will emerge from this act. It is in doing this that we really become the image of God, who created the world by love and in this way permeated it with his presence. We become the image of Jesus Christ, who gave his life for all men, including the sinners, so that they should be saved.

In this, we are not unaware of the problems that may arise for anyone who really wants to be present for God, himself and his brothers. These three ways of being present are undeniably necessary if any form of apostolate is to be fruitful. Priests have above all to be present in these ways. How adaptable they have to be, changing themselves and their approach to suit the time and place and above all the different kinds of men and women whom they meet! The priest is, after all, everyone's father and yet at the same time he must always take care never to forget the God whom he serves when he serves his fellow-men or the total transcendence of eternal values.

What is the great virtue, apart from charity, in which all the virtues are rooted, that helps us especially to be present for others? Surely it is purity, the virtue that Louis Lavalle called "the childlike quality that provides us with all forms of power before these are inhibited or corrupted." Purity can penetrate everything and fill it with its rays. It can pass through all the uncleanness of the world. It is both strength and clarity and evil cannot prevent its activity. It sees people and things in their authenticity and objective reality and has no prejudices. It cannot compromise. It places all its hope in its influence, but does not rely on itself. It counts only on God, whom it humbly reflects by virtue of his grace. In this way, its transparent quality can be communicated to others and, since it is a mirror reflecting God, it can also become a mirror reflecting others, who may thus discover their true face in it and begin to recognize what is authentic and true in their being.

If we are quite pure in God's presence and in the presence of our human brothers, we shall anticipate here on earth the universal presence of the elect in paradise where we shall, in the fullness of the unique presence of God in the Holy Trinity, all be quite translucent to each other. There too, the joy of one will be completed by the joy of all and everything will be communication and unity.

We would like to conclude this chapter with the words of Saint Catherine of Siena, who experienced in her own life the blessedness of having a pure heart:

> How brotherly this charity is! How closely it unites all these souls to me and how it binds them to each other, since it is from me that men have and know this purity with holy fear and perfect respect and it is from me that they have received it. This

sets them on fire with love for me and from that moment onward they see and recognize in me the dignity to which I have
raised them. The angel communicates with man, with the
blessed soul, and the blessed themselves communicate with the
angels, united as they are with them by the bonds of charity.
Everyone rejoices in the happiness of everyone else and all exult
in possessing me. There is jubilation, cheerfulness without sorrow and sweetness without sorrow and sweetness without bitterness, because they have tasted me in their lives and their
death. They have tasted me in and through the feeling of love
experienced in their love of their neighbor.[23]

NOTES

1. See, among others, the works of those who followed Matthias Joseph Scheeben, *La Mère virginale du Sauveur:* J.-M. Nicholas, for example,
and Fathers Laurentin, Bernard and Dillenschneider.
2. The originator of this idea is Saint Gregory Nazianzen, in his poem
in praise of virginity; *PG* 37. 523.
3. The relationship between our Lady and the Father inspired Paul
Claudel to write these lines of verse in his *La Messe là-bas: Pater Noster:*

"Who has ever known the Father better than the woman whom he
    once desired?
It was she who knew him before all others
and, with her heart, she was the first in the plan to give life.
Without her, he could not have been the Father and those could not
    have been his sons.
They only knew his strength, but she knew his weakness."

4. Benedict XIV in his bull *Gloriosae Dominae*, 1747.
5. In his encyclical *Ad diem illum*, 2 February 1904.
6. See the quotation from Father Montchanin's writings in Cardinal
Daniélou's book, *Le Mystère de l'Avent:* this will be found in his chapter
on the Virgin and time.
7. Saint Gertrude, *The Herald of Divine Love;* Saint Mechthild, *The
Book of Special Grace;* Saint Mechthild of Magdeburg, *The Flowing Light of
the Godhead.*
8. See her *Cahiers de la Vierge*, No. 15: *L'Union Mystique à Marie*,
translated from the Flemish by L. van den Bossche.
9. Cardinal Daniélou, *op. cit.*, pp. 136ff.
10. This term is Saint Catherine of Siena's.
11. The hymn sung at the Feast of the Dedication of a Church speaks
of being "crowned with angels like a bride with her procession."
12. Taken from his *Fourth Letter to a Young Woman of Metz on the
Mystery of the Church;* see also Bossuet's "Panegyric preached in 1659 on
the Guardian Angels" (Lebarcq, Vol. 3).

13. *Homily on John*, 10. 6; *Contra Celsus*, 8. 31.

14. See his Parochial Sermons: "The Powers of Nature."

15. *Le livre des anges*, Part 3.

16. This is taken from the oration on the spiritual marriage that the Abbess of Sainte-Cécile of Solesmes, Mother Claire de Livron, wanted to hand on and which appeared in the *Revue d'ascétique et de mystique*, Vol. 8, July 1927.

17. *Treatise on Purgatory*.

18. See his Sermon in commemoration of the dead: "Although they can do nothing for themselves, the souls in purgatory can do a great deal for us. Hardly anyone has ever invoked them without having obtained the grace for which he asked."

19. *Sermon on Purgatory*.

20. *Treatise on Purgatory*.

21. *Sermon on the Invisible World*.

22. See Saint Augustine, *In Evang. Ioh. Tract.*, 10. 3; 35. 2060: "If you want to love Christ as he ought to be loved, spread your love over all the parts of the globe, for the members of Christ are scattered over the whole world. If you love only one part, you will be divided, you will not be in the whole body and you will not be under one head."

23. *Dialogue*, translated by Hurtaud, Part 2, pp. 222–223. In the first part of this dialogue, the saint speaks about this mystery of love; see pp. 131–132. In this quotation, it is, of course, God who is speaking.

Epilogue

Now that we have reached the end of this book, we can ask an important question. It is this. Is there not perhaps one act that includes every possible divine and human presence? Is there not one act uniting heaven and earth, time and eternity and man and the whole universe to God? To express this same question in a slightly different way, is there not one act that is raised above the whole of history and human progress and that also transcends time and space?

Yes, there is such an act. It is in fact the supreme religious act. It is the act of an exceptional presence in all its universality and depth. Although it is unique, it can be repeated again and again throughout history until the second coming in glory of the Lord: "Until the Lord comes" (1 Cor. 11. 26). This act, which is at the heart of the *mysterium fidei,* comes from the word of the one who is the Word: "This is my body."

This act corresponds on earth to the eternal generation of the Word and in it every mystery is present—the Trinity, the incarnation, the redemption and the death on the cross of the one who rose again bringing infinite life. In this supreme act, everyone dies with and in Christ in order to live forever fulfilled in and united with him, even though everyone continues to live and to die here on earth. Jesus himself shines in and through this act as what Saint Ignatius of Antioch called "our inseparable life." This is above all because we eat his flesh in this act. This is the final expression of his love for us.

The author of this book regrets very much that she is not a poet, since she would like to conclude with a hymn to life. Life, love and presence are, after all, aspects of the same reality. God is love and, in and through his presence, which is always active, he calls on us to enter into the mystery of his infinite life, which makes him Father, Son and Holy Spirit.

Scripture, and especially the gospel and the Apocalypse of Saint John, is full of the life of God, which is the beginning and the end of our life. He lives and we live. He came among us so that life itself, his life, might be superabundantly present in us. His life, moreover, is his being and his being is love. The book of the Apocalypse, which appears at the end of the biblical account of revelation and is the book that presents in a unique way God's being with us in heaven and on earth, is filled with life. This life is unfolded in the last book of the Bible in great scenes of unparalleled splendor and with a magnificence, a power and a vigor that often astonishes us on the one hand and with a gentleness, privacy and intimacy on the other. A foretaste of the intimate nature of this writing can already be gained in the gospel composed by the same author, who was, of course, the disciple whom Jesus loved.

Everything in the Apocalypse is filled with the presence of the invisible majesty of the one who is seated on the throne, the living one who lives "forever and ever." This presence is inseparable from that of the Lamb and that of the royal and victorious horseman followed by his white armies. The Lamb and the royal horseman are the same as the one presented to us at the beginning of the book in the imposing figure of the high-priest, with eyes like flames of fire, a voice like the sound of many waters and a face like the sun shining with all its force. This "figure like a son of man" declares: "I am the living one. I was dead and now I am to live forever and ever" (Apoc. 1. 14–18). Gathered all round this presence there is life in profusion, a life that expresses itself in worship, praise, thanksgiving, religious gestures and, at times, silence (see Apoc. 4. 8–11; 5. 8–14; 7. 9–13; 15. 2–4).

The unity of heaven and earth is achieved in this unique and radiant presence, in which we are all present for each other, even before the wedding of the Lamb and his bride, the Church, is consummated in the unity of life. In this presence too, are we not invited to blend our own note into that of the great symphony of the many waters? We have, after all, been written in the book of life from all eternity (Apoc. 21. 27), been allowed to drink from the fountain of the water of life (21. 6) and have lived in a city through which the river of life passes (22. 1–2). Yes, "let all who are thirsty come; all who want it may have the water of life and have it free" (22. 17). Let them look forward to the second coming of Jesus, calling out without ceasing with the Spirit and the Bride: "Come, Lord Jesus" and "may the grace of the Lord Jesus be with all of us. Amen" (22. 20–21).

As we have already said several times in this book, God's presence is his very being. For us, however, his presence is also the object of an experience that takes different forms and is undergone at different degrees and levels. But how is it possible for us not to want this experience to be as full and as profound here on earth as it will be in eternity, when we see God face to face? And has God, in his omnipotent love, not ordered everything toward this end?

At this point, we are bound to quote the words of the Apostle Paul: "Since God did not spare his own Son, but gave him up to benefit us all, we may be certain, after such a gift, that he will not refuse anything he can give" (Rom. 8. 32). The literal translation of this text reads: "how will he not give with him all things to us." We shall never be able to fathom the complete meaning of these words: "with him all things." This Christ, whom the Father has given to us and with whom we are united in the unity of the Spirit whom he sent to us, is now alive and totally deified in the heart of the Trinity. Since the ascension, the manhood of the divine and risen Christ, which is inseparable from the eternal Word and the glory of the Father, has achieved its supreme longing: "Father, it is time for you to glorify me with that glory I had with you before ever the world was" (John 17. 5).

We live no longer for ourselves (2 Cor. 5. 15), but have been taken up into heaven (Col. 3. 1), since God has given us his glorified Son, who has, through his sacrifice, made us his body. In this way, we are able to enter into the life of the three consubstantial persons of the Trinity and make our home there. It is therefore sufficient for us to lose our life, going beyond the reality of creation and beyond ourselves (Matt. 10. 39), just as God lost his life, by going beyond himself and becoming man (John 1. 14), when he himself was beyond all men and all things.

He came down to us so that we could go up to him, but this ascent is at the same time also a descent into our most profound depths, down into that source of our being which springs from the heart of our creator and enables us to flow into the boundless ocean of his being. Because of this, we can really be God in God. Because of this admirable interchange, which extends that of the incarnation, we can go beyond the presence of God that we perceive through the windows of our soul—our senses in general and our eyes in particular. We can even go beyond God's providence and the countless movements of his grace. Passing beyond these visible signs, we can then contemplate in faith the invisible presence of the three who are only one.

These three persons are together the family of which we form a real part (see, for example, 1 John 1. 3; John 14. 23). With the Father, we beget the Son. With the Son, we are begotten and we point exclusively to the Father. With the Spirit, we are inspired by breathing him, Christ extending in us the same breath of love that comes from the Father and enters him in the Spirit's proceeding from him and the Father. It is in this way that we are able to share in this unending flow of life which makes the three divine persons circulate within each other—in circumincession—and rest in each other—in circuminsession.

We are completely lost and yet totally personalized and at the same time everything is given to us in the Son who is everything to us and also beyond us and whom the Father wants to receive from us in a mutual interchange that is beyond expression. We become sons in the one Son and are able to say truthfully, inspired by the Spirit: "Abba, Father." We are allowed then to give God to God and have become quite transparent to God. God also shines through us.

What an unfathomable mystery of love this is! God creates me with a sovereign freedom in an act of infinite and gratuitous freedom. He has no need of me or the goods that he has given me. Yet he keeps me so firmly enclosed within the mystery of his being and his life that he only gives himself to me in order to receive everything from me and wants me with the same love with which he loves himself. So, if we take this text of Saint Paul to its ultimate limit and experience this presence that is so consuming and yet so gentle by stripping ourselves bare, we may be able to understand the words of Master Eckhart, which at first sight seem so strange and almost blasphemous: "Let God be God; I am a cause. God derives his being from the soul." Having entered the Son, I point to the Father, who would not be the Father without me. He has really given me that Son for me to be able to offer him to the Father in the Spirit, whom I breathe with the Son and whom he has given to me so that I can breathe him with them.

This, then, is the highest point of the mystery of the presence of God, who makes himself present for us only in the presence that he has of himself and who consequently reveals to us his presence for the whole of creation only in this great light. As soon as the soul has descended into its most intimate inner depths and as soon as it has been overwhelmed and penetrated by the presence of God, it is impossible for it to go back. The experience is one of awakening after death, in which the soul has been taken, gradually or suddenly, to the shore of eternity. We are men and not angels and we must live as men, even if we continue to long for that light in which God lives. At the same time, however, that light is friendly and bracing. It may be fleeting, but it is always there as a backcloth on which is reflected everything that happens in our life of nature and grace and which provides evidence of the true value or the vanity of that life.

In this experience, we have gone far beyond reason and concepts. We can only look and love. We are in that sphere where there are no more barriers. Everything is in love and everything is for the love of God's love. The old man has disappeared in an immensity in which hatred of evil is at one with a love that includes the whole of creation. We are in the homeland of those who can endure the divisions brought about by sin, but who go beyond them and overcome them and who can only be checked by them in order to combat them and heal them.